INTO THE CLASSROOM

RELIGIOUS EDUCATION IN THE LEAVING CERTIFICATE

The Search for Meaning and Values

Eoin G. Cassidy

Series Editors
Eoin G. Cassidy and Patrick M. Devitt

VERITAS

First published 2004 by
Veritas Publications
7/8 Lower Abbey Street
Dublin 1
Ireland
Email publications@veritas.ie
Website www.veritas.ie

ISBN 1 85390 689 1

10 9 8 7 6 5 4 3 2 1

Copyright © Eoin G. Cassidy, 2004

The material in this publication is protected by copyright law. Except as may be permitted by law, no part of the material may be reproduced (including by storage in a retrieval system) or transmitted in any form or by any means, adapted, rented or lent without the written permission of the copyright owners. Applications for permissions should be addressed to the publisher.

A catalogue record for this book is available from the British Library.

Cover design by Bill Bolger
Printed in the Republic of Ireland by Betaprint Ltd, Dublin

Veritas books are printed on paper made from the wood pulp of managed forests. For every tree felled, at least one tree is planted, thereby renewing natural resources.

Contents

Series Introduction ... 7

PART ONE: **REFLECTING ON THE CONTEXT**
Introduction ... 19
1   The Contemporary Context ... 26
    Contemporary expressions of the search for meaning ... 36
    Key questions that emerge in contemporary culture ... 40
    Hindering the search for meaning and values ... 47
    Contemporary expressions of indifference to the search for meaning ... 50
2   The Tradition of the Search ... 52
    The nature and purpose of philosophy ... 52
    The development of philosophy in ancient Greece ... 54
        The Sophists ... 56
        Socrates ... 57
        Plato ... 64
        Aristotle ... 70
    Key moments in the development of philosophical thought ... 76
    The emergence of a Christian philosophy ... 76
        Augustine ... 77
        Aquinas ... 84

		The rise of modernity and the turn to the subject	88
		René Descartes	90
		Immanuel Kant	93
		Contemporary Continental philosophy	96
		Martin Heidegger	97
		Emmanuel Levinas	102
		Edith Stein	108
		Jean-Luc Marion	110

PART TWO:	THE RESPONSE TO THE QUEST	
	Introduction	119
3	The Language of Symbol	121
	Forms of symbolic language	121
	The importance of symbols	123
	The power of symbolic language	126
4	The Tradition of Response	129
	Myth and early cosmologies	129
	Evidence of religious and spiritual behaviour in ancient societies	133
	The sense of the sacred in contemporary culture	139
	The humanist tradition	146
	Erasmus	149
	Karl Marx	150
	Albert Camus	154
	Hannah Arendt	161
	The dialogue between religion and science	164
	Non-religious responses to the questions of life	167

PART THREE:	CONCEPTS OF GOD	
	Introduction	173
5	*Gods of the Ancients*	176
	Descriptions of Gods in ancient myths	176
	Polytheism and the emergence of monotheism	181
	The concept of God in key monotheistic traditions	186
	Judaism	186
	Christianity	187
	Islam	189
6	*The Concept of Revelation*	192
	Divine revelation: God as known through self-revelation	192
	The significance of revelation in different religious traditions	193
	The meaning of the transcendent in some religious traditions	196
7	*Naming God, Past and Present*	200
	Images of God in traditional and contemporary cultures	200
	Religious and spiritual interpretations of experience	203
	Establishing the credibility of religious belief	208
PART FOUR:	RELIGION AND THE EMERGENCE OF VALUES	
	Introduction	227
8	*Religion as a Source of Communal Values*	230
	The relationship between concept of God and the person	230
9	*Secular Sources of Communal Values*	239
	The emergence of a secular world with its own value system	239
	The Enlightenment	239
	John Locke	240

David Hume	245
Existentialism	252
Friedrich Nietzsche	253
Jean Paul Sartre	258
A secular world-view critiqued	263
Iris Murdoch	263
Shaping communal values: sources other than religion	267
Liberal individualism	267
Liberalism and the shaping of communal values	268
Liberal individualism critiqued	270
Robert Bellah	270
Alasdair MacIntyre	274
Shaping communal values: a challenge to the Christian community	280
Appendix	283
Different relations between religions and the secular world	283
Select Bibliography	286

Series Introduction

September 2003 saw the introduction of the Leaving Certificate Religious Education Syllabus by the Department of Education and Science. For those concerned to promote a religious sensibility in young Irish adults it is hard to exaggerate the importance of this event. It both represents a formal recognition by society of the value of religious education in the academic lives of second-level students, and it also reflects the importance which Irish society attaches to promoting the personal growth of students, including their spiritual and moral development. Religious education offers young people the opportunity to understand and interpret their experience in the light of a religious world-view. Furthermore, in and through an engagement with the RE Syllabus at Leaving Certificate level, students will learn a language that will enable them both to articulate their own faith experience and to dialogue with those of different faiths or non-theistic stances.

The Department of Education Syllabus is to be welcomed in that it gives recognition to the role that religious education plays in the human development of the young person. It is not an exaggeration to say that religious education is the capstone of the school's educational response to the young person's search for meaning and values. In this context, it encourages students to reflect upon their awareness of themselves as unique individuals with roots in a community network of family, friends and parish. Furthermore, it allows students to acknowledge and reflect upon their relationship to a God who cares for them and for the world in which we live. Finally, it gives students access to the universal nature of the quest for truth, beauty and goodness. Most of these themes are addressed sympathetically in the section entitled *The Search for Meaning and Values*. In particular, this section is to be welcomed because it offers the possibility for students to grapple with theistic and non-theistic world-views in a context that is hospitable to religious belief.

A critical dimension of the young person's educational journey is the growth in understanding of their own culture and the manner in which culture shapes their outlook on the world. The Religious Education Syllabus not only addresses the manner in which religion (and in particular Christianity) has shaped Irish culture over many centuries, but it also provides an extremely valuable platform from which to critique aspects of the relationship between faith and culture in the contemporary world. The section entitled *Religion: The Irish Experience* addresses the former concern by showing pupils the manner in which the Christian religion has contributed to the belief patterns and values of Irish society. It also alerts them to the depths of religious belief that predate by many centuries, even millennia, the arrival of Christianity in Ireland; and it also connects them to the cultural richness that links Ireland to the European continent. In this context, the devotional revolution that took place in Ireland (including the extraordinary growth in religious orders from 1850-1930) is a topic that could be expanded. The missionary outreach of the Catholic Church in Ireland in the last hundred years is worthy of special mention. Finally, students studying this section should be encouraged to acknowledge the ambiguities that have attended the presence of religion in Ireland over the centuries; to see on the one hand the image of an island of saints and scholars, and on the other hand to note how 'lilies that fester smell far worse than weeds'.

In examining the manner in which faith and culture interact, the sections entitled *Religion and Science* and *Religion and Gender* make a valuable contribution to the Syllabus. These sections address topical issues that were controversial in the past and continue to be problematical even today. In treating of these two topics it is obviously important to avoid stereotypes – the acceptance of unexamined assumptions that mask or over-simplify the truth to such an extent as to do a disservice to the seriousness of the issues involved. Likewise, the section on *World Religions* should be taught in a manner that is sensitive to the dangers of cultural and religious stereotypes. This section not only gives students a valuable introduction to the main religions in the world, but it also provides a cultural context for an awareness of the fact that the phenomenon of religion and the experience of religious belief is something that shapes people's understanding of themselves and their lifestyles across all cultural boundaries. Furthermore, it should never be forgotten that if, as Christians believe, God's Spirit is present in and through these religions, there is a need to study these religions precisely in order to discover aspects of God's presence in the world that has the capability to continually surprise.

In the Irish cultural context, Catholicism shapes the religious sensibilities and practices of the majority of young people. The Syllabus offers a generous acknowledgement of the importance of Christianity in the Irish context by providing two sections that focus on core aspects of the Christian faith. These are: *Christianity: origins and contemporary expressions* and *The Bible: Literature and Sacred text*. In this context, the Syllabus section on the Bible is to be welcomed. However, greater attention could be given to the role and significance of the Prophets in the Old Testament and to Paul in the New Testament. Furthermore, in studying the Bible it should never be forgotten that the primary reality is not the 'book' but rather the person of Christ and the community tradition grappling with this reality that is revealed in and through the Bible.

What is often in danger of being forgotten in an academic context is the importance of the fostering of attitudes and practices that promote personal growth. Religious education cannot be focused only on knowledge and understanding, because religion is primarily a way of celebrating life and, in particular, the spiritual dimension of life in and through the practices of worship, ritual and prayer. The Syllabus's recognition of this critical dimension of religious education through the section entitled *Worship, Ritual and Prayer* is to be welcomed. In addressing this section of the Syllabus it would be important to alert students to the great variety of spiritualities, prayer forms, mysticisms, rituals and styles of music that are to be found within the Christian tradition in order that students may have the possibility of exploring the richness of the spiritual dimension of their own tradition.

A key remit of the educational process is the fostering of moral maturity through a syllabus that allows students to engage in moral education. Not only is religious education particularly suited to facilitating this educational imperative, but the ethical character of human life is a core feature of all religions. The importance of this dimension of religious education is recognised in the provision of two sections entitled *Moral Decision Making* and *Issues of Justice and Peace*. There is nothing optional about the challenge to promote justice and peace. However, it is a topic that can all too easily be ideologically driven. Therefore, there is a special responsibility on those teaching this section to ensure that the instances of injustice cited, and the causes of injustice proposed, are grounded in solid research.

The challenges to Catholic religion teachers

Though religious education has been an integral part of Irish second-level schools long before the foundation of the state, it has not until now been possible to assess this work under the State examination system. The reason for this anomaly is the Intermediate Education Act (1878) which allowed for the teaching but forbade the State examination of religious education. The removal of this legal constraint on State examination of RE has provided the impetus for the introduction of the Junior Certificate Syllabus in September 2000 and the introduction of the Leaving Certificate Syllabus in September 2003. These changes are to be welcomed but they provide a number of major challenges to Catholic religion teachers that should not be minimised.

In the *first* place, Catholic religion teachers have to attend to the danger that the new Syllabus will lead to a weakening of a commitment to catechesis in second level schools. The catechetical project of faith formation is built around six key pillars: knowledge of the faith; liturgical/sacramental education; moral formation; learning to pray; education for community life, including a fostering of the ecumenical character of Christian community, and finally, missionary initiative and inter-religious dialogue. Clearly, the RE Leaving Certificate Syllabus does give attention to many of the above themes, including the key catechetical concerns of attitude or value formation and the development of commitments. However, the emphasis in the Syllabus is undoubtedly upon the acquiring of knowledge, understanding and knowledge-based skills, all of which undoubtedly place it under the rubric of religious education rather than catechesis. The religion teacher ought to value the distinctive approaches to religion reflected in both catechesis and religious education. Both are important because both contribute in distinctive ways to the religious development of the young person. Catechesis aims at maturity of faith whereas religious education aims at knowledge and understanding of the faith.

From the point of view of the religion teacher, the teaching can have a different tone at different times. On one occasion, it might have a 'showing how' or catechetical tone, one that assumes a shared faith experience and encourages active participation. At another time it can have an educational or 'explaining' tone that invites pupils to stand back from religion to a certain extent, so that they can gain a more objective understanding of what is being taught. The Religious Education Syllabus should be taught in a manner that keeps both of these approaches in balance. In a similar vein, the presence of RE on the Leaving Certificate curriculum should not distract teachers from acknowledging that the religious development of young people happens in many contexts, which are distinct, though complementary. It can take place at home, in the parish, with friends as well as in school. Furthermore, even in the school it can take place at a whole series of levels including liturgy, prayer and projects that encourage an awareness of the need to care for those in most need.

In the *second* place, teachers have to attend to the scope and range of the aims of the Syllabus, one that seeks both to introduce students to a broad range of religious traditions and to the non-religious interpretation of life as well as providing students with the opportunity to develop an informed and critical understanding of the Christian tradition. In this context, teachers have to balance the need to promote tolerance for and mutual understanding of those of other or no religious traditions, alongside the need to give explicit attention to the Christian faith claims that Jesus is the Son of God and that he died to save us and to unite us with God and one another. Similarly, in teaching Christianity, teachers need to give attention to the role and significance of the Church from a Catholic perspective. It should never be forgotten that the idea of the Church as 'people of God', 'body of Christ' and 'temple of the Holy Spirit' is one that is at the heart of Catholic self-understanding.

In a similar vein, the Syllabus encourages students to engage critically with a wide variety of ethical codes with a view to the development of a moral maturity. Teachers will have to balance this approach with the way in which morality is viewed within the Christian tradition under the heading of discipleship – Jesus invites people to follow *him* rather than an ethical code or vision. Furthermore, from a Christian perspective, morality is never simply or even primarily concerned with a listing of moral prohibitions, rather it situates the ethical dimension of human nature within the context of a belief in a forgiving God. Finally, it should not be forgotten that it does not make sense to teach morality in too abstract a manner. Morality is something preeminently practical and at all times needs to be brought down to the level of real people – those who struggle with the demands of conscience in their lives. From a Catholic perspective, one has in the lives of the saints a multitude of examples of the manner in which people have attempted to follow the call to discipleship that is Christian morality.

Finally, nobody concerned with the seriousness of the challenge facing schools to promote moral maturity could be unaware of the importance of the contemporary challenge posed to the promotion of societal and religious values by the rise of a relativist and/or subjectivist ethos. In this context, the teaching of the broad variety of moral codes will have to be done in a manner that draws students' attention to the importance of acknowledging the objective nature of morality as opposed to accepting uncritically either a relativist or a subjectivist standpoint. In the light of the need to critique an exaggerated acceptance of pluralism, there is also a need to acknowledge that not all theories are equally valid, and moral decision-making is not simply a matter of applying one's own personal preference.

What is proposed in these commentaries

Given the breadth and scope of the Syllabus it is undoubtedly true that teachers will have to attend to the wide variety of sections in the Syllabus which demand a breadth of knowledge that some may find a little daunting. Even though it is not envisaged that teachers would attempt to teach all ten sections of the Syllabus to any one group of students, nevertheless, the Syllabus will make demands upon teachers that can only be met if there are support services in place. For example, apart from the need to ensure the publishing of good quality teaching and learning resources, the schools themselves will need to ensure that appropriate resources – books, CDs, internet and videos – are provided. Finally, teachers will need to be provided with appropriate in-service training. It is to furthering this goal of providing good quality teaching and learning resources that the present series of volumes is addressed.

The eleven volumes in this series of commentaries comprise an introductory volume (already published, *Willingly To School*) that reflects upon the challenge of RE as an examination subject, along with ten other volumes that mirror the ten sections in the Syllabus. These commentaries on the Syllabus have been published to address the critical issue of the need to provide resources for the teaching of the Syllabus that are both academically rigorous and yet accessible to the educated general reader. Although primarily addressed to both specialist and general teachers of religion and third-level students studying to be religion teachers, the commentaries will be accessible to parents of Leaving Certificate pupils and, in addition, it is to be hoped that they will provide an important focus for adults in parish-based or other religious education or theology programmes. In the light of this focus, each of the volumes is structured in order to closely reflect the content of the Syllabus and its order of presentation. Furthermore, they are written in clear, easily accessible language and each includes an explanation of new theological and philosophical perspectives.

The volumes offered in this series are as follows

Patrick M. Devitt:	*Willingly to School: Religious Education as an Examination Subject*
Eoin G. Cassidy:	*The Search for Meaning and Values*
Thomas Norris and Brendan Leahy:	*Christianity: Origins and Contemporary Expressions*
Philip Barnes:	*World Religions*
Patrick Hannon:	*Moral Decision Making*
Sandra Cullen:	*Religion and Gender*
John Murray:	*Issues of Justice and Peace*
Christopher O'Donnell:	*Worship, Prayer and Ritual*
Benedict Hegarty:	*The Bible: Literature and Sacred Text*
John Walsh:	*Religion: The Irish Experience*
Fachtna McCarthy and Joseph McCann:	*Religion and Science*

Thanks are due to the generosity of our contributors who so readily agreed to write a commentary on each of the sections in the new Leaving Certificate Syllabus. Each of them brings to their commentary both academic expertise and a wealth of experience in the teaching of their particular area. In the light of this, one should not underestimate the contribution that they will make to the work of preparing teachers for this challenging project. Thanks are also due to our publishers, Veritas. Their unfailing encouragement and practical support has been of inestimable value to us and has ensured that these volumes saw the light of day. Finally, we hope that you the reader will find each of these commentaries helpful as you negotiate the paths of a new and challenging syllabus.

Eoin G. Cassidy
Patrick M. Devitt
Series Editors

Part One

REFLECTING ON THE CONTEXT

Introduction

Respecting the complexity of the title
At first glance the title appears unproblematic. What could be more straightforward than to explore the contours of the search for meaning and values, a quest with which everyone is familiar? And yet, the very simplicity of the title masks an intuition that is audacious and profound, audacious in the scope of its claims and profound in the consequences of its acceptance. The presumption is that there is meaning and that there are values and that since the beginning of time all of us have engaged in a search for these goals – a quest that transcends all racial, cultural, generational and physical differences. In other words, the presumption is that there is such a thing as a human nature and that this nature is in some way constituted by the search for meaning and values in a way that privileges these goals over any others that one can imagine. Do all human beings search for meaning and values and, even if they do, is there any guarantee that the search will prove any more fruitful than the proverbial quest for the elusive crock of gold? Perhaps the quest for meaning and values is built on a false premise, namely, that there is coherence or an order to the world in which we live. The question as to whether there is a meaning to life and even how one would be able to answer such

a question is something that touches on key philosophical themes. Even more problematical is the question as to whether one can expect answers to these questions to be culturally invariant. If different cultures or even different generations arrive at widely divergent answers to the quest for meaning and value, are these answers all equally valid, and if not, on what basis can one discriminate between them? These questions raise further questions: is there an objective horizon within which all responses to the questions of meaning and values can be adjudged? Is everything purely relative and subjective?

There is another obvious question that is presupposed in the title, namely, why do we engage in this search, and how important is it relative to other quests that one could list, such as the search for good health, prosperity, adventure; the quest for a person with whom one could live happily, or the search for a peaceful and a prosperous life? Is this search just one among many or is it one that in some way defines every person? Clearly, the search for meaning is closely allied to the quest for identity or the search for self-understanding that everyone undertakes at some stage in his or her life. It would seem, at least at first sight, that the quest for values is also about the search for self-identity, one that suggests that there is an ethical core to human nature. If this is correct it would also seem to imply that this ethical realm is something that transcends mere personal preference: values are to be sought after, or searched for, rather than invented.

There is a further presumption about human nature that is in danger of being masked by the unproblematic structure of the title, namely, the restlessness of the human spirit suggested by the motif of searching or questioning. Why are we restless, why do we have to search for self-understanding? What is it about human beings that they have to seek to find or to shape or to create their own identity? Is human identity something that is received by us or created by us, or both? What are the building blocks of personhood? The significance of the search for meaning and values is clearly to be located in the context of this constellation of questions. Now what is particularly interesting is that there is no other species that engages in this type of questioning, no other species that engages in the search for meaning and values. This fact alone raises the most profound questions about what it is to be a human being and whether one can ever satisfactorily accommodate human existence within a purely materialistic world-view.

Finally, there is the presumption in the title that the quest for meaning is in some way related to the quest for values. If this is correct, what does this say about human nature? Clearly, it suggests that the quest for self-understanding cannot be undertaken in isolation from that which probes the extent to which the ethical realm is an intrinsic dimension of human nature. Furthermore, it is not only ethics that is encompassed by this search for meaning and values but also religion. At root, this quest raises precisely those issues that are not only at the heart of all religions but could be said to give rise to the religious impulse that has marked human civilisation since the beginning of time. If the quest is to be successfully pursued, this will only happen by acknowledging a transcendent dimension to human nature: giving recognition to the religious, spiritual and moral dimensions of life that direct human beings to strive for a goal beyond a purely materialist and this-worldly horizon.

The restless heart: the person as a searcher

One of the few things that we all share in common is that we are questioners. None of us can avoid the foundational questions such as why were we born, why will we die, and perhaps most difficult of all, why do we suffer? No young person arrives at adulthood without wondering what it is that makes us attractive to others or what attracts us to others – issues that raise the question as to how one would explain the nature of beauty. Likewise, we all at one stage or another question whether there is any such thing as the good life and wonder how to explain the feeling that one ought to be good. There are theoretical questions such as, is the world intelligible or how does one explain the possibility of science? These related questions give rise to the first of all questions, why is there something rather than nothing? Then there are the more practical questions such as, can one ever be truly happy or wherein lies the path to human happiness? These questions remind us that there is something that all of us desire, i.e. happiness. This issue raises another fundamental question, namely, how do we account for human desire? How do we explain the restless heart – a restlessness that is unique to the human species?

Where would we begin to look in order to find answers to questions that touch upon such diverse issues as the intelligibility of the universe or the elusive quest for happiness? Perhaps there is a prior question, namely, to what extent should we be preoccupied with the concern for answers? While not denying the validity of seeking answers to foundational questions, nevertheless the dimensions of the search for meaning can never be fully grasped if one is solely preoccupied with the quest for answers. Furthermore, to succumb to the temptation to rush headlong into a premature answer is to fail to respect the understanding of the person either as a questioner or as one who is a searcher. This caveat is not meant to deny that, where possible, questions deserve to be answered; it is rather to draw attention to the need to allow questions to interrogate us. The problem about a premature answer is not that it may be wrong, but rather that it does not allow the questioner truly to question or the searcher truly to seek. Neither does it allow us to stand in awe before the majesty of the insight that gives rise to the question or to wonder at the infinite horizon that the question exposes. To question truly is to be attuned to the question or to be in harmony with that which is being questioned. It is to enter into a relationship with that which is questioned. It is only by giving space to awe and wonder that we allow the question to interrogate us and in this manner to open up dimensions of our being that can all too easily remain hidden.

The ability to name human questions and the desire to articulate our own questions is the first step in what is commonly called the search for meaning. The second step is to recognise that the desire to engage in that search for meaning is constitutive of what it is to be a human being. The third step is not to be in too much of a rush to seek to supplant awe and wonder with answers. The fourth and most important step in the search for meaning is the recognition of the transcendent character of foundational questions. Not every question can be posed in the manner of a problem to be solved. What is the answer to the question as to the beauty of a Rembrandt painting or indeed the beauty of an old woman bowed down with age and yet radiant? There is something mysterious – something inexhaustible about these questions, and yet who would deny that they are still worthy of being asked.

In the last analysis, the search for meaning is not one that can be addressed as a problem-solving exercise but rather as one that allows us to enter into relationship with that which is being sought. From a Christian faith perspective the quest for meaning is nothing less than the quest to meet God, and the only path that will provide for the possibility of this relationship is the one that allows space to question and to search. God draws us along that path to him by giving us the priceless gifts of questioning and seeking. Nothing should be done to stunt the growth of these precious gifts. Ultimately, in the context of a Christian faith perspective, we recognise that the only answer to the question of meaning and values is that which is provided by one who is present to us; the presence of one who is not overly concerned with answers, but nevertheless, one who by his very presence responds to our questions in ways that answers could never do. The truth that is often missed is that it is only to the extent that we recognise that someone is present for us that we can glimpse the possibility of meaning.

Religion as a source of meaning
Religion is a source of meaning because it provides a way of addressing such diverse foundational questions as those raised by the facts of life and death or the very existence of the universe. Even more importantly, in terms of the meaning of everyday life, all religions provide a value structure within which the quality of human life or human progress can be measured. Finally, religion acknowledges the validity of the quest for human happiness and all religions attempt to offer a map that traces the path by which happiness can be attained.

Common to all religions is the ritualising of the key moments in the cycle of life. By providing a context within which the rhythms of nature and human life can be celebrated, religion can be a powerful source of meaning. Furthermore, by creating and sustaining sacred symbols, all religions work to highlight a particular sense of time and place that provides an indispensable scaffold for the construction of an ordered life. Most importantly, religious symbolism helps people uncover a sense of the sacred that provides space for reverence, awe, respect and hope.

The question of the meaning of life is bound up with how one perceives one's human identity. All religions provide a sense of personal identity within which human life can be structured. They also provide a social context that allows us to understand ourselves as part of a community with rights and responsibilities to that community and ways of relating to other communities. Obviously it is possible to find alternative ways of shaping one's personal and social identity. However, history suggests that there are few ways that can match religion in catering for this key requirement in the search for meaning.

All religions have in common a concern with foundational issues that define human existence. However, each religion has a particular focus that is unique; and Christianity is no exception. The particular insight that Christianity brings to an understanding of human nature revolves around the mystery of sin and reconciliation. The experience of the need for forgiveness is something that defines human beings in a manner unlike any other experience. Christianity offers a vision of a loving God and more especially, a forgiving God. In this context, the Paschal Mystery is a source of meaning that has few parallels.

To conclude, the importance of facilitating a reflective awareness among young people of the universal character of the search for meaning and values is not something that should be underestimated. It both promotes the personal growth of students, including their spiritual and moral development, and it also encourages students to reflect upon their awareness of themselves as unique individuals with roots in a community network of family, friends and parish. The section of the Leaving Certificate syllabus devoted to exploring this theme provides a broad and inclusive perspective that does justice both to the foundational significance and also to the wide parameters of the search for meaning and values.

I

The Contemporary Context

Introduction

It is a truism to say that no search for meaning and values takes place in a vacuum. Whatever one might say about the universal character of the search for meaning and values, each person undertakes this quest in a particular cultural context and this milieu not only shapes the answers but also shapes the questions that are asked. The first step in uncovering the contemporary context for the search for meaning and values is to be attentive to the importance of culture – that cluster of assumptions, values and ways of life that both create and give expression to the identity of each human community. All questioning takes place in a particular context, but because culture determines what we regard as normal and abnormal, we are, for the most part, unaware of the extent to which our questioning is predetermined.

Educators charged with the responsibility to foster in young people a reflective awareness of the search for meaning and values need to be attentive to the main themes of the contemporary ethos. They need to be cultural meteorologists – proficient readers of the signs of the times; otherwise they risk being blind to the manner in which the contemporary milieu shapes the contours of these fundamental questions. The problem facing educators in reading the signs of the times or spotting the straws in the wind lies precisely in the fact that there is no neutral vantage point from which to survey any culture. We are all creatures of a particular ethos and each one erects a highly selective screen that makes it difficult to see with clarity our own or any other culture. To some extent we are all 'prejudiced' in that we inevitably bring a pre-judgement to bear on any act of cultural analysis. Educators, therefore, need to be people of discernment. This is a task that demands an ability to be sensitive to the cultural presuppositions of the students and an awareness of the presuppositions that we bring to any encounter.

Asking questions in any milieu is difficult, but asking questions in a youth culture is a particularly challenging task. Not only does it demand sensitivity to the cultural parameters within which we question and those within which young people live their lives, but it also requires alertness to the developmental factors that are at work in young people's lives. Each society is composed of a mixture of light and shadow. There are factors in contemporary culture that can block young people's search for meaning and values, but equally young adults have the potential to re-imagine the quest in ways that would have been inconceivable to an earlier generation. Ultimately, the challenge is to strike a balance that neither dismisses nor naively accepts as normative the value system and beliefs of any particular culture. The educator needs to be both a respectful and a critical listener.

The world of classical culture
It is often said that the most enthusiastic disciples of post-modernity are the marketing executives of publishing houses; 'what is new sells' is a good post-modern maxim. Whatever about the truth of that allegation, it reminds us of the need to be wary of uncritically accepting the newest label by which contemporary culture is described. While not denying that

western society is changing and that this is most evident in what might be described as youth culture, nevertheless, it would be foolish to presume that all vestiges of previous culture no longer holds sway with a significant segment of the youth population. Despite the all-pervasive nature of pop culture, all the evidence suggests that the dominant behavioural influence on young people remains the parents or extended family. Furthermore, it must be recognised that cultural change seldom, if ever, happens through a sudden or indeed a complete rejection of all features of the previous ethos. For the most part it occurs incrementally and over an extended period of time. Despite the 'market' driven perceptions of the increasing pace of change in western society, our world-view is to a surprisingly large extent still shaped by ideas and values of the classical world of Judaeo-Christian and Greco-Roman civilisation.

The classical vision of human nature was one that placed emphasis on characteristics of the search for meaning and values that highlight the transcendent and social dimensions of human experience. With few exceptions, the classical world was one that never doubted the existence of a transcendent and objective horizon for the search for meaning. It was also a culture that defined human beings as social beings and would have been convinced that this quest for meaning could only be successfully undertaken by those who accept their status as members of a community and the inheritor of a tradition.

Modernity
Modern culture, or modernity, is an umbrella term for a number of cultural developments that took place primarily in Europe and North America over a period of roughly two hundred and fifty years between the seventeenth and nineteenth centuries. Four of the core themes that have shaped modernity have been <u>secularisation, the acceptance of an individualist anthropology, the emergence of a technological</u>

world-view that accompanied the rise of instrumental rationality to a position of preeminence, and finally, the development of a Liberal culture that flowed from an increasing societal acceptance of liberal democracy.

Secularisation is the process by which culture progressively defines itself in a 'this-worldly' context. Although its origins can be traced to the rise of secular humanism during the Renaissance in the fifteenth and sixteenth centuries, its development is closely associated with the growth of the empirical sciences. With its focus on the material world the secularisation process has given an impetus to the development of science that has brought considerable benefit to humankind. However, from the point of view of human progress every cultural development is a mixed blessing, and the movement to a more secular society is no exception. The 'this-worldly' focus of the secularisation process in western societies has encouraged the belief that the parameters of the search for meaning and values are those defined by a materialist world-view. Furthermore, the secularisation of culture has also been accompanied by the growth of an individualist ethos. Taken to extremes this trend encourages the privatisation of core beliefs and values and the progressive loss of engagement with a social context for the quest for meaning and values. The secularisation of culture has also given impetus to the rise of a belief system entitled secularism, which holds that the progress of civilisation can be measured by the extent to which societies are able to free themselves from all religious/superstitious belief patterns.

An individualist anthropology can be traced back to the early philosophers of the Enlightenment, but its development is for the most part associated with the emergence of a Protestant ethos in the sixteenth and seventeenth centuries. This cultural development is by its very nature anti-authoritarian and its growth has in no small measure led to the acceptance of a human rights culture. Today this individualist ethos has the potential to create an ethical environment that espouses the positive ideal or ethic of authenticity, one that stresses the importance of self-esteem and the need to be responsible. On the negative side, it also has the potential to lose sight of the larger community within which human beings can and ought to live. In extreme forms of individualism, the appropriation of oneself as an individual can be accompanied by a withdrawal from any engagement with the community – a stance that is inimical to all values associated with social solidarity.

The rise of individualism is often linked to that of capitalism. In fact, many would argue that capitalism, as an indicator of a cultural ethos as well as an economic theory, would never have successfully inserted itself into the cultural fabric of contemporary western society if it were not for the rise of an individualist anthropology in the seventeenth and eighteenth centuries. Whatever about the merits of the argument, it is undoubtedly true that capitalism is an individualist doctrine that, in its extreme forms, divides the world into winners and losers. The modern development of a technological view of the world, reflected in the rise of instrumental rationality, can be traced to the industrial revolution and the development of capitalism. In its pragmatic concern with efficiency it has promoted a confident self-mastery over our environment. However, the 'can-do' attitude that is typical of a culture that is shaped by the success of instrumental reason could very easily lead to an over-valuing of the logic of the market place, a consumerist ethos where everything and everybody has an economic price, to the exclusion of all other values. In such a milieu, there is little place for what might be described as virtue ethics; foundational issues of meaning and value tend to be set to one side in favour of more short-term pragmatic concerns.

One of the developments in western society closely associated with the instrumentalist goals of economic effectiveness or personal satisfaction is the emergence of the manager and the therapist as cultural role models. In a managerial ethos the goal of economic effectiveness supersedes ethical considerations. Too tied to the extrinsic utilitarian goal of effectiveness, too tightly dependent on the methodology of cost-benefit analysis, the managerial model is not ideally suited to transcending the narrow boundaries of self-interest. What is not often recognised is that an instrumentalist world is also one that has fostered the emergence of a therapeutic culture. In this milieu people are led to believe that human happiness is achievable without the need to advert to any ethical considerations that might relate the individual to the larger context of their life. Therapy is concerned to assist clients to become well-adjusted persons. That in itself is a most worthy goal. However, in bracketing out consideration of the ethical character of human happiness or the consideration of duties or responsibilities to the wider community, therapy can never embrace the very virtues that alone will promote a well-adjusted personality.

Liberalism emerged at a point in European history that marked the break-up of western Christendom, and with that break-up the loss of a shared understanding of the values, beliefs and practices that define human existence. Five centuries later, the distinguishing feature of a liberal culture continues to be a tolerance of many divergent and in some cases incompatible world-views. From a liberal perspective pluralism is a fact of life, and over the last two hundred years liberal democracy has been developed as a political system that can accommodate pluralism. In this context, a liberal culture may inadvertently encourage the acceptance of a relativist ethos that has little sympathy for either the importance of tradition or the belief in the objectivity of moral values.

In any attempt to summarise a cultural movement as disparate as modernity one runs the risk of neglecting divergent strands or counter-cultural forces at work in that culture. The rise of Marxism is a case in point. Fiercely opposed to both an individualist and a capitalist ethos, its appeal in the early part of the twentieth century testified to the enduring desire for relationships that are based on more than their market value. Although the totalitarian character of the communist regimes corrupted the emancipatory ideals of Karl Marx, nevertheless the desire for social liberation is one that is at the heart of modernity as is evidenced by the French revolutionary ideals of liberty and fraternity. Furthermore, one can point also to another characteristic of Marxism that is not captured in the themes listed above, namely its utopian character. The belief in the progress of history was ingrained into Marxist theory and reflected not only the messianic character of Marxism but also the extraordinary cultural optimism that characterised the culture of modernity. The industrial revolution and the colonial exploits of the European powers gave rise to an unquestioned belief in the onward march of civilisation that only met its nemesis in the trench warfare of the Great War.

Post-modernism

As it has emerged in the latter half of the twentieth century, post-modernism has been marked by a rejection of some of the key themes of modernity and a deepening of others. On the one hand, there is evidence of an increasing acceptance of a pluralist and/or relativist cultural ethos, whereas, on the other hand, there is evidence of a growing reserve with regard to the twin beliefs in history and human progress. Both of these trends are linked to a rejection of the over-exaggerated claims of scientific rationalism that characterised modernity. From another perspective, there is evidence that, despite the pervasive presence of a 'this worldly' secular outlook, a post-modern culture is ill at ease with an exclusively materialist world-view. In the developed world today one witnesses a mushrooming of small communities that stress the importance of attending to the spiritual dimension of the search for meaning. Finally, while there is evidence of a deepening of the individualism that was characteristic of modernity – the emergence of a radical individualism shorn of any contact with institutions and traditions – there is also some evidence of a questioning of this trend, evidence of a yearning for the relational.

Undoubtedly, the most noticeable feature of an emerging post-modern ethos is the de-legitimising of horizons of significance – both the vertical objective framework of meaning and values and the horizontal self-definition constituted by the dialogue with others as a member of a community. With the adoption of this stance post-modernism finds itself in conflict with the classical world-view. Rejecting the classical belief in the existence of a transcendent and objective horizon, truth is proposed as something provisional and contextual; pluralism is absolute and there is a rejection of dogmas, institutions that suggest otherwise. Post-modernism rejects the belief that the quest for meaning can be successfully undertaken only by those who accept their status as members of a community and the inheritors of a tradition. In this context, it can be said to be the bearer of a culture that has both jettisoned tradition and absolutised a subjectivist and/or emotivist standpoint.

Post-modernism and youth culture

In and through its rejection of classical reservoirs of tradition, many would hold that post-modernist cultural developments are lending themselves to the creation of a new youth culture where pluralism is absolute and cultural isolation a fact of life. Those who would embrace this development clearly see it in a different and more positive light, as a culture that for the first time can be truly said to be accepting of plurality, novelty, exciting possibility and play. In this scenario, the fleeting and ever changing horizons that mark post-modernity are perceived as embracing an idea of infinite capacity rather than marking the demise of any belief in an ordered and coherent world. Despite the obvious merit in this argument, there is a case to be made that there is a difference between cherishing the playful side of human nature and embracing play as the primary mode of being or belonging. Furthermore, it could be argued that the contemporary preoccupation with play, as reflected in so-called 'Reality TV', may mask something much more serious. Just as indifference or apathy can be a mask that hides a deep-seated anger, so too the contemporary preoccupation with play may be a protective screen that masks a sense of powerlessness – political powerlessness in the face of the global outreach and power of major multi-nationals. No serious treatment of the contemporary context of cultural change can afford to ignore the influence of these economic realities.

From another perspective, there are those who would argue that contemporary cultural developments are facilitating the creation of an anchorless or rootless generation. From the opposite perspective, those embracing the idea of a post-modern youth culture may not be as ready to accept the idea of disappearing anchor points as the critiques of post-modernism might argue, or at least they might question whether the idea of an anchor is the correct metaphor to describe the idea of a 'rooted' person. Perhaps a more appropriate metaphor is that suggested by the rhizome. From this perspective, it is arguable that youth culture has roots but ones that lie on the surface – roots that spread out and interconnect rather than go deep. Observers of the contemporary context of youth culture will recognise here the signs of the post-modern reinterpretation of the 'rooted' person. However, there is clearly the danger that an unqualified acceptance of this perspective will lead to an ethos marked by the loss of place or history or any sense of cultural memory. It must be remembered that no search for meaning and values can successfully occur in the absence of a sense of the larger picture within which human identity is constructed – one that includes one's history and the community within which one's earliest formative years were lived. To deny one's cultural memory is to discard the furniture of one's identity and to trivialise the significance of the search for meaning and values.

The radical individualism that is characteristic of the postmodern generation has been criticised for contributing to the growth of what has been described as the 'Me' generation, a culture that is perceived to be both egotistical and hedonistic in that it places undue emphasis on the related goals of self-realisation or self-fulfillment. But is this valid? One of the consequences of the growth of an individualistic culture over the past two hundred years is a greatly increased awareness of freedom and responsibility. In this context, the related goals of self-fulfilment and self-realisation cannot necessarily be dismissed as instances of a selfish mindset as they could just as easily be understood in terms of an ethic of personal responsibility. Furthermore, the contemporary importance attached to the need 'to be true to oneself' is an instance of this concern to use freedom in a responsible manner; the ethical ideal that is here espoused is the ideal of authenticity. There are very few young people today who would deny that they have a duty to be authentic, just as there are very few who would not place hypocrisy at or near the top of their list of unethical behaviour.

Unfortunately, an individualist anthropology shorn of any contact either with a community or with an objective horizon of meaning and values has the potential to become enclosed in the pretence of a self-made world. In a world of absolute freedom all choices are valid, but, paradoxically, none is of any value, because there can be no reason for one's choice of one alternative over another other than the mere fact of desiring to so choose. In such a world, where no choice carries any significance, the quest for authenticity risks being trivialised. To be truly true to oneself is to recognise that my identity as an individual is one that has been sculpted by me – but only out of the material that is the history of my dialogue with significant others, namely my family, community and friends. Furthermore, to be truly authentic is possible but only to the extent that one is conscious that there is an ethical ideal worth attending to, namely, one that transcends the parameters of personal preference.

No sketch of post-modernism and youth culture, however brief, could conclude without making reference to the evidence of the dominance of instrumental reason in the post-modernist world. Associated with the rise of a capitalist or consumer ethos, there is little doubt of the all-pervasive presence of this feature in the contemporary world of post-modernity. In fact, all the evidence points to the increasing dominance in western society of what has been described as the culture of the marketplace. It is a virtual reality largely created by the world of advertising and marketing, where the consumer rules and what is real is new. It is an ethos in which youth culture is at home; one that has embraced novelty – makes purchases and forms relationships with careful attention to 'sell by' dates. No serious investigation of the contemporary context of the search for meaning and values can ignore the implications of this phenomenon that makes it increasingly difficult to offer a rationale for commitments or to comprehend the idea of life-long fidelity.

Contemporary expressions of the search for meaning
The challenge of exploring the quest for meaning is one that has shaped artistic creation in the world of music, art, and literature since time immemorial and the study of the history of any of the artistic disciplines offers a privileged point of entry into the manner in which the contours of the quest for meaning have been shaped by successive cultures. Likewise, in search of contemporary expressions of the search for meaning one could hardly do better than to interrogate the contemporary world of artistic creation. There will inevitably be an element of arbitrariness in the choice of such material.

However, in the context of a syllabus geared to leaving certificate students, these choices ought to be guided by the possibilities that it offers for cross-curricular reflection. In what follows, we will briefly reflect on the manner in which a few selected artistic works from the fields of music, art, literature, and youth culture could be profitably introduced to foster an awareness of the scope and significance of the contemporary search for meaning.

Music
As in all forms of artistic creation, the sheer range of compositions makes any set of choices appear arbitrary. For a valuable guide to worthwhile material one could profitably explore the contemporary music centre website, cmc.ie. The following is suggested simply as a guide for reflection:
- *Ultima Rerum*, Gerard Victory
- *The Prayer Cycle*, Jonathan Elias
- *Innocence*, John Tavener
- *The Protecting Veil*, John Tavener
- *A Child of Our Time*, Michael Tippett
- *Requiem*, John Rutter
- *Mass of the Children*, John Rutter
- *Quattuor pour la Fin du Temps*, Olivier Messiaen
- *Fratres*, Arvo Pärt

Art
One could profitably explore the political as well as the artistic masterpiece that is Picasso's *Guernica* – a painting that portrays in stark detail the horror and suffering of war. The searing critique of violence on canvas has seldom if ever been surpassed. As a meditation on suffering its significance transcends the context of the Spanish civil war. It offers an unsurpassable statement of the consequences that flow from a warped sense of the search for meaning that seeks fulfilment in the desire for power. Irish students would benefit from a study

of the permanent collection in the Hugh Lane Gallery of Modern Art in Dublin . I am drawn to highlight the following three works of art:
- *There is no Night* (1949), Jack B. Yeats. The title is adapted from Revelation 22,5, 'And there shall be no night there'. It is the indomitable spirit of the horse that suggests a biblical prophetic image of hope.
- *Isolated Being* (1962), Louis le Brocquy. The inner person is expressed with remarkable sensitivity in this reflection on the loss of connectedness that is such a feature of contemporary life.
- *Drawing from the Tank* (1989), Edward and Nancy Reddin Kienholz. The title of this work of art relates to a young girl from a poverty stricken area of Houston. Part of a larger work that does not shirk from the challenge of political commentary.

Literature
For the majority of students the possibility of learning from cross-curricular reflection will be provided by drawing on texts that feature on the English Leaving Certificate syllabus. Although the content of this syllabus does not and cannot be expected to remain constant, nevertheless there are a significant number of writers and poets whose presence on the syllabus can be fairly guaranteed for the foreseeable future and whose writings offer valuable insights into the scope and significance of the search for meaning. Poems that reflect the bias of this particular author include:
- *A Prayer For My Daughter,* W.B Yeats
- *The Great Hunger,* Patrick Kavanagh
- *By Candlelight,* Sylvia Platt
- *Tell all the Truth but tell it slant,* Emily Dickinson
- *Digging,* Seamus Heaney
- *Hard Berries,* Brian Power

Youth culture

The place where youth culture resides is one named 'now'. There is nothing that is more guaranteed to date a publication than to suggest artistic representations of youth culture, and yet one writes for now and not just for posterity, albeit that it is the now of one's own world that may have little access to that created by today's youth culture. There are many reasons that suggest the importance of the virtue of reticence about attempting to enter into the world of youth culture; however, some conversations can be cross-generational and indeed cross-cultural, and a dialogue surrounding the search for meaning and values is one of those.

A search for meaning that is shaped by the world of adolescence is one of limitless possibilities, hope, joy, and pain, and above all the sense of confusion sometimes expressed as boredom that attends all process of growth. Since music plays such a large role in youth culture, the two suggested resources that could encourage reflectiveness in this area are taken from the artistic world of music. The two groups/individuals chosen are U2 and Eminem.

Apart from articulating issues particular to the world of adolescence, many of the lyrics from U2 give expression to universal themes, such as a yearning to be accepted, a longing for relationships that are not purely instrumental, dissatisfaction with an exclusively materialist world-view, the desire for justice, and the importance which ought to be attached to issues surrounding care for the world. From amongst the prodigious output of U2, I am drawn to highlight the following four pieces:
- *I Still Haven't Found What I'm Looking For* (1987)
- *If God Will Send His Angels* (1997)
- *Last Night On Earth* (1997)
- *One* (1990)

A yearning to be authentic, a desire to test the limits of the possible and an abhorrence of hypocrisy are some of the themes that one finds in the lyrics of the Kansas City born 'Rap' artist, Marshall Mathers, better known as Eminem. There is no doubting his unrivalled ability to write lyrics that penetrate the psyche of the 'post-modern' adolescent, evoking a sense of the cultural reality for young people, albeit the darker side of adolescent life. The poet Seamus Heaney has recognised this ability and in a recent interview said of Eminem, 'He has sent a voltage around a generation. He has done this not just through his subversive attitude but also his verbal energy.' (*Irish Independent*, 1 July 2003). Whether one could recommend any of his songs is, however, debatable because some of his lyrics could be interpreted as condoning behaviour that is unacceptable. Two of the less violent but nonetheless disturbing pieces are:
- *Lose Yourself* (2002)
- *Brain Damage* from *The Slim Shady LP*

The choice of material in this area is inevitably subjective, but other songs that are worth a mention include, *I Say A Little Prayer* by Aretha Franklin, *Smells Like Teen Spirit* by Nirvana, *Independent Women Part 1* by Destiny's Child, *Live Forever* by Oasis and *River Deep Mountain High* by Ike and Tina Turner.

Key questions that emerge in contemporary culture

The goal and purpose of life
The search for meaning is intimately linked to the manner in which one envisages the goal and purpose of life. Anyone concerned with exploring examples of the goal and purpose of life that emerge in contemporary culture could do worse than to begin by reflecting on a question such as 'What do people hope for in life?' For many the short answer to this question would be 'happiness'. If pressed to explain what would make

them happy they might respond by speaking about their hopes for a loving relationship with God or their spouse, a happy family life, a good job, a life free of money problems and a life free of serious illness. Another valuable point of entry into this issue might be a question such as 'What type of person would we like to be?' or 'On whom if anyone would we like to model our lives?' A curriculum vite for such a person might read: 'He/She is a beautiful, good, caring, intelligent, creative and successful person'! Popular role models are those who are perceived to possess some or all of the ideals of beauty, goodness, love, intelligence and creativity, and/or those who would seem to have achieved success that is defined in monetary terms as well as in terms of a loving relationship and/or happy family life. Undoubtedly, contemporary examples of the goal and purpose of life would include such ideals as the attainment of happiness and success, however these might be defined. The list is endless and depends entirely on one's anthropology – one's understanding of human nature. Is the desire for a happy life identical with the desire for a successful life? Not necessarily, in that the former as classically understood places emphasis on the ethical and social dimensions of human nature, whereas the latter is used more to draw attention to the importance of goals of achievement such as work or career. While the adoption of a success-oriented model to depict the goal of life does not necessarily downplay the significance of the ethical character of human nature, nevertheless there is always the danger that, with such a model, the good life will be defined in terms of success rather than that success would be defined in terms that acknowledge the primacy of the ethical.

What is striking about the contemporary culture is the manner in which the terms happiness and success are almost interchangeable. This suggests that, in our contemporary society, the goal of life is increasingly perceived as something that lies within the competence of personal achievement. The alternative suggested by the classical view of happiness is of a goal that is essentially relational and one that is received as a gift within the ambit of love or friendship. It is questionable whether a success-oriented model of the goal of life can do justice to the reality that the goal of life is only achieved to the extent that it is received. What is abundantly clear is that the only adequate model for describing the goal of life is one that can successfully counter that timeless reproach from the author of the book of Ecclesiastes: 'vanity of vanities! All is vanity'. The existential self-doubt that is revealed by the desire for happiness cannot be assuaged by any goal that is dependent upon personal achievement, because all personal achievement can be critiqued by 'so what?' or 'what's the point?' In the last analysis the challenge of the preacher in Ecclesiastes is one that can only be met in response to the question 'does anyone love me?', a context that acknowledges the foundational nature of the desire to love and to be loved. In the light of the challenge posed by the author of Ecclesiastes one can appreciate the approach taken by a belief system such as Christianity, one that holds fast to the viewpoint that the goal of life is only achieved to the extent that one receives the gift of love or grace.

The meaning of good and evil
The search for meaning and values suggests that the ethical dimension of human existence is something that cannot be ignored. Thus, there are few who would deny the truth of the maxim that 'good should be done and evil avoided'. Unfortunately, there is no such consensus on what constitutes good and evil, although from a religious perspective the meaning of good and evil is understood in the context of the believer's relationship with God: a good act is one that is in conformity with God's law. Thus, the commandments to love God and love thy neighbour shape the Christian understanding of good and evil. From a Jewish perspective the meaning of good and evil is determined by the law as set out in the Torah;

similarly, from an Islamic perspective the Qur'an provides Muslims with a precise understanding of the nature of good and evil.

Prescinding from a religious faith perspective, how can one understand the meaning of good and evil? One of the most celebrated attempts to address this issue was the Natural Law theory as proposed by the thirteenth-century philosopher Thomas Aquinas. From this perspective, a good act is defined as that which is in accord with human nature or that which promotes the attainment of the goal or purpose of human nature. It is arguable as to whether there has ever been a more insightful description of the meaning of good and evil. However, the problem with the theory is that there is no consensus as to what constitutes human nature. In the light of this reality two very different theories emerged in the seventeenth and eighteenth centuries, one of which placed emphasis on the consequences of an action and the other on the intention of the action. Moralists of a Utilitarian persuasion affirm that it is the consequences of an action that determine its goodness; whereas Deontologists, including many human rights theorists, believe that to determine the ethical character of an action emphasis should be placed on the intention that motivated the action.

Up until the advent of modernity it was generally accepted that the meaning of good and evil was objectively determined, something that could be discovered by paying careful attention to first principles. Increasingly, this view has been called into question as a more subject-centered world-view, with an emphasis on human freedom, has attained greater credence, a world-view that increasingly supports a subjectivist and/or relativist ethos. In such a milieu there are some who adopt an emotivist ethical stance, one that distinguishes between the rightness and wrongness of an action on the basis of what might be described as a 'feel good' factor. To what extent emotivism is characteristic of the contemporary cultural ethos is a matter for debate but there is no doubting the manner in which the primacy of the human subject is accepted over and against any objective horizon of meaning. In this context, the meaning of good and evil is defined in the light of the opposing ideals of sincerity and hypocrisy. A good life is an authentic life – one that is marked by sincerity, the acceptance of personal freedom and the need to live in the light of, and in conformity with, one's fundamental choices.

Apart from Natural Law theory, one of the major contemporary counterbalances to emotivism comes from the increasing acceptance today of a human rights perspective. Appealing to a concept of the inalienable dignity of each individual, both the idea and the understanding of what constitutes human rights emerged largely from a Judaeo-Christian understanding of the person. One of the most celebrated appeals to human rights is to be found in the American constitution, but its widespread acceptance cannot be said to predate the 1948 UN declaration of human rights. Unlike all forms of emotivism, a human rights perspective acknowledges the existence of an objective standard by which good and evil can be assessed, i.e. one that is shaped by an acceptance of the inalienable dignity of each individual.

The experience of suffering
As has been stressed above, no search for meaning takes place in a vacuum, each person's search takes place in the context of an engagement with the prevailing culture. However, it must be acknowledged that, although culture exercises an influence on the manner in which the quest is perceived, there are other factors such as family, social status and, most importantly, health, that both influence the manner in which the prevailing culture is received and in no small manner determine how the search for meaning is pursued.

The reference to health reminds one that it is almost impossible to underestimate the manner in which the experience of suffering shapes the contours of the search for meaning. Indeed, in some cases the experience of suffering can effectively block all attempts to seek any meaning in life. Furthermore, many would argue that in the absence of some way of addressing the meaning of suffering it is not possible to accept that we live in a rational world. From the perspective of a belief in a loving God who is the creator of the world, this is a challenge that is particularly acutely felt. In short, how is it possible to reconcile belief in an omnipotent and loving God with the experience of suffering?

In order to come to some tentative understanding of the experience of suffering, and to address these and other related questions, it is necessary to make a distinction between what might be described as existential or natural evil and that described as moral evil. The former draws attention to suffering that is not directly due to the actions of human beings, the latter pinpointing suffering that owes its origin to the misuse of human freedom. Examples of the former might include suffering that is the result of natural disasters or illnesses whose cause cannot be laid at the door of human negligence. Examples of the latter include the suffering caused by the multitude of crimes that scar the human landscape. The challenges posed to a theistic world-view by these two examples of evil are quite different.

It could be argued that suffering caused by events such as natural disasters ought to be addressed in the context of an evolutionary vision of creation that situates such events in the context of a world that is growing towards perfection. Such a perspective has the added merit of envisaging human beings as co-creators rather than spectators of an already finished project. This viewpoint also has the potential to give recognition to the responsibility that human beings have to care for the natural environment. Much of the suffering caused by so-called natural disasters undoubtedly carries a human imprint. This line of reasoning can be extended to include some but not all of the illnesses that are the cause of so much of the suffering in the world. However, at some point one is faced with the inescapable reality of the incurable illnesses that lay waste the lives of so many young children. The issue is not that of the existence of incurable illnesses because the effect of these illnesses on the lives of the very old is not necessarily perceived as evil in the same sense as when the very young suffer. One might even suggest that these illnesses had merely contributed to bringing the lives of the very old to their natural end. Rather, the issue is that the death of a young child is perceived as unfair in a manner that is not applicable to one who is very old. There are no easy answers to questions surrounding the suffering and/or death of the young and to pretend otherwise would be to do an injustice to the seriousness of the issue. However, it is a reminder of the folly of too closely identifying the quality of a life with its length. One should never presume that the short life of a child is of any less value than that of the person who has lived a long life. From a theistic, and in particular, from a Christian perspective, the life of every human being is held to be of equal value.

The issue of what has been described as moral evil poses a different but equally daunting challenge to the coherence of a theistic, and in particular, a Christian perspective. The challenge is often posed in the following manner, namely, how could a loving God who is all-powerful permit the mass murder of innocent people? In this case one is brought face to face with the issue of human freedom. How could God create people who both desire and are free to commit such unspeakable crimes? The short answer is that a creature that is not free is also one that is not capable of love and the greatest privilege of human nature is the ability to love. The paradox is that freedom is often perceived as both a curse and a blessing. However, it is more correct to say that freedom is a blessing; its misuse is a curse. Just as with the issue of existential or natural evil the challenge posed to a theistic world-view by the existence of moral evil is not one that can easily be surmounted. In the last analysis, if one were to argue from a Christian point of view all that one can point to is the figure of Christ on the cross, a reminder that the Christian God is one who is not only not indifferent to human suffering but is one who knows at first hand what it is to experience suffering as an innocent victim. In this context, Christians can with reason argue that the God in which they believe is closest to innocent people who are the victims of crimes against humanity.

Hindering the search for meaning and values

Questions that touch on human meaning are those that raise issues of the most profound anthropological import. Ultimately, the question of the cultural factors in contemporary society that can block the search for meaning and values is one that cannot be addressed outside of a consideration of the larger question that inquires into who we are as human beings. Traditionally, philosophers have highlighted the love of beauty, truth, goodness and love as those that provide parameters for understanding human nature. Furthermore, all with few exceptions have stressed the social nature of human beings, that happiness will not be achieved outside of a community setting or in the absence of friends.

In more recent times there has been a renewed stress on the importance of the related themes of individuality, freedom and creativity. Furthermore, the emergence of a more instrumentalist culture has given rise to the view that success, measured in material or monetary terms, is the key that will open the door to a happy life or at least that, in the absence of this measure of success, happiness cannot be attained. The secularisation of culture that is also suggested in this redefinition of happiness is a process that is assisted by the fact that people in the 'developed' world can confidently expect to live longer and experience less poverty than would have been conceivable as recently as one generation ago. However, redefining happiness in these more short-term and pragmatic, secular and materialist categories can block the search for meaning and values or at least reshape it in a manner that illegitimately foreshortens the dimensions of the quest. The assumption that the answer to the search for meaning and values is to be found in the attainment of a high material standard of living or some such marker of success leaves little room for either a relational, spiritual or an ethical dimension to human happiness.

Two of the great achievements of modernity were the cultural acceptance of the person as an individual and the acceptance of the value of instrumental reasoning. The former would give rise to an era that would be marked by a renewed appreciation of the possibilities of human freedom and creativity as well as the development of a human rights culture. The latter would herald an era of unparalleled prosperity as the power of instrumental reason was put at the service of the technological mastery of the universe. However, as with all cultural developments, if taken to extremes both of these developments can have serious negative consequences for society. As the contours of a post-modern world crystallise it is becoming increasingly evident that we are witnessing a significant radicalisation of both individualism and instrumentalism without the counter-balancing influence of either tradition or the community. This is leading to the growth of an individualism shorn of all contact with family or community and the increasing dominance of the instrumentalism of the marketplace in setting the parameters within which all relationships are assessed.

Both of these emerging influences on the shape of contemporary society have the potential to block the search for meaning and values because they deny two key premises upon which this quest is based. Radical individualism denies the horizon of meaning that is framed by one's membership of a community, whether that be constituted by the bonds that link one to one's family, society or religious community/Church. The instrumentalism of the marketplace denies the existence of any objective values other than commercial effectiveness that can be brought to bear on any evaluation of the good or indeed the happy life. In such a milieu the search for meaning and values can appear as an esoteric pursuit that fails to comprehend that the answer to this quest is before our very eyes, namely material prosperity.

The relatively recent emergence in the 'developed' world of the phenomenon of religious indifference is symptomatic of this changed cultural environment. Extreme individualism allied to an instrumentalist culture inevitably leads to the loss of anchor points, both horizontal and vertical. Affiliation to either Christianity or any of the other major world religions cannot be sustained in the absence of the horizontal bonds that link us to significant others such as family, neighbours, friends, community and society and the vertical bonds that link us to the Good or God.

Religious affiliation and people's sense of identification with either the local or institutional church has always been closely bound up with the role of the Church as an important symbol of the community. In an individualist culture, particularly an urban culture, in which a traditional form of community such as the parish is no longer perceived to nurture personal identity, the significance of the presence of the church is less obvious. Religious belief is also linked to a sense that there is an objective horizon of meaning and values within which human life can and ought to be lived. In the context of the emergence of an increasingly subjectivist and instrumentalist ethos, marked by the failure to appreciate the need to attend to any horizon of meaning and values that transcends pure personal preference, the relevance or even the appropriateness of religious belief is at best questionable.

Contemporary expressions of indifference to the search for meaning

Indifference to any search for meaning, including religious indifference, is a complex attitude that may take different forms. As discussed above, there is increasing evidence of the growing influence in contemporary culture of instrumental reasoning – that consumerist type of reasoning that promotes the 'logic of the marketplace', where everything and everybody has a price and a shelf life. Such an ethos marginalises the type of values that are to be found in a virtue ethics; foundational issues of meaning and value tend to be set to one side in favour of more short-term pragmatic concerns. Obviously, this cultural ethos can contribute to a climate of indifference. In this scenario, a belief system such as Christianity would be treated very much in the same way that one would treat a shelf of goods in a supermarket. It is not a cultural ethos that leaves much room for an appreciation of the value of the ideal of an unconditional commitment to the person of Christ or indeed anybody else.

From another perspective, namely the ideology of secularism, there are those who would be indifferent to religion but not necessarily indifferent to secular values such as honesty, truthfulness, social justice, etc. Repudiating any reference to the sacred either as a result of a belief in the self-sufficiency of science and technology or as a result of the perceived ineffectiveness of religion when faced with social, economic and political evils, this form of indifference reflects the viewpoint that religion is literally irrelevant to life. This secularist opinion is accentuated in an increasingly individualistic environment that seeks to privatise religious beliefs and that has lost any sense of the importance of the social role of the Church as a builder or sustainer of community values.

Finally, there are those who are indifferent to all values and beliefs. This expression of indifference can be a mask that hides anger and/or a deeply pessimistic attitude to life – an experience of emptiness or the failure to find any meaning in life. It may have its origins in the experience of illness, loneliness, unemployment or the experience of rejection in a relationship. Expressing itself in phrases such as 'so what' or 'it does not matter', it proclaims not just that there is nothing to believe in, but no one to believe. This form of indifference could reflect the sense of rootlessness in a culture that is increasingly marked by the loss of essential social/community contexts within which lives can and must be anchored.

2

The Tradition of the Search

The nature and purpose of philosophy
Human beings are motivated by an innate sense of wonder, a yearning to grasp the 'how' of an experience and a desire to know the reason why. The nature and purpose of philosophy is to reflect on this reality, giving recognition to the viewpoint that what is unique to the human species is the search for wisdom, a quest that defines the human species in a manner that distinguishes it from all other species. In this light, one way of understanding the history of philosophy is to see it as the record of human beings' search for wisdom as the foundational questions of meaning and value are re-shaped by each successive generation.

Aristotle believed that all human beings by nature share a desire to know and that the most noble of all human activities is the pursuit of learning. Thus philosophy has its origin in a sense of wonder – the passionate desire to uncover the secrets of the universe. What distinguishes philosophy, however, is the belief that it is possible to attain this goal by the unaided use of reason. The birth of philosophy in the Greek city of Miletus in 585 BCE is attributed to a critical breakthrough in the development of human self-consciousness that heralded a belief in reason – a movement away from the world of mythic culture to one that is founded on the power of logic. Not only did they believe that there was coherence to reality, but they also believed that reality is intelligible, that it is accessible to reason. In short, their philosophical speculations were based on the belief in a law-governed universe rather than one that is lawless, random and irrational.

Writing over two and a half thousand years after the birth of philosophy it is hard to grasp the significance of this breakthrough, but it was one that not only gave birth to philosophy, but also made possible the development of science. Prompted by this desire to know and by the refusal to accept either that the universe is absurd or that its laws are inaccessible to human reason, scientists in all ages have given expression to this human impulse. In their struggle to unlock the secrets of the universe they offer eloquent testimony to the intuition that the universe which we inhabit is intelligible, a stance that is framed by the rejection of both nihilism and scepticism. In opposition to the claims of nihilism, science rests upon the belief that the universe is ordered; in contrast to the claims of scepticism science rests upon the conviction that these laws are accessible to human reason and that scientific experimentation is capable of uncovering the complex matrix of laws that govern the universe. If this two-fold intuition of an ordered and intelligible universe is the bedrock upon which science is based, the dialogue that takes as its focus the acceptance or rejection of either nihilism or scepticism is the special concern of philosophy. The task of philosophy is to enquire as to whether the universe is law-governed, and if so, whether the human mind is capable of penetrating the shroud that veils these laws. It is philosophy, or more precisely, that branch of philosophy aptly called metaphysics (meta-physics) which takes as its remit this study of the very possibility of science.

The role of philosophy is to inquire into the nature of the universe, to seek to uncover the laws that govern the world and to seek answers to the foundational questions that define human existence. Philosophy is thus all-embracing in its scope and this is reflected in the classical divisions into which it has traditionally been divided. Metaphysics inquires into the nature of Being or that which exists. Epistemology is the study of knowledge and reflects on questions such as 'how do we know?' and 'what are the limits of human knowledge?' Anthropology or philosophical psychology examines foundational questions surrounding human nature such as 'what is a person?' 'are human beings free?' and even 'is there such a thing as human nature?' That branch of philosophy called ethics continues the focus on human nature by reflecting on the nature of good and evil and what it is to be an ethical person. Core questions would include, 'is there such a thing as the good life?' and if so, 'what is it?' and 'how can we know it?' Political philosophy takes as its starting point the social character of human living and reflects on key issues surrounding the nature and purpose of a political community. Finally, there is that discipline that carries the name that is almost synonymous with philosophy, namely, logic. This branch of philosophy takes as its focus the structure of rationality and seeks to uncover the basis upon which rational discourse is possible.

The development of philosophy in ancient Greece

The most valuable entry point into the world of ancient Greek philosophy is to reflect upon the extraordinary beginnings of philosophy in that small geographical region in the eastern Mediterranean that lies between Ionia on the western seaboard of present day Turkey and the small communities that populated southern Italy and Sicily. As mentioned above, in the sixth century BCE the Greek culture of that area gave rise to a breakthrough in civilisation that has few if any parallels. The idea that the universe is open to rational rather than mythological explanation is what marks the early Greek thinkers as being truly epochal. Reflecting on the world around them, the earliest philosophers raised the question as to the ultimate nature of things, looking for a unifying principle or element in the midst of diversity. In seeking this unifying principle, these earliest Pre-Socratics focused upon material elements such as water, air and fire. The first philosopher of whom we are acquainted is Thales. He believed that the origin of all things was water; something not so extraordinary when one adverts to the importance of water as a source of life and growth. Another of these earliest philosophers from Miletus was Anaximenes. Possibly reflecting on the origin of rain, he proposed air rather than water as the basis of creation. Philosophising at a more abstract level, later Pre-Socratic philosophers reflected on the ultimate principles underlying reality such as 'being' and 'becoming'. One of the most famous of these philosophers Heraclitus argued that everything is in flux; that nothing is stable but that everything is in process. The phrase attributed to him is 'everything flows' (*panta rhei*), and his most famous argument for this position is that it is not possible to step into the same river twice. Another of these philosophers, Parmenides, disagreed with Heraclitus' views. Noticing that at any one moment something either is or it is not, he argued that an intermediate state such as 'becoming' or movement is an illusion. On a related issue philosophers differed as to whether the cosmos was ultimately harmonious or strife-torn. Heraclitus argued that strife or the conflict between opposites is the motor that generates change and suggested the motif of fire as an appropriate symbol for the unity of the cosmos. Taking a very different approach, the philosopher Pythagoras argued that there is a harmony underlying all that exists. As a rationale for his position he pointed to the aesthetic beauty and harmony that underlies both mathematics and music.

    Whatever one's views about the logical quality of the Pre-Socratic arguments it would be ungenerous not to acknowledge the contribution that they made to the search for meaning. Their love of wisdom was born of astonishment at or before being, and as the philosopher Heidegger correctly observed, the font of genuine thought is astonishment before the mystery of being and its unfolding is that careful translation of astonishment into action which is questioning. It could be argued that our contemporary problem-solving culture is one that is marked by the loss of astonishment and therefore of the loss of an ability to genuinely question. If this is correct, we have much to learn from these earliest philosophers.

The Sophists
In the confident belief in the power of the human mind to unlock the secrets of the universe, the ancient Greek culture of the sixth century BCE can truly be said to be the birthplace of European civilisation. The following century saw the rise of Athens to become the undisputed centre of Greek culture. In the latter part of the fifth century BCE there appeared in Athens a class of thinkers (Sophists) who found employment as itinerant teachers. Among the practical arts that the Sophists taught, the most important was rhetoric – the art of persuasion. Their influence on early classical education was significant although not universally perceived to be beneficial. Some of their oft-quoted comments on the nature of morality and the best way for a city to be governed include: 'Man is the measure of all things' (Protagoras), and 'justice is simply the interest of the stronger' (Thrasymachus). These viewpoints would seem to offer grounds for the accusation that the Sophists favoured a society that would be prepared to sacrifice all commitment to truth, goodness and justice on the altar of moral relativism and political expediency. Whatever the truth of this criticism, there is no doubting the seriousness of the struggle between the Sophists and their most implacable opponent, Socrates who was arguably the most famous of all the classical Greek philosophers.

Each of these philosophers is grappling with issues that are part of universal human experience. One could argue that in the Socratic dialogues such as the *Gorgias* (treated in some detail below) we witness a struggle between two diametrically opposed ways of viewing the world that is played out daily on our contemporary world stage. Against the Sophists, Socrates argues that: (i) it is better to suffer evil than to inflict evil, (ii) justice cannot be regarded as the set of rules laid down by the strong on the principle that might is right, (iii) we are obliged to seek the truth rather than simply to persuade others that our views are true, and (iv) the good life is not identical with pleasure. In all cases, Socrates, in opposition to the Sophists, argued for the objectivity of values such as justice, goodness and truth. Furthermore, he believed passionately that the human person is both capable of discerning the true nature of these values and is obliged to adhere to them. The alternative as he saw it is a type of moral anarchy that enshrines the power principle that only the fittest survive. Today, we can without too much difficulty see that this debate is just as relevant as society seeks to challenge the presumptions of the subjectivist standpoints of both emotivism and power politics.

Socrates (470–399 BCE)
Philosophising in Athens in the second half of the fifth century BCE, Socrates was the first of the great Greek philosophers and unquestionably one of the most influential philosophers of all time. His philosophical contribution to ethical reasoning has few parallels in the history of philosophy and is only matched by his life commitment to these ideals that was to result in his death. He was also a peerless exponent of the art of dialogical reasoning and the teacher and mentor of Plato.

Remarkably, for a philosopher of such eminence, Socrates left us no written record of his philosophy and we are dependent upon the early dialogues of Plato to give us a sense of the richness of his philosophical discourse. We are also indebted to Plato for our knowledge of the life and death of Socrates, a death that was to become immortalised in a dialogue entitled the *Crito*. Socrates' death arose directly as a result of the challenge that his ethical philosophy posed to the newly established democracy in Athens. Accused falsely of introducing new gods and corrupting the youth, Socrates was found guilty by an Athenian court and sentenced to death. He could have saved his life by appealing for leniency and agreeing to go into exile or by escaping from prison but his conscience would not allow him to follow this course of action. In a memorable line that addresses the purpose of life, Socrates says, 'the really important thing is not to live but to live well' (48b)[1]. What he means by living well is to live honourably or rightly even if it means accepting the inevitability of death. In another passage (48e-50a) Socrates argues that it is not permissible to do wrong, i.e. to escape from prison, no matter what the circumstances, even if one has been wronged oneself. In this instance, Socrates offers a spirited defence of the state and the duty of citizens to obey its laws. As he says (50b-51c), a city cannot continue to exist if the legal judgments which are pronounced in it are nullified by private citizens.

Arguably the most famous of all the Socratic dialogues is the *Gorgias*. In this dialogue one comes face to face with the core ethical teaching of Socrates. As Socrates himself said of this dialogue,

> The subject we are discussing is one which cannot fail to engage the earnest attention even of someone of small intelligence; it is nothing less than how one should live. (Gorgias, 500c)[2]

The background to the dialogue is Socrates' criticism of the high value placed on the art of rhetoric or the skills of persuasion by those aspiring to public office at the expense of a commitment to truth. The dialogue sees Socrates in conversation with three of the most well known Sophists or teachers of rhetoric in Athens: Gorgias, Polus and Callicles. The question being discussed is who gives the greater service to both the individual and the state, is it philosophy or sophistry/rhetoric? The former teaches the truth, the latter how to persuade. The dialogue is divided into three parts. Each represents a more intensified statement of the argument. In the last and most extreme of the three, Callicles attacks conventional morality completely and claims that the courageous and intelligent person will devote himself to the ruthless pursuit of pleasure.

The dialogue opens with a spirited defence of the art of rhetoric or persuasion as the most noble of all the arts 'which confers on every one who possesses it not only freedom for himself but also the power of ruling his fellow-countrymen. (452e). In a sharp riposte to the argument of Gorgias, Socrates compares rhetoric to fancy cookery and cosmetics – forms of flattery, which in contrast to physical training and medicine, aim to please the customer rather than giving them what is really good for them. In a remark that foreshadows Socrates' own trial, he conjures up the image of a doctor being prosecuted by a confectioner before a jury of children (464e). Socrates' reasoning here is that there is a gap between what pleases us and what is actually good for us: food can appeal to people's taste or 'fantasies' because the manufacturer ran a clever advertising campaign, but the food could actually be bad for us. The mere fact that it appeals to our fantasies does not give us a proper reason to think that it is 'good'. The problem comes when we fail to see this distinction, and think that what merely pleases us is also what is good for us. Socrates is convinced that this is precisely what is happening with orators. Just because we are pleased by their way of speaking, so we are persuaded by their speeches about subjects such as justice and injustice.

In his conversation with Polus, Socrates puts forward the view that the orator/rhetorician is more to be pitied than envied because the one who does not will the good has no real power. Polus disagrees, and boasts that orators have the power in society to wield tremendous influence: they can have people put in prison, have their property confiscated, and even have them put to death (466c). Socrates wonders why we might want to exercise this ability. Power for its own sake is not a legitimate goal. Polus is incredulous that Socrates would not envy a person with such power. Here Socrates replies that he definitely does not envy people who have other people put to death, and if they do it unjustly they are miserable and are to be pitied. He concludes with the memorable response that, 'it is better to suffer wrong than to do wrong' (469d). This is the idea that virtue is necessary and sufficient for happiness. It means that you cannot be happy without being virtuous, and if you are virtuous you are bound to be happy. This does not mean that other things besides virtue, e.g. physical health or wealth, have no contribution to make to a happy life, but it does mean that, on their own, such things cannot transform an unhappy person into a happy person; conversely, taking away riches or health cannot make a happy person unhappy. Polus regards this as nonsense because it would imply that the man who expires among torturers is happier than the successful tyrant. Nevertheless, Socrates pursues his line of thought and argues that happiest of all is he who is just; happy in the second degree is he who is delivered from injustice by punishment and the most deluded and unhappiest of all is he who lives on, enjoying the fruit of his crimes (478d-478e).

In the final section of the dialogue we see an application of these moral principles to a theory of statesmanship and government. The new speaker is Callicles who was a prominent figure in Athenian public life. The section commences with Callicles asking in amazement if Socrates is really serious, because if what he says is true the whole world order would be turned upside down. To make his point he introduces a distinction between nature and convention, saying that

Socrates who pretends to be engaged in the pursuit of truth is in fact only articulating convention – that set of laws that has been devised by the weak to protect themselves from the strong, and what we call justice or the desire for equality has no basis in the natural order (483-484). According to the laws of nature 'the better man should prevail over the worse and stronger over the weaker – right consists in the superior ruling over the inferior and having the upper hand' (483d). He concludes by referring approvingly to what he regards as the Greek poet Pindar's view that in the natural order 'might is right' (484a). For Callicles, the worthwhile life is about excelling at no matter what cost to others; the law of nature admires, above all else, strength, courage and power. It is a philosophy that reminds us that empires were not founded on humility and that history remembers the winners not the losers, the victors not the vanquished.

In a further development of his doctrine of the natural order, Callicles reasserts his opinion that the esteem in which virtue and justice are held can be explained by the efforts of the weak to conceal their weakness. The thesis of Callicles, and indeed all moralists who follow Nietzsche's theory of the will to power, is that the truly virtuous life consists in pleasure and passion and no one who has the power to enjoy himself/herself practises self-control. He concludes with the following ringing endorsement of his position:

> Luxury and excess and licence, provided that they can obtain sufficient backing, are virtue and happiness; all the rest is mere flummery, unnatural conventions of society, worthless cant. (*Gorgias*, 492b)

As the recapitulation of the debate at the end of the dialogue makes clear, the argument of Socrates against Callicles focuses on a discussion of the question of what should people aim for in life, i.e. pleasure or goodness (506d-507a), an argument whose contemporary relevance is not difficult to discern. However, to engage in this discussion he has to first successfully challenge the presumption of Callicles that the pleasurable life is identical with the good life and that the subjective standard of pleasure is the barometer by which we measure the Good. Socrates engages in a complex series of arguments to challenge this presumption, one of which is to point out that, unlike goodness, the desire for pleasure is never ending. He comments that the intemperate person is like a vessel full of holes because passions and pleasures can never be satisfied (493d-494b). Once this position has been secured, Socrates addresses the core question as to whether the good should be sought for the sake of a pleasurable life or whether pleasure is to be sought after for the sake of the good life. He argues for the latter on the basis that only the search for the Good can justify human striving (499a-500a). It is this conviction that established the bedrock on which the classical view of morality would be constructed.

Having established that the subjective standard of personal pleasure cannot function as the measure of the good life, Socrates proposes an alternative objective standard based on the concept of order. His key point is that order is good and disorder evil, and that health in any organism reflects the existence of order or harmony among the parts. In this vein, Socrates defines temperance and justice in terms of order and argues, in contrast to Callicles, that lives that are lived to excess are thus disordered and sick. In his opinion, intemperate people can neither be friends of themselves, others or God because they are at war with themselves, others and God (508a). Socrates condemns injustice because it destroys the order and harmony that constitutes both the soul of the individual and the soul of the state. But in a reprise of an earlier discussion, he comments that it is an even greater evil not to be punished for doing an injustice because punishment at least helps to restore the balance, order and harmony of the relationships that have been sundered. In this sense, Socrates can truly maintain that it is better to suffer injustice than to inflict it even if this means one's own death. This dialogue comes to a conclusion with a reflection on the fact that worse things could befall a person than to die in the cause of righteousness:

> Renouncing the honours at which the world aims, I desire only to know the truth and to live as well as I can and when I die, to die as well as I can. (*Gorgias*, 526e)

By any standards the *Gorgias* is a masterful dialogue, but in terms of the questions that it poses for our contemporary culture it is peerless. It is hard to believe that it was written almost two and a half thousand years ago, something that reflects the timelessness of core issues that define human existence. For Socrates, how we live is the crucial question, the big issue behind all his philosophy. He was convinced that we should not just live according to appetite, pleasure, appearance or 'mere persuasion' because we have reason, a rational capacity that allows us to discern essences and to define the nature of concepts such as truth, goodness and justice. It is this rational capacity to discern the essence of things which makes us human and should set the standards for us rather than an over-reliance on appearance. Accordingly, we should try to live by the dictates of reason, a doctrine that leads to very different conclusions than that which presumes that 'better' is a mere synonym of 'stronger' and 'worse' of 'weaker'.

It is this vision that marked Socrates' conception of the moral good and the purpose of life. As he said himself, the purpose of life is not just to live but to live well – to live in accordance with reason. From this perspective, to live a good life is to live an ordered life, one that is marked by temperance or moderation – the Greek word here is *sophrosyne*. It is a vision of life that is in sharp contrast to the consumerist ethos of contemporary culture. Similarly, for Socrates, the moral good is not only objective but is both capable of rational discernment and universally binding. Again one is conscious of the contrast with an increasing tendency in our contemporary western culture to define the good in terms of a subjective standard such as pleasure. Paradoxically, it is precisely these contrasts that point to the importance of a philosopher such as Socrates in any attempt to clarify today the nature of the quest for meaning and values.

Plato (428-347 BCE)
Classical Greek philosophy emerged, so to speak, on the coat tails of the intuition that the universe is ordered and that this order is accessible to human reason. What core experiences need to be satisfactorily addressed if this intuition is to be sustained? Two come readily to mind: (i) the experience of movement, change and becoming, coupled with the desire for permanence, and (ii) the experience of diversity and individuality, coupled with the desire for unity. No one who is sensitive to the universal experience of birth, growth, decay and death allied to the desire for permanence or immortality can be unaware of the significance of this first issue. Similarly, no one who is sensitive to the unity of the cosmos and the interrelatedness of all species, and is yet aware of the desire to affirm the uniqueness of each individual species and each individual in a species, can be unaware of the significance of this latter issue.

What is truly remarkable about the earliest Pre-Socratic philosophers is that it was precisely these two issues, (i) the relation between Being and Becoming and (ii) that between the One and the Many, which would provide the focus of their speculations. These issues would in turn provide a key focus for classical Greek philosophy. These philosophers recognised the importance of the issues raised by the universal impulse to change or to become and the relation of Being to beings or the One to the Many. If one cannot satisfactorily address the dialectic created by change and permanence as well as identity and difference, there is little possibility of confirming the intuition that gave rise to philosophy, namely, that the universe that we inhabit is both ordered and intelligible to human reason. For Plato and the later Neo-Platonist tradition this intelligible context is provided by his theory of ideas/forms that gives prominence to the idea of the 'Good'. In Plato's celebrated simile of the sun in a dialogue entitled the *Republic*, the 'Good' is proposed as the origin of existence and the goal for which all beings strive. According to the Neo-Platonism of Plotinus, the 'Good' or the 'One' is the source from which multiplicity flows by necessity like light from the sun or heat from a fire.

Born into an old Athenian family, Plato is regarded as one of the greatest teachers of philosophy of all time. The dialogical method that he used is justly celebrated, and the school of philosophy that he founded called the Academy had a reputation that was unrivaled in the world of classical culture. Plato's philosophical output was prodigious and we are very fortunate that we possess intact his whole corpus, a total of thirty-six dialogues. Profoundly influenced by his teacher and mentor Socrates – Plato was twenty-nine years old when Socrates died from the hemlock poison – many of Plato's dialogues are written as a record of the ethical ideals for which Socrates lived and died. The influence of Socrates on Plato is most evident in the most famous of all Plato's dialogues entitled the *Republic* where he argues that the health of the state is crucially dependent on its being governed by those who love wisdom; those whose lives are lived in the light of the Good rather than by those whose lives are blinded by their own illusions.

Nowhere is the distinction between reality and illusion better expressed than in a small section from book seven of the *Republic* where Plato introduces the allegory of the cave (*Republic*, 514a-519c). The allegory is situated in the context of the task of education, pointing out the nature of the challenge that awaits all those who seek to model their lives in the light of the Good. It begins with a description of a cave that is inhabited by prisoners. From their earliest childhood they have been in chains facing a wall with their backs to the entrance. Behind them is a fire and between them and the fire is a screen that displays puppet-like figures. All that those in chains can see are the shadows of these puppet-like figures that the light of the fire throws on to the back wall. To them, the shadows are real; for them, truth is the shadows of the figures – the only reality of which they are aware. What happens if one of the prisoners is released from his chains and forced to turn towards the fire? He will be distressed by the glare of the light and perplexed because he will think that the shadows, which he formerly saw, are more real than the objects that are now shown to him. Suppose once more that he is dragged up to the entrance of the cave. He is likely to be irritated and he will have to grow accustomed to the light of the sun. Gradually he will begin to see the real world and to recognise the world in the cave for what it is – a world made up of shadows. Finally, out of pity for his former friends, he will return to the cave to enlighten them. However, they will not welcome his visit and he will be received with hostility as someone who threatens their world-view. Furthermore, any attempt to release them and to lead them up to the light will likely meet with violent opposition that could end with his death.

This deceptively simple allegory captures a number of core Platonic insights, most notably the distinction between the real world and an illusory one that is shaped by public opinion – the distinction between truth and opinion, reality and shadows/illusions. For Plato, the sun symbolises the Good, and it is only a life lived in this light that is capable of either seeing reality or living in the real world. In this context, the allegory of the cave charts the journey that must be taken by all who strive to live the good life. As is evident from the allegory, this journey is not one that ought to be taken lightly as it is involves a personal conversion – a radical reshaping of one's vision that will demand the shedding of cherished images of fulfillment shaped by the desires for pleasure or power. The symbolic potential of the image of sight/blindness is powerfully used by Plato to reflect the manner in which prejudice is a form of blindness. As Plato perceptively recognised, to see the real world – to see and to love truth – is a moral achievement. All too many people are content to live in the illusory world that is shaped by their own prejudices. The reference to the person who returned to the cave to free the prisoners reflects Plato's conviction that those who love wisdom have a responsibility to contribute to the education of society. The likely death of the person who would return to the cave to free the prisoners is undoubtedly meant to refer to the death of Socrates, a sobering conclusion to the allegory and a reminder of the obduracy of all who are captive to their own illusions.

The writings of Plato highlight the manner in which the goal and purpose of life, the search for meaning and values, is shaped by the universal love of truth, goodness beauty and love. These concepts are not just figments of imagination or subjective creations; beauty is not simply in the eye of the beholder, nor can the good life be determined simply by what is felt to be good. Plato's celebrated theory of Ideas is an expression of the conviction that there is an objective order that transcends a transient and illusory material world. Based on an intuition that what is worthwhile, valuable and real must be (a) something which is eternal rather than finite, (b) something that is objective not subjective (c) something which is immutable not transient; it was Plato's conviction that the universal or the form or idea is that which really exists. The individual or the particular is merely a copy of the universal form and exists only to the extent that it participates in it. Beauty, truth, goodness, justice are forms that are eternal, objective, immutable, spiritual and real.

There is no finer exposition of Plato's understanding of love and beauty than in Socrates' speech in *Symposium* 199c-212c.

The setting for this dialogue is a banquet and the topic for discussion is the nature of love. Socrates begins his address by engaging in a dialogue with the previous speaker, Agathon. He makes three points: (a) there is no such thing as love, but only love of somebody or something; (b) love is to be perceived as desire of that which we lack; (c) love is not to be identified with beauty or goodness but rather the desire for beauty or goodness. Socrates (202a) now proceeds to introduce one of the key concepts in his treatment of the nature of love, namely the realm of the 'between' *(metaxis)*: between beauty and ugliness, between good and evil and between knowledge and ignorance. It is in this realm of the 'between' that love belongs; it is the realm also where human beings belong, where our mythical parents 'plenty' and 'poverty' are revealed. As Socrates recognised, human nature exists between plenty and poverty; both of these parents are necessary if one is to succeed in either loving or desiring. If one already possessed beauty there would be nothing to desire, and if one were ignorant of beauty one would not be able to desire it. Through these passages, Plato unveils a vision of human nature understood through the lens of love or desire. It is love as desire that defines the person; a remarkable definition of human nature, the importance of which has never been more acknowledged than in the contemporary world of psychoanalysis.

In his address, Socrates (204a-208c) now begins to reflect on the nature of the goal that is the object of desire and argues convincingly that happiness is to be found in the possession of beauty and goodness forever, a theme that reflects his belief in immortality (206a). Plato here introduces the idea of love being directed at the procreation of that which is beautiful, a theme that suggests some acute psychological observations. As he says,

> There is something divine about the whole matter; in procreation and bringing to birth the mortal creature is endowed with a touch of immortality.[3]

In the passages that follow, the reader is drawn into a hierarchy of being that finds expression in the need to ascend from the contemplation of physical beauty to the beauty of the soul that is identified with virtue. Plato is here pursuing the idea that it is the vocation of the philosopher to nurture beauty in the souls of the young through fostering an education in the nature and importance of virtue. In the final section (210d-212c) the ascent passages are repeated and explained in a manner that leaves no doubt but that Plato envisaged the goal of human desire as the contemplation of absolute beauty that is unique, eternal and unchangeable. In the attainment of this goal he believed that 'one is beloved of God, and becomes, if ever one can, immortal' (212a). The speech of Socrates concludes with a ringing endorsement of the importance of love or desire as the essential pre-requisite for any search for beauty. As he says: 'I try to persuade others that in the acquisition of this blessing, human nature can find no better helper than love' (212c).

Even the briefest survey of the dialogues allows the reader to see the link that Plata discerns between the search for meaning and the desire for beauty and goodness. Furthermore, the *Symposium* highlights Plato's conviction that in loving that which is beautiful one is drawn to ascend from a world that is material and transient to one that is both spiritual and eternal. It is a conviction that is replicated in the history of artistic creation. To quote W.B. Yeats: 'No man can create as did Shakespeare, Homer, Sophocles, who does not believe with all his blood and nerve, that man's soul is immortal'[4]. Why is there beauty rather than banality, or why is there artistic creation rather than mere technological efficiency? As Plato recognised, the motif of beauty and artistic creation puts us in touch with the fundamental mystery of existence, that is, transcendence.

Plato's *Symposium* leaves us with another legacy, namely the importance of understanding love as desire. Arguably one of the most important contributions ever made to the attempt to understand the dynamics underpinning the search for meaning, it is an insight that is replicated in the writings of that most celebrated of early Christian philosophers, Augustine of Hippo. The *Confessions* of Augustine begin with that oft-quoted reference to 'the restless heart' that defines human nature: 'you made us for yourself and our hearts find no peace until they rest in you.' (*Confessions* 1.1)

Despite its obvious attractions, Plato's theory of Ideas is not without its critics. In particular, many would have little sympathy with its dualist character – the creation of two separate worlds of Form (immaterial/universal) and Matter (material/particular). Furthermore, no less a philosopher than Aristotle, Plato's student, fundamentally disagreed with Plato's contention that it is the universals or the Forms/Ideas that really exist. For Aristotle what is primary is the individual: it is the individual substance that really exists; the universal is an abstraction that has no separate existence. For Aristotle, whiteness *per se* is an idea we can arrive at by abstracting from real entities such as white walls or white paper.

To conclude, even if one were to accept these criticisms of Plato's philosophy it does not take away from his genius and his contribution to the history of European civilisation. His conviction that there is a higher rational standard according to which we can judge human behaviour is one that is not only held by Aristotle, but one that is shared by Aquinas and the Natural Law theorists that follow in his path to this day. This is a radical standpoint that directly challenges an increasing acceptance of relativism in the contemporary western world. The relevance of objective standards continues to manifest itself in such matters as their application by international jurists in cases of crimes against humanity.

Aristotle (385–322 BCE)
Born in 385 BCE, Aristotle studied under Plato as a pupil of his Academy. As a young teacher he was tutor to Alexander the Great. Returning to Athens in 335 BCE he taught philosophy at

the Lyceum. He later founded his own school of philosophy that subsequently became known as the Peripatetic school (Aristotle was reputed to walk as he taught). Regarded by many as the greatest philosopher that has ever lived, Aristotle wrote on an extraordinarily diverse range of subjects, much of which tragically has not survived intact. In many respects Aristotle's contribution to the natural sciences could be said to rival even that of his philosophical output. In particular, mention must be made of his work in the related areas of zoology and biology. He is widely regarded as having laid the foundations of the biological sciences, and his contributions to these sciences were not superseded for many centuries.

The search for meaning cannot be divorced from the larger issue of an ordered world, one that is amenable to scientific exploration. Aristotle is universally recognised for his contribution to this issue in his work entitled *Metaphysics*. Despite its rough style, the first book (*Alpha*) is in effect a lengthy meditation focused on (i) the dignity of the human species that is distinguished from all others in its capacity to know, to seek for wisdom, to seek the answer to the question 'why?' – to search for the cause of that which is experienced, and on (ii) the nobility of that science that seeks the first cause, namely metaphysics. Despite strong disagreement with the materialist bias of the earliest Pre-Socratic philosophers, Aristotle acknowledged their contribution to the subsequent development of philosophy. It was they who first recognised that the intelligibility of the cosmos is dependent on our ability to structure it in terms of a complex matrix of cause and effect. Furthermore, it was they who were the first to explore systematically the universe in terms of these categories.

It is hard for us today to comprehend the enormity of the breakthrough initiated by these earliest philosophers. The belief that every experience can be investigated because it can be understood as an effect underpins the possibility of all scientific enterprise. Science of every kind is dedicated to explaining the reason for experiences through the process of uncovering the existence of a cause or causes of these experiences. It was Aristotle's unique contribution to the history of philosophy that he not only provided the first systematic analysis of the nature of causation but also recognised that the intelligibility of the cosmos, and thus the possibility of physics, depended on the existence of a first cause.

The most famous book of the *Metaphysics* is book twelve, entitled *Lambda,* which contains in summary form the main features of Aristotle's metaphysical theory. In the first five chapters of the book Aristotle reflects on the nature of being as substance. The first chapter of *Lambda* opens with a short summary of the reasons why Aristotle accords primacy to substance rather than the universal form, a stance that is in sharp contrast to that adopted by Plato. For Aristotle, what is primary is the individual. It is his most deeply held conviction that only an individual substance really exists. In Aristotle's opinion, white things are prior to whiteness, a common sense opinion that contradicts Plato's theory of forms. According to Aristotle, the universal so beloved by Plato is an abstraction that has no separate existence: universals exist only to the extent that they modify substances. For example, individual substances can be modified by accidents of quantity, quality and relation.

If the intelligibility of the universe is to be affirmed, Aristotle was convinced that one had to make sense of the experience of movement, change or becoming. In this context, his metaphysics is directed to showing that this issue of intelligibility will only be satisfactorily resolved if one successfully addresses the related questions concerning both the origin and purpose of movement or change, something which he endeavours to do through an elaboration of his theory of 'Potency and Act'. In chapter two it is this issue that is the focus of Aristotle's reflections. As he perceptively observed, one is only able to explain the possibility of movement if every sensible substance is composed of both act and potency: the act reflecting the being as it is, the potency reflecting the being as it could become (its potential). The only being that has no potency is the one who is the first cause of all movement – the unmoved mover (the Creator or God). It is this that explains Aristotle's description of God as 'Pure Act'.

For Aristotle, to understand something's essence is to grasp its potentiality. He urges us to think beyond immediate experience and to attend to the goal, end or purpose (*telos*) of all living beings, and, as he recognised, we only grasp our goal in life if we are conscious of the species to which we belong. Thus just as in biological terms we only understand an acorn if we grasp its potentiality to become a fully developed oak tree, so too, in terms of the meaning and value of an individual human life, Aristotle would urge us to look beyond the immediate horizon and to think instead of the human form – the potentiality of human nature.

The distinction between matter and form that is introduced in chapter three is also one that is necessary if change or movement is to be explained. There are two types of change, accidental change and substantial change. In the former, the substance is changed accidentally, such as in the example of a change of light, whereas in the latter, the substance changes substantially, as in the change brought about by a fire where a tree is reduced to a pile of ashes. In each case of change, as distinct from annihilation, something remains after the change has occurred. In the case of substantial change this means that every sensible substance must be complex – composed of what Aristotle called prime matter and substantial form. The matter is what makes me unique and survives any substantial change, whereas the form tells me the species to which I belong and does not survive a substantial change. In the case just mentioned, the species (tree) is replaced by a new species (ash). One of the great contributions that Aristotle made to the development of science was to provide the first systematic analysis of the nature of causation. He was the first to recognise that there are four ways of asking the question why; four ways and only four ways of understanding what could be meant in seeking to explain the reason for an experience or an event. When one enquires into the reason for the universe or anything in the universe one could be asking one of only four possible questions. These are reflected in four possible types of causation: material, efficient, formal and final. In chapters four and five Aristotle summarises his theory of causation. One can explain a substance in terms of its matter (material cause), its form or essence (formal cause), its parentage (efficient cause), and its purpose (final cause).

The two great themes of Aristotle's metaphysics were (i) the study of the nature of being as substance, and (ii) the study of the first cause of being or movement. If the first part of *Lambda* (chs 1-5) focused on the first of these two themes, the second part of *Lambda* (chs 6-10) took as its subject the study of the first cause of being or movement, namely God. In chapter six, Aristotle argues for the existence of God as the creator/first cause of movement and thus of being. The stages in the argument are as follows:
- Since substances are primary amongst existing things it follows that if all substances are perishable so is everything else.
- Therefore, for anything to exist there must exist a substance that is eternal, immaterial and yet capable of generating motion.
- That being must be immaterial because only an immaterial being could be immutable (all material substances are subject to movement/change) and thus the first cause of all movement. Such a being can be termed God.

In the following chapter Aristotle seeks to explore the nature of God as the prime mover. In an insight that is very Platonic in character, Aristotle identifies God with the Good, which is the object of desire and thought. With this insight Aristotle shifts the direction of our thoughts from the origins of movement to the purpose or goal of movement – the Good. It is a remarkable change in perspective that directs attention, away from a God who is the guarantor of the possibility of science, to a God of love who draws all beings to him. As he says: 'The final cause, then, moves by being loved, while all other things that move do so by being moved.'[4] (1072b, 5) The chapter continues with a number of sublime passages that reflect on the nobility of human life and the divine/human relationship and concludes with a reflection on the goal of life as the contemplation of God.

After the majesty of these passages, the final three chapters read almost like a post-script. However, they contain some interesting observations on the mode of existence of the supreme intellect (ch. 9) and on how the Good as the principle of order exists in the world (ch. 10). In this final and very Platonic chapter, Aristotle offers a confident restatement of the reasons for his belief in the existence of God as the cause of order, generation and movement – prerequisites for the belief in a world that is intelligible. The chapter concludes with a concise critique of both the materialist bias of the Pre-Socratic philosophers and the inconsistencies underlying Plato's theory of forms.

To conclude, Aristotle is universally recognised for his contribution to scientific thought and principles. His studies in the natural sciences had convinced him that every living organism exists for a purpose and he saw this as a powerful argument in favour of an ordered universe and the existence of an intelligent being, God, who is the creator/cause of this order. Finally, in common with Plato and in contrast to all forms of relativism and/or subjectivism, he also maintained that there is a right, rational and natural order to the quest for individual and social self-realisation, an order that finds its articulation in an analysis of the substantial form, i.e. human nature. Aristotle would never have been in any doubt about the existence of an objective horizon for the search for meaning and values.

Key moments in the development of philosophical thought
Over the centuries the direction of the search for meaning and values in Europe has been altered by a number of changes in the cultural fabric of European society. Developments in the world of philosophy document these movements and provide us with a way of assessing their effect on the manner in which perennial questions are shaped. In this study we will limit ourselves to a brief analysis of the following three developments in philosophical thought:
- The emergence of a Christian philosophy in the late classical and medieval cultures: Augustine and Aquinas;
- The rise of modernity: Descartes and Kant;
- Contemporary continental philosophy: Heidegger, Levinas, Stein and Marion.

The emergence of a Christian philosophy
For nearly three hundred years after the death of Jesus the emerging Christian community suffered intermittent persecution. The last and most savage of these persecutions took place between 303 and 311 under the emperor Diocletian. Upon the death of Diocletian in 318, Constantine became emperor and declared Christianity to be the official religion of the Roman Empire. This was a *volte-face* of remarkable proportions that can truly be said to have both transformed the fortunes of Christianity and given rise to a re-shaping of European culture. As a direct result of this newly found freedom, there arose a profusion of Christian preaching and writing that would lead to the rapid Christianisation of much of the Roman culture in both its Greek and Latin spheres. Figures such as Athanasius, Basil, Gregory of Nyssa and John

Chrysostom are indelibly associated with the flowering of a Christian culture in the Greek world of the late fourth and early fifth centuries. In the Latin west, Christians recorded the contributions of Ambrose of Milan and of Jerome, who is identified with the Vulgate translation of the Bible into Latin. However, despite the eminence of these and other Christian writers of this period, there are few who would dispute the contention that Augustine of Hippo was the key figure responsible for shaping the 'Christian' culture that emerged in late classical and early medieval Europe.

Augustine (354–430)
Born in Thagaste, a small city in the Roman province of Africa (modern day Tunisia), Augustine lived in the twilight of the Roman Empire. He was converted to Christianity in 387, became bishop in 395, and died just as the Vandals were laying siege to Hippo, the city of which he was bishop. His early life was influenced by a materialist and Gnostic sect called Manichaeism, which proposed a determinist view of reality that had much in common with astrology. Through contact with Ambrose the celebrated bishop of Milan and his reading of Neo-Platonist philosophy, Augustine was led to reject Manichaeism. In particular, he was to reject their materialism and determinism, arguing for the existence of a spiritual dimension to reality and for the viewpoint which affirms that human beings are free and therefore responsible for the quality of their lives – both of which themes are cornerstones of Neo-Platonist philosophy. While not wishing to exaggerate the extent to which Augustine was a Neo-Platonist, it is nevertheless true that the Christian philosophy that emerges in the writings of Augustine is one that owes much to the links that he discerns between the classical world of Platonism/Neo-Platonism and the Christian faith, the worlds of Athens and Jerusalem. It is a legacy that was to shape the subsequent history of philosophy and indeed European culture.

The most celebrated of Augustine's writings is the *Confessions*, a book that attempts to chart not just his own spiritual journey but also that which must be taken by every person. It is a journey motivated by the desire for happiness, a conviction reflected in the opening paragraph of the *Confessions*, 'that our hearts are restless until they rest in you O Lord' (Conf.1:1). It is also a pilgrimage that is marked by the painful recognition of the need for a personal conversion if one is to truly desire to trace the path that will lead to happiness. In fact, one of most striking aspects of Augustine's writings is the link that he makes between this motif of conversion and the challenge to nurture desire. It is an insight that is beautifully expressed in the following passage:

> These men were far from the bread of heaven and they did not know how to hunger for it. They had weak jaws of the heart; they were deaf with open ears; they saw and stood blind. For indeed, this bread searches out the hunger of the interior man. (*Commentary on the Gospel of St. John* 26:1)

What Augustine so successfully evokes in this passage is the sense of interior or spiritual paralysis that affects those unable to desire God's love. They do no know how to hunger for it; they have lost the ability to desire God's love. It is not just disordered desire but, even more importantly, the failure to desire which ultimately destroys the human potential because it constricts the soul. It was Augustine's abiding conviction that it is possible to lose the knowledge of desire if and only if one believes oneself to be self-sufficient. If he is correct, there are only two categories of people that cannot desire, those in despair and those whose lives are shaped by pride. The former are fixated on the futility of desire, the latter on its irrelevance. From Augustine's point of view the most destructive effect of pride is that it prevents one even commencing the journey to

Christ because it strangles the impulse to desire. From the perspective of this reflection on the nature of the search for meaning and values, Augustine's contribution could be summarised by the insight that the quest will neither be undertaken nor even comprehended unless there are people prepared to nurture the restlessness, the longing, the desire that is in every person's heart. It is an insight with particular relevance in a culture that, many would suggest, is marked by an over-confidence in its own prowess.

In many respects, the *Confessions* can be read as Augustine's portrayal of the universal search for self-identity, one that reveals the person as a profound puzzle to himself/herself. The restlessness of the human heart, as portrayed in the *Confessions*, testifies to the difficulties that humans experience in their quest to find anchor points to construct their identity. Similarly, the detailed analysis of the psychology of sin that one finds in the *Confessions* (2:4-10) and the often tortuous detail that Augustine uses to describe his own struggle – 'my inner self was a house divided against itself' (Conf.8:8) – is eloquent testimony to his recognition of the struggles that face all who seek some assurance in answer to the questions that define their existence.

Augustine was in no doubt but that it is the quest for truth that defines the person. No other theme comes near to matching in detail and intensity this 'bewildering passion for the wisdom of eternal truth' (Conf.3:4) that is etched into the pages of the *Confessions*. However, the key insight that for so long eluded Augustine's grasp was the correct manner of pursuing this quest. Fifteen years under the influence of the Manicheans was to teach Augustine a hard won lesson: that the quest for truth can never be satisfied unless one is conscious of the difference between an obsessive curiosity (*curiositas*) and true or holy desire. It is nothing less than the difference between the desire to appropriate knowledge as one would appropriate an object and the desire to know the person who is the subject of one's love: to know that and only that which love reveals. The insight that marks Augustine's conversion as recounted in the *Confessions* is that the only appropriate focus for the quest for truth is a person in and through whom I receive the gift of truth. Augustine was in no doubt that this person is God: it is God as truth who is the true focus of his love or desire. Furthermore, he recognised that the only question capable of making sense of desire or the experience of a restless heart is the one that asks whether there is someone who loves me, a question which alone can ensure that I in turn am capable of loving. The phrase 'to love and to be loved was sweet to me' (Conf.2:2 and 3:1) acts almost as a refrain that shapes the early books of the *Confessions*. It is a reminder that, for Augustine, the only way to understand the restless heart that shapes human nature is to see it in the context of the desire to love and to be loved.

The distinction between curiosity and desire has another focus that draws attention to the direction of the path illuminated by desire. A central premise of the *Confessions* that is shaped by Augustine's emphasis on interiority is that curiosity or disordered desire is marked by a love that is both directed at that which is lower rather than higher and, most importantly, is 'inflated with desire for things outside the self.' (Conf.7:16) The whole structure of the *Confessions* is modeled on the imagery of the biblical account of the Prodigal Son (Lk 15:11-32) – a structure that is well expressed in this well known passage:

> I have learnt to love you late, Beauty at once so ancient and so new! I have learnt to love you late! You were within me, and I was in the world outside myself. I searched for you outside myself and, disfigured as I was, I fell upon the lovely things of your creation. You were with me, but I was not with you … .You called me, you cried aloud to me; you broke my barrier of deafness. You shone upon me; your radiance enveloped me; you put my blindness to flight. You shed your fragrance about

me; I drew breath and now I gasp for your sweet odour.
I tasted you, and now I hunger and thirst for you. You
touched me, and I am inflamed with love of your peace.
(Conf.10:27)

This lengthy passage highlights a number of key themes that mark Augustine's anthropology. First, in the emphasis on interiority reflected in the motif of the return to the self, one is confronted by the central insight that shapes Augustine's understanding of the divine/human relationship; the one who is loved, God, although he is infinitely above me, he is also closer to me than I am to myself (Conf.3:6). Secondly, in that sustained evocation of the motif of 'calling', Augustine reminds his readers in no uncertain manner that the possibility of seeking God is dependent upon God seeking us first – one can only desire God because he has first desired us (Conf.1:1). It was Augustine's abiding conviction that one cannot confer significance on oneself. A person can only love because he/she is loved first. One is drawn to desire by the profoundly affective character of the gift of one who is beautiful – the one in whom I delight. Finally, the passage offers us an evocative portrayal of the person as a lover – the passionate desire of a lover for God.

In one of the most memorable sections in the *Confessions*, Augustine describes the death of a close friend whom he had known since early childhood. Not only does this section mark the moment, at the age of nineteen, that he first became conscious of his own mortality but also, in the course of this section, Augustine offers his most extended treatment of the nature of love and the significance of friendship (Conf.4:4-9). Indeed, there are few passages in classical literature that offer the reader either a greater sensitivity to the intimacy that constitutes the love between friends or a more profound acknowledgement of the significance of this love for the life of each human being. In recounting this moment of awakening to his own mortality occasioned by the death of his friend, Augustine offers the following comment:

> I wondered that other men should live when he was dead, for I had loved him as though he would never die. Still more I wondered that he should die and I remain alive, for I was his second self. How well the poet (Horace) put it when he called his friend the half of his soul! I felt that our two souls had been as one, living in two bodies, and life to me was fearful because I did not want to live with only half a soul. Perhaps this, too, is why I shrank from death for fear that one whom I had loved so well might then be wholly dead. (Conf.4:6)

It is an evocative passage that reflects the interpersonal character of Augustine's anthropology; love of the other for his own sake, whether described as neighbour or friend or lover, is at the core of his understanding of the human person. Furthermore, it not only shows Augustine's familiarity with the classical understanding of friendship, but it also reveals the true nature of the challenge to the 'self' posed by the reality of death. For Augustine, death is not something that poses the ultimate challenge to my significance as an individual. Death is rather experienced in the context of the challenge that it poses to love. It is the loss of a friend rather than my own mortality that provides the lens through which death is viewed. The phrase quoted above, 'for I had loved him as though he would never die', is one that will deeply preoccupy Augustine. As he says in another passage, 'What madness to love a man as something more than human ... I had poured out my soul upon him, like water upon sand, loving a man who was mortal as though he were never to die.' (Conf.4:7) Augustine never doubted that, at some foundational level, the intimacy of love demands to be eternal and resists all rational attempts to constrain it within the boundaries set by death. How then does

Augustine attempt to address this paradox posed by the fact of human mortality? He does so in and through his reflections on the nature of true love:

> Blessed are those who love you, O God, and love their friends in you and their enemies for your sake. They alone will never lose those who are dear to them for they love them in one who is never lost, in God. (Conf.4:9)

One of the hallmarks of the distinction that Augustine makes between ordered and disordered love hinges upon the difference between a love that is exclusive and one that is inclusive – a love that generously includes a 'third'. In the faith perspective of Augustine this openness to the generosity of love is always described as a love that is 'in God'. It is a love that is both all-embracing and eternal because it is a love that extends even to enemies and because it participates in God who is eternal.

Augustine's intellectual life was lived at the crossroads of the classical Graeco-Roman and Christian worlds and his writings can in many respects be seen as an attempt to create a bridge between Athens and Jerusalem. However, there are critical differences between the two cultures. Nowhere is this more evident than in his treatment of love – a motif that would forever remain prominent in his philosophical and theological writings. No one familiar with the traditions of Platonism and Neoplatonism could be unaware of the importance of the motif of *erôs* or desire – a tradition that contributed in no small way to the emphasis that Augustine would place on it. However, unlike Neoplatonism Augustine would never lose sight of the grace or gift dimension of love that is reflected in the passage from the First Letter of St John, 'This is the love I mean; not our love for God, but God's love for us.' (I Jn.4:8-10) Augustine was always conscious that it is the gift of love that enables one in turn to love. Another of the very obvious differences between the classical Greek and Christian ideals of love or friendship is that the former is founded upon only the experience of the attractiveness of a shared likeness in respect of virtue, whereas the latter extends even to enemies. As the quotation above suggests, it is the love of enemies that is the touchstone of a love that is 'in God'.

Aquinas (1225–1274)

Eight centuries separate Augustine from Aquinas and yet one can see in their writings the twin pillars upon which a Christian philosophy was constructed, one that was to shape European civilisation for close on thirteen hundred years. If Augustine was to highlight the links between Platonism, Neoplatonism and Christianity, it was left to Aquinas to suggest a synthesis between the philosophy of Aristotle and Christian revelation. While having great respect for Augustine, Aquinas was to largely substitute Aristotle's philosophy for the Platonism/Neoplatonism of Augustine.

In the period between the fifth and twelfth centuries it was the monasteries that were largely responsible for the promotion of learning, and in particular, the development of philosophy and theology. Towards the end of this period, Europe witnessed the rise of universities such as Paris, Oxford and Bologna. They would continue to nurture the study of these disciplines. In these monasteries and early universities the development of philosophy was largely Neoplatonic and Augustinian, and it was studied principally as a companion to theology. The recovery of the importance of Aristotle's philosophy as a counterbalance to Neoplatonism can be dated to the twelfth century. Much of his works were re-discovered through the influence of Arab scholarship and Islamic philosophy, and the importance of his philosophy was to be seen in the writings of Ibn Sina (Avicenna) and Ibn Rushd (Averroes). However, the immense standing of Aristotle's philosophy in the world of medieval Christendom and beyond is the unique contribution of Thomas Aquinas.

Born in the small Italian town of Aquino from which his name is derived, Thomas Aquinas both studied and lectured in Paris as a member of the Dominican order. Widely regarded as one of the greatest Christian philosophers and theologians, he combined the philosophy of Aristotle with Christian revelation to provide a remarkable synthesis of the Christian faith. He was a prolific writer and his most famous book, the *Summa Theologiae,* has inspired the writings of both philosophers and theologians over many centuries.

In the context of a reflection on the search for meaning and values one could do no better than to examine the manner in which Aquinas treats of the subject of human happiness. As we have seen, friendship, happiness and death are interwoven in the narrative of Augustine's life, and when writing about friendship and love he thought also about misery, obsession and illusion. However, notwithstanding the wounded state of the human heart, Augustine never lost the Christian hope that sustained his trust that happiness is to be found in the love that unites us to a friend – a friendship that is 'in Christ'. Although the style of Aquinas, a 'question and answer' format, is very different from that of Augustine, his reflections on happiness contained in the *Summa Theologiae (ST* 1.2.1-5) reflect many of the same themes that are to be found in Augustine's writings.

The treatise begins with Aquinas offering cogent arguments which seek to establish that 'properly human action is action that pursues goals'. *(ST* 1.2.1:1). In fact, he will argue that it is not just reasoning creatures such as human beings that pursue goals but all nature does so. The argument is deceptively simple, 'an agent not aimed at its effect will not do one thing rather than another'. *(ST* 1.2.1:2). In other words, the possibility of movement is dependent on having a goal – a reason to move and/or a reason to move in one direction rather than another. Furthermore, not only does every action have a goal but also it is the goal of the action that determines its quality, i.e. whether it is worthy of praise or blame. Aquinas then argues for the notion of an ultimate goal. While acknowledging that a single human action can have more than one goal or end he argues that 'you cannot have endless ends' (*ST* 1.2.1:4); there must be an ultimate goal/end in the context of which all other goals or 'sub-goals' are deemed attractive. He concludes:

> So all men agree in pursuing an ultimate goal and seeking their own fulfilment, but they disagree as to where this fulfilment can be found; just as all men like their food tasty, yet disagree as to which food is tastiest.... [Even] sinners turn away from the true ultimate goal, but not from an ultimate goal as such, since this is what they seek falsely in other things. (*ST* 1.2.1:7)

In the context of a reflection on the search for meaning and values there are a number of valuable points here to be noted. Firstly, Aquinas like Aristotle before him is arguing that a search for meaning is only intelligible if the universe is purposeful rather than the product of chance, i.e. a universe where all actions can be explained in terns of goals that are in principle rationally intelligible. Secondly, Aquinas argues that the concept of freedom alone cannot explain human nature, because unless there is some goal to which humans can freely aspire, there is no way that one can explain why one would choose one eventuality over another, or even why one would choose at all. Finally, while Aquinas is realistic enough to acknowledge that there is disagreement as to where fulfilment is to be found, he never deviates from the belief that there is an objective goal to human nature and that it is rationally discernible. It is a stance that places him in opposition to much of contemporary liberal opinion.

In sections two and three of this treatise Aquinas proceeds to argue that God is our ultimate goal. In a series of questions he asks, does happiness consist in riches, in honours, in fame and glory, in power, in bodily endowment, in pleasure, in any endowment of soul, or in any created good? His reply is that happiness cannot consist in riches, because as he says, 'man is wealth's goal rather than wealth man's' (*ST* 1.2.2:1). It cannot lie in honours because (with Aristotle) honour is external to the person receiving it. Nor can happiness be identified with glory, which is something extrinsic to the real worth of the person.

Power does not define it either, being morally ambivalent, and dependent upon virtue for its good use. The human body is for the sake of the soul; it cannot be the focus of happiness any more than sense-pleasure can be. Happiness cannot be realised in any created good, since by definition the latter cannot include everything the human being can desire. Therefore, only God, the complete good, can satisfy the innate desire for happiness. For Aquinas, the journey that will lead to happiness is not diverted by attractions that are external or extrinsic but rather seeks a goal that is intrinsic to human nature, namely a virtuous or a good life. Ultimately, it is a journey towards the contemplation of God, the one who is both the origin and the end of all that is (*ST* 1.2.3:8).

In sections four and five Aquinas reflects on what happiness brings with it and whether happiness is possible at all. He has no doubt but that happiness is possible for those who seek the good and that happiness will be accompanied by delight/pleasure. However, he cautions against making pleasure one's goal (*ST* 1.2.4:2-4). Paradoxically, those who aim for pleasure will not achieve it. Aquinas argues convincingly that it is only those who live virtuous lives – those who seek after the good – who will achieve happiness. It is a viewpoint that more than anything else shows the affinity between the philosophies of Aristotle and Aquinas. Both of these philosophers were in no doubt but that all human beings act towards an end that is rationally intelligible, namely, happiness, and that it is the precise function of ethics to direct us towards that goal.

In the course of this discussion Aquinas raises the issue as to whether the happy man needs friends. It is a question that is to be found in both the Classical Greek and Christian worlds. In company with Aristotle and indeed Augustine, he is in no doubt as to the importance of friends in the journey towards happiness, and he is also convinced that the happy person in this life will only be happy in the company of friends. Although conscious that friendship is not a prerequisite for the contemplation of God in eternal life, Aquinas argues convincingly that friendship always accompanies perfect happiness.

The rise of modernity and the turn to the subject

The sixteenth century saw a gradual movement of culture that would transform European society and undermine the premise upon which both the philosophy of Augustine and the scholasticism of Aquinas were based, namely the close link between philosophy and theology, one that reflects the conviction that human beings can only successfully find their meaning and purpose in terms of a sacred world-view. Influenced by a renewed interest in the self-confident humanism of classical antiquity that marked the artistic world of the Renaissance, this century was to usher in a new secular and person-centered world – a turn to the human subject that would alter the center of gravity within which the search for meaning and values would be understood. No longer would human beings automatically seek to situate their sense of self-identity in the larger context of an objective horizon of meaning suggested by their relationship to God or the world, rather it would be the focus on the human subject which would determine the manner in which either God or the world would both be understood and assessed. This development was accompanied by a shift of interest from theological themes to a study of the person and of Nature without explicit reference to God. This movement marked the shift from a theocentric or cosmocentric world-view to one that is anthropocentric – one shaped by a focus on the human being as a creator of meaning and value rather than on his/her status as a creature subject to God.

This shift to an anthropocentric world-view in the sixteenth and early seventeenth centuries was aided immeasurably by a number of related factors, the most important being the development of a new spirit of human enquiry that flowed from the renewed acceptance of an inductive or an empirical methodology by the scientific community. The scientific achievements of Kepler, Galileo, Copernicus and Newton owed much to their enthusiastic acceptance of a method of enquiry based upon the belief that knowledge is attained in and through sense perception – observation and experimentation. Under the influence of this scientific revolution society would increasingly be of the opinion that the focus for knowledge and self-understanding ought to be the world of scientific experimentation rather than sacred texts.

Alongside the development of modern science, another factor that gave rise in Europe to a renewed self-confidence in human nature was the wealth generated through the discovery and colonisation of the 'new' world. Many would argue that modernity would never have taken the course that it did if it were not for the discovery of the compass, the development of gunpowder and the invention of the printing press. It was this latter invention that was to be so instrumental in ensuring the widespread dissemination of the ideas of the Reformation.

There was no more important crisis in sixteenth-century European society than that provoked by the Reformation. Its effect was to sunder in the West the unity of Christendom that had shaped European culture for more than a thousand years. In both its rejection of the established institutions of authority and its espousal of the rights of individual interpretation of scripture, the Reformation was responsible in no small manner for the birth of individualism – a cultural trait that is almost synonymous with modernity. However, what is not so often recognised is that alongside the demise of the old certainties of Scholasticism the Reformation gave rise to a revival of scepticism, particularly one that questions the possibility of attaining metaphysical and theological truth by the use of reason. A rejection of the scepticism of the French philosopher Montaigne was to be the catalyst for the philosophical output of René Descartes – the philosopher who is the father of modernity.

René Descartes (1596–1650)
Born in a small French town on the Loire that now carries his name and educated by the Jesuits of La Flèche, Descartes was a mathematician, an applied scientist and a philosopher of the first order. He was particularly critical of the educational and philosophical milieu of the time, which he felt fostered a sceptical culture. As he once famously remarked:

> Philosophy teaches us to speak with an appearance of truth about all things and causes us to be admired by the less learned, and that though it has been cultivated for centuries by the best minds no single thing is to be found in it which is not a matter of dispute and which in consequence is not dubious.[5]

Descartes was to devote his adult life to the goal of creating a secure foundation for philosophy. His concern was with the question of knowledge and he was determined to prove that the human mind could know things with absolute certainty.

Clearly, the subject that Descartes addresses is of the first importance to anyone concerned to explore the parameters of the search for meaning and values because, if sceptics such as Montaigne are correct, the search would be pointless. If the human mind is simply not capable of finding answers to foundational questions such as are implied by the search for meaning and values then there is no point in engaging in what could only be regarded as a futile exercise. In this context, there are parallels with the struggle of Socrates against the Sophists' scepticism and/or lack of interest in the idea of objective truth.

In part one of the *Principles of Philosophy*, I-XVIII, Descartes put forward in summary form the manner in which he countered the challenge of scepticism.

Devoted to an exploration of the principles of human knowledge this treatise opens with the following statement:

> In order to examine into the truth, it is necessary once in one's life to doubt of all things, so far as this is possible. (*Principle one*)

This is a classic formulation of Descartes' methodology, what has become known as 'Methodic Doubt'. Descartes believed that there is only one way to prove that the human mind is capable of attaining knowledge with absolute certainty and that is to doubt methodically everything that it is possible to doubt. If nothing remains that cannot be doubted then the position of the sceptics is vindicated. If on the other hand there is something which it is not possible to doubt, then there exists something that is objectively true and furthermore, the human mind is capable of knowing that truth with absolute certainty. The stakes could not be higher; the issue is nothing less than the existence of truth and the power of human reason to grasp the truth. *Principles* two to five reveal the lengths to which Descartes is prepared to go in his pursuit of methodic doubt. This includes doubting the evidence of the senses (*Principle* four) and even the truth of mathematics (*Principle* five). When everything possible has been doubted does anything remain? In *Principle* seven Descartes pronounces the following:

> While we thus reject all that which can be possibly doubted, and feign that as false, it is easy to suppose that there is no God, nor heaven, nor bodies ... but we cannot in the same way conceive that we who doubt these things are not; for there is a contradiction in conceiving that what thinks does not at the same time as it thinks, exist.

And hence this conclusion *I think, therefore I am*, (*Cogito ergo sum*) is the first and most certain of all that occurs to one who philosophizes in an orderly way.

With the ringing affirmation of '*I think, therefore I am*', Descartes can truly be said to have inaugurated the modern age. The spirit of modernity is one that is characterised above all by confidence in the power of reason – the ability of humans to unlock the secrets of the world by their own unaided power. It is a rationalist and scientific age, one that harbours few doubts as to the reasonableness or the coherence of the universe.

In *Principles* eight to eleven Descartes reflects on the distinction between the soul and the body that would seem to be implied by the *'Cogito'*, a distinction that highlights the idea of the person as a conscious being. One of the consequences of this dualism, the opposition between soul and body, is that the physical body would seem to have little significance. This is not a position that can be easily sustained.

In *Principles* fourteen to eighteen Descartes puts forward a number of proofs for the existence of God that hinge upon the idea of God as a perfect being. In *Principle* fourteen he argues that 'the existence of God may be rightly demonstrated from the fact that the necessity of His existence is comprehended in the conception which we have of Him.' As he understands it, both necessary and eternal existence is contained in the idea of an absolutely perfect being. Therefore, God who is this absolutely perfect being must exist. This argument is a variation of the 'ontological argument' put forward by Anselm, the eleventh century abbot of Bec in Normandy. In *Principles* seventeen and eighteen Descartes argues that God must exist if one is to be able to explain the origin of the idea that we have of a supremely perfect Being. As he says,

> It is impossible for us to have any idea of anything whatever, if there is not within us or outside of us, an

> original, which as a matter of fact comprehends all the perfections. But as we do not in any way possess all those absolute perfections of which we have the idea, we must conclude that they reside in some other nature different from ours, and that is in God. (*Principle* eighteen)

Many times over the centuries the coherence of these proofs for the existence of God has been called into question, and yet they exhibit a fascination for the human mind. Undoubtedly, this is because they give expression to the widespread desire to affirm that there is a goal to human striving, and that this goal can be grasped by the unaided use of human reason. However one evaluates Descartes philosophy, there is no question but that he gives expression to this characteristic of the spirit of modernity.

Immanuel Kant (1724–1804)
If the focus of Descartes' philosophy is on the human subject rather than on the objective world outside of the subject, this emphasis is continued and deepened in the following century. The eighteenth century, the 'Age of Reason' or the 'Enlightenment', gives expression to the confidence of the period in the power of the human mind for speculative and scientific enquiry. The spirit of the age was intellectual freedom in opposition to all forms of dogmatism, and one of the great monuments to this intellectual confidence is the *Encyclopedia* – an enormous work in twenty-eight volumes published between 1751 and 1772 that sought to catalogue the whole spectrum of knowledge. The social and political expression of the renewed focus on human autonomy was in no small measure responsible for the 1789 revolution in France, an event that would transform the political and cultural landscape of Europe. Born in the East Prussian town of Konigsberg, the German philosopher Immanuel Kant was the age of reason's greatest advocate and one of the greatest philosophers of all time. He

was a prolific writer and his most famous book is the *Critique of Pure Reason* that was published in 1781.

Under the direction of Kant's philosophy the turn to the subject as knower attains a critical impetus. In what he describes as a Copernican revolution in philosophy he invites the reader to accept that instead of considering knowledge as a conformity of the mind to the given structure of objects we ought to consider it rather as a conformity of objects to the structure of the mind. The raw material of knowledge is transformed into intelligible reality by the activity of the mind. The forms of space and time as well as a category of the understanding such as causality are not to be found in the objective world. They are activities of the human subject that render sense perception intelligible. Furthermore, in a radical re-statement of empiricism Kant draws a distinction between the world as it is (*Noumena*), and the world as it appears to me (*Phenomena*). We can only know what the world is like for me; we cannot know for certainty what the world is like in itself.

Kant once famously described the Enlightenment as 'the courage to use your own intellect', a statement that reflects a confidence in the ability of the human intellect. However, if the Enlightenment is characterised by a cultural optimism, it is also the moment in European culture that gave birth to the widespread acceptance of the belief that there is no objective horizon of meaning that can be known with any certainty. Faced with the loss of this traditional anchor, Kant nevertheless was never predisposed to adopt a subjectivist world-view. As the following quotation illustrates, the opposite was in fact the case.

> Two things fill the mind with ever increasing admiration and awe, the oftener and the more steadily we reflect upon them: the starry heavens above me, and the moral law within me.[6]

This celebrated statement in the conclusion of Kant's *Critique of Practical Reason* brings into poignant juxtaposition the two realms of reason, the theoretical (concerned with the possibility of science) and the practical (concerned with the possibility of ethics). In many respects Kant's philosophical output was focused on the deceptively simple issue, namely, how to provide a rational justification for the possibility of both science and ethics. The issue is of course anything but simple because it raises foundational questions concerning the limits of human reason. Traditionally, a rational justification for the possibility of both science and ethics was supplied by metaphysics – arguing rationally for the existence of a God who is the creator of an ordered logical world and one who is both the author and the incarnation of the Good. However, under the influence of an empiricist scientific world-view this solution became culturally less and less acceptable. Increasingly, the limits of human knowledge were perceived to be coterminous with the limits of scientific observation and experimentation. In this scenario the possibility of meta-physics was rejected because by its very nature it seeks to go beyond the limits of physics or science. Kant agreed with the empiricist position that nothing could be known that went beyond the limits of sense perception – the boundaries of our material world.

In keeping with empiricist principles as outlined in the *Critique of Pure Reason*, Kant was to argue that not only can we not prove the existence of God but that, even if God exists, we cannot have any knowledge of him. And yet, paradoxically, Kant believed that if science is to be possible it is necessary to posit the existence of a regulative ideal, namely God, to unify the world of sense into an ordered system.

In the realm of the practical reason (ethics) as in the area of pure reason (science) Kant was firmly opposed to the attempt to base his rationalism upon the existence of God. He refused to believe that God was necessary either as a basis of moral obligation or as a motivating source of moral action.

Nevertheless, in the final analysis, Kant was forced to postulate the existence of God because, as he recognised, only if such a being exists who would judge the world fairly could the good person be certain of attaining his or her just rewards. The existence of God is necessary to guarantee the union of virtue and happiness and Kant was never in doubt but that this outcome was implied as the final end of morality.

How then does Kant seek to justify the possibility of science and morality in the limited areas that seem to require a theistic horizon of meaning and values? The response of Kant to this dilemma is contained in the following sentence from the *Critique of Pure Reason*: 'I have denied reason to make room for faith'. It is a remarkable statement that invites the reader to acknowledge that the answers to foundational questions of meaning and value are not to be found within the boundaries of knowledge but rather in the realm of faith. As a devout Lutheran, Kant had no interest in undermining belief in the existence of God. On the contrary it was his conviction that it was only by freeing belief in God from what he regarded as spurious attempts to prove God's existence that one could begin to appreciate the true setting for belief in God, namely in the realm of faith – an eminently reasonable faith, but nonetheless a stance based on faith rather than reason.

Contemporary continental philosophy

In many respects, modernity can be characterised by its anthropocentric focus. In its final phase between 1850 and 1975 this turn to the subject took on its most radical form. Ill at ease with the limitations of an epistemological focus – the preoccupation with the subject as a thinker/knower – that was characteristic of both the philosophies of Descartes and Kant, the newly emerging philosophical schools in continental Europe in the late nineteenth and early twentieth century sought to broaden the concerns of philosophy to embrace the whole spectrum of life as it is concretely lived. Chief among these schools was phenomenology founded by Edmund Husserl, which was characterised by a desire to take as its focus the concrete human experience in all its richness. The phenomenological method proposed by Husserl was to exercise an unrivaled influence on the course of twentieth century philosophy. From his phenomenological perspective, philosophy is the work of reflection that is brought to bear on unreflective, everyday life. In essence it is a systematic and scientific analysis of the common, shared features or structures of conscious life that both underlie everyday existence and give it meaning. The influence of phenomenology is particularly noticeable in the writings of Martin Heidegger, Edith Stein and Emmanuel Levinas, all of whom were students of Husserl. A more recent student of the school of phenomenology is the French philosopher Jean Luc Marion. What they have in common is a focus on the everyday structures of being in the world that both shape human existence and distinguish human beings from all other beings.

Martin Heidegger (1889–1976)
Born in Messkirch in Germany, Martin Heidegger was a leading exponent of both phenomenology and existentialism and he is widely regarded today as one of the most important philosophers of the twentieth century. Any assessment of his life however is not without controversy, because of Heidegger's brief espousal of the National Socialist movement in Germany in the early 1930s, and his later refusal to comment on issues connected with the holocaust. Heidegger's major work *Being and Time* was published in 1927. Its phenomenological analysis of human existence (*Dasein*) reflects the influence of the turn to existentialism in phenomenology in the period between the two world wars – a shift of emphasis that, among other things, drew attention to the nature and significance of individual freedom. As Heidegger observes, the linguistic derivation of the verb 'to exist' is to stand apart, a stance that emphasises

freedom, responsibility and also aloneness. The understandable and yet morally reprehensible reluctance to embrace one's aloneness and to accept personal responsibility for one's life is responsible for what Heidegger describes as the appeal of the 'they' world – the collective embrace described as the 'they-self' where I can attempt to lose myself and pretend that it is not I but 'they' who are responsible for the shape of my life. Heidegger's phenomenological analysis of 'everyday existence' draws attention to the reality that it is marked by 'falleness' – human beings all too often fail to live up to the ideals of an authentic life.

One of the most powerful reflections on the meaning of human existence (*Dasein*), and indeed, the aloneness of the individual, is to be found in the chapter in *Being and Time* devoted to an existential analysis of death, one that highlights the manner in which the category of time structures the quest for meaning. As the title *Being and Time* suggests, life is lived in the shadow of our temporal and historical existence, and in particular, human finitude – the fact that 'as soon as we are born we are old enough to die'. He begins the chapter by acknowledging the difficulty of experiencing or understanding ourselves as a 'whole' because we have not yet reached the end of our lives (§46). Not only can we not experience our own death but we cannot even experience the death of others (§47). At best we are always just 'there alongside'. However, even though we cannot experience 'Being-at-an-end', we can nevertheless experience ourselves as a 'Being-towards-the-end'. As he says:

> Death is a way to be which Dasein takes over as soon as it is. As soon as one comes to life, he/she is at once old enough to die. (§48)[7]

It was the genius of Heidegger to recognise that one's stance before death defines the manner in which one lives one's life.

He contrasts the inauthentic collective, or the 'they-self,' with the authentic individual. The former stance is marked by evasive concealment in the face of death; death is spoken of as a mishap – someone or other dies, as if to say, 'one of these days one will die too, in the end: but right now it has nothing to do with us.' (§51) In contrast to this evasive concealment in the face of death the authentic individual lives in the light of the possibility of death. He/she does not brood on death, but rather anticipates it, and thus becomes conscious of the true nature of human existence. Firstly, the anticipation of death reveals the non-relational character of human existence: the radical aloneness of each individual in this world. As Heidegger reminds us, just as no one can do my dying for me, likewise, no one can do my living for me. Secondly, the anticipation of death reveals the transitory nature of human existence, and finally, it frees itself for accepting this reality. In this act of freedom, the authentic person becomes truly liberated, because the freely chosen anticipation of death 'shatters all one's tenaciousness to whatever existence one has reached.' (§53)

Heidegger's reflections on the meaning of human existence is only one part of a larger interrogation of the meaning of Being itself, one that comes to the surface when one asks the first of all questions, namely 'why is there something rather than nothing?'. As early as 1927, in the opening lines of Heidegger's *Being and Time,* one reads, 'The Question [of Being] has today been forgotten'. (§1) The question as to the meaning of Being is equally evoked by the question 'Why is there something rather than nothing?' posed by Heidegger in his 1935 lecture series, *An Introduction to Metaphysics*:

> Why are there essents rather than nothing? That is the question. Clearly it is no ordinary question ... obviously this is the first of all questions, ... Many men never encounter this question, if by encounter we mean not merely to hear and read about it as an interrogative

> formulation but to ask the question, that is, to bring it about, to raise it, to feel its inevitability. And yet each of us is grazed at least once, perhaps more than once, by the hidden power of this question, even if he is not aware of what is happening to him. The question looms in moments of great despair, when things tend to lose all their weight and all meaning becomes obscured ... it is present in moments of rejoicing, ... The question is upon us in boredom when we are equally removed from despair and joy...[8]

When we acknowledge the finitude of human existence this question as to the meaning of Being becomes inescapable. However, in Heidegger's opinion, the effects of a death-denying culture – an ethos that pretends that death does not have anything to do with me – mark western society. His concern is that in such a culture, where the finitude of human existence is bracketed out of the contemporary consciousness, the question as to the meaning of 'Being' is also forgotten or marginalised. According to Heidegger, the modern cultural triumph of what he describes as 'the technological spirit', made possible by the loss of the question of 'Being', signals the spiritual decline of the 'West' with potentially catastrophic consequences for humankind. He sees his critique of the roots of this culture as nothing less than an appeal to win back our history – to arrest this spiritual decline.

Throughout his writings, Heidegger is concerned to situate the origins of the modern cultural triumph of the technological spirit in the context of the history of philosophy. According to him, the preoccupation of the modern scientist/technologist with finding answers to every question or ignoring questions that do not seem to have definitive answers reflects both the desire to control reality and a reluctance to admit to any mysterious or transcendent dimension to reality. From Heidegger's perspective, this is a serious error because it fails to heed the difference between Being and individual beings and it presumes that Being can be studied as substance, an object of science like any other being.

The question of the meaning of Being has nothing to do with the composition of individual existents. Rather, it draws attention to the question as to 'why is there something rather than nothing?' To authentically ask this question is to be open to the reality of nothingness, and it is this feature of the question that shows just how far removed philosophy is from science. For science the question of nothingness is simply a non-question.

The work of philosophy is to listen to Being rather than to seek answers. To question truly is not to seek answers, rather it is to seek attunement. In this context, Heidegger contrasts a knower or a user with someone who is a listener or a respondent to existence. According to Heidegger, the technological spirit gives priority to the 'ego' driven faculties of knowing and using. In this technological culture, we deliberately forget or more precisely we conceal from ourselves the need to be astonished before the mystery of Being. With Heidegger, the stress not only falls on the question of 'Being' but on the way of asking that question. To question truly is to enter into harmony with that which is being questioned. Furthermore, according to Heidegger, that which is worthy of questioning is literally inexhaustible. There are no terminal answers to the meaning of human existence or of a Mozart sonata or a painting by van Gogh.

The manner in which Heidegger's philosophy calls us to stand humbly before the mystery of Being suggests parallels between the Heideggerian conception of Being and the Judeo-Christian understanding of God. Heidegger's philosophy offers a trenchant critique of the death denying ethos of western society and the attempt within this cultural ethos to situate the quest for meaning and values within the exclusively materialist parameters of scientific or technological power. His exploration of the question of the meaning of Being draws attention to the necessity to acknowledge the existence of a transcendent horizon, a stance that has much in common with traditional theism – the belief in the need to affirm a divine source for the search for meaning and values. Just because there can be no end to genuine questioning that does not mean that the search for meaning and values is futile or aimless. If Heidegger is correct, we must recognise the dignity of the unanswerable; we must respect the mystery of God or the mystery of Being and yet, nevertheless, enter into dialogue with it.

Emmanuel Levinas (1906–1995)
Emmanuel Levinas was one of the most prominent philosophers in the phenomenological tradition in the twentieth century. Born in Lithuania of Jewish parentage, Levinas moved to France at the age of seventeen and in 1930 he became a French citizen. In 1928 and 1929 he briefly studied under both Husserl and Heidegger. Between 1940 and 1945 Levinas was a prisoner of war in Germany; his status as an officer in the French army being the only thing that saved him from the fate that befell so many of his co-religionists in the concentration camps. The experience of the Holocaust was to leave an indelible mark on his subsequent life. After the war he returned to France where he devoted himself to promoting the thesis that 'ethics is first philosophy', where ethics is understood as a relation of infinite responsibility to the other person. It was a stance that he believed would challenge the whole tradition of Greek or Western philosophy which he argued fails to accept the obligation to respond to the claims of the other because it suppresses the separateness or the transcendence of the other person, a relationship to which I am exposed when confronted by the face of the other.

Levinas's *Totality and Infinity* which was published in 1961 contained a searing critique of Greek or western philosophy which has consistently sought to suppress 'infinity' – the transcendence or the otherness of the other. Furthermore, while acknowledging the influence of Heidegger on his philosophy, Levinas is nevertheless of the opinion that Heidegger is but the most recent example of this tradition that has contributed to the marginalisation of the other. In a telling comment on Heidegger's celebrated phenomenological analysis of death he observes that:

> There is a fundamental difference between my ethical analysis of death and Heidegger's ontological analysis. Whereas for Heidegger, death is my death, for me it is the other's death.[9]

For one who had survived the Holocaust, for one who was conscious of the ethical challenge posed by the vulnerability of the 'face', it would never be acceptable to tolerate a reduction of the other to a faceless face in the crowd; the death of the other could never be a matter of indifference. For Levinas, an ethical philosophy is one that does not seek to avoid the face of the other because 'the face is the other who asks me not to let him die alone.' (*Dialogues*, 60) Ultimately, the face of the other is a reminder that the other always exceeds any idea that I may have of it and can never be integrated into systems of knowledge, power or control.

There is a strong religious dimension to the philosophy of Levinas and he is one of those credited with being responsible for what has been described as the theological turn in contemporary French phenomenology. As a Jew who had lived through the Holocaust, God could never simply or even primarily be understood as the God of nature or the all-powerful God of creation. As he says:

> The God of ethical philosophy is ... the persecuted God of the prophets who is always in relation with men and whose difference from man is never indifference. (*Dialogues*, 68)

In both 1983 and 1985 he contributed to a serious of dialogues hosted by Pope John Paul II in his summer residence at Castel Gandolfo. He died in 1995 at the age of eighty-nine.

A valuable overview of Levinas' philosophy is to be found in an interview that he gave to the Irish philosopher, Richard Kearney. Some passages from this interview have already been quoted. The following is a brief summary of the other points that were raised in the course of that interview.[10] It commences with a question as to the influences on his philosophy. First and foremost Levinas acknowledges his debt to the phenomenological tradition and, in particular, the contributions of Husserl and Heidegger. He credits the latter with showing the most far-reaching potentialities of this method that, for the first time, gave due prominence to the emotional character of human existence. The emotional states such as guilt, fear, anxiety, joy or dread, are 'the ontological ways in which we feel and find our being-in-the-world.' (*Dialogues*, 51)

Increasingly, in the post-war years, the other major formative influence on Levinas' philosophy was his Jewish faith. In acknowledging the importance of this influence he allows himself to be drawn to reflect on contrasting features of the Greek and biblical approaches to meaning and truth. In his opinion, western philosophy and indeed western culture has inherited a specifically Greek way of thinking, the distinguishing feature of which is:

> the equation of truth with an intelligibility of presence ... that which can be gathered into a totality which we would call the world or cosmos. (*Dialogues*, 55)

In the ethical or biblical perspective the focus is on the theme of justice and concern for the other as other, a theme of love and desire that carries us beyond the finite being of the world as presence. It is in this ethical perspective that God must be thought and not in the ontological perspective of our being-there or of some Supreme Being and Creator. As he says,

> God or *alterité* (otherness) and transcendence, can only be understood in terms of that interhuman dimension ...that cuts through and perforates the totality of presence and points towards the absolutely Other. (*Dialogues*, 57)

In answer to the question as to whether the path to God as the absolutely 'Other' is the path towards the human other Levinas acknowledges that the ethical exigency to be responsible for the other undermines any claim that a philosopher such as Heidegger would place on the primacy of the question of the meaning of Being.

> 'Going towards God' is meaningless unless seen in terms of my primary going towards the other person. I can only go towards God by being ethically concerned by and for the other person. (*Dialogues*, 59)

The introduction of the idea of the primacy of the ethical gives Levinas the opportunity to reflect on the symbol of the other for which he is most remembered, i.e. the symbol of the face. As he says:

> The approach to the face is the most basic mode of responsibility ... . The face is not in front of me but above me; it is the other before death ... it is the other who asks me not to let him die alone. (*Dialogues*, 59-60)

Although Levinas acknowledges Heidegger's contribution to phenomenology, nothing so graphically exposes the gulf that separates their philosophies as this reflection on the face – the symbol of an ethical philosophy. As he says,

> To expose myself to the vulnerability of the face is to put my ontological right to existence into question. In ethics, the other's right to exist has primacy over my own ... the ethical rapport with the face is asymmetrical in that it subordinates my existence to the other. (*Dialogues*, 60)

In contrast to Heidegger, the ethical philosophy espoused by Levinas is based upon the primacy of love for the other and the belief that the self cannot survive or find meaning within its own being-in-the-world. One of the most valuable contributions that Levinas has made to contemporary philosophical debate is to critique the radical individualism that is characteristic of twentieth century portraits of human identity, subjectivity and freedom. As he says,

> I am defined as a subjectivity, as a singular person, as an 'I', precisely because I am exposed to the other. It is my inescapable and incontrovertible answerability to the other that makes me an individual 'I'. (*Dialogues*, 62-63)

In contrast to a philosophy that focuses the quest for meaning and values on the individual autonomous subject, Levinas proposes a philosophy that de-centres the subject and acknowledges that meaning is not so much achieved by the subject as received from another:

> For me, the freedom of the subject is not the highest or primary value. The heteronomy of our response to the human other, or to God as the absolutely other precedes the autonomy of our subjective freedom ... I can never escape the fact that the other has demanded a response from me before I affirm my freedom not to respond to his demand. (*Dialogues*, 63)

In the context of a reflection on the search for meaning and values Levinas' philosophy provides an important reminder of the ethical nature of the quest – the centrality of values in any search for meaning. In point of fact, Levinas' philosophy is premised upon the belief in the primacy of ethics – that 'ethics is first philosophy'. Ethics does not flow from the nature of the quest for meaning, rather it is only an ethical life that is capable of revealing either the possibility of meaning or the contours of the search for meaning that is nothing less than a quest for authenticity or full humanity. Furthermore, his view that 'ethics is first philosophy' is an implicit critique of the view that the search for meaning is one characterised primarily by the search for knowledge or understanding. Most importantly, his philosophy is a reminder that the 'I' or the ego is not the only or even the primary source of meaning in the world – the other is not merely a step on the path to meaning but rather the source and the goal of that search. As mentioned above, Levinas' ethical standpoint is based upon the conviction that the self cannot either survive or find meaning within the confines of its own individual autonomy – its own 'being-in-the-world'. Finally, the philosophical perspective of Levinas allows one to understand the link that Christians make between the love of the neighbour and human fulfillment. From both a Christian and Levinasian perspective, it is only in and through the acceptance of responsibility for the poor and the dispossessed that human identity can be articulated and meaning attained.

This final reflection on the contribution of the phenomenological movement to the search for meaning and values will briefly examine the writings of Edith Stein and Jean Luc Marion. Although from widely divergent backgrounds, these two philosophers have in different ways contributed to a contemporary re-awakening of the transcendent and/or theistic dimension to the search for meaning. In addition, alongside Levinas, Marion is one of those philosophers responsible for the increasing respect that is shown for theological discourse in contemporary phenomenology.

Edith Stein (1891–1942)
Born in Germany of Jewish parents, Edith Stein's passionate quest for truth led her initially to abandon Judaism, becoming as early as 1904 a self-proclaimed atheist. Directing her attention to philosophy she traveled to the university town of Gottingen and commenced her studies under Husserl under whose direction she obtained her doctorate in philosophy in 1916 with a dissertation on the theme of empathy. She subsequently became Husserl's assistant and worked in close collaboration with him for two years. This period was also marked by an increasing interest in the Catholic faith and she was baptised on New Year's Day, 1922. The following years were marked by her increasing reputation as a scholar and an educator, one who forcibly promoted the status of women in society. She correctly recognised that education was a key to women's fulfillment and she strove against the educational and societal barriers that prevented women from attaining their true potential and from exercising leadership roles in social and political life.

With the rise to power of Hitler in 1933 laws were instituted that barred Jewish people from the professions. This brought to an abrupt end Edith Stein's public lectures. However, at the same time, she had begun to become increasingly drawn to the ascetic and contemplative life of St Teresa of Avila, and in May 1933 she entered the Carmelites. Although cloistered in the convent she continued her study of philosophy and completed *Finite and Eternal Being*, a major work that in many respects attempts to reconcile the phenomenology of Husserl with the medieval genius of Aquinas. In 1938 the anti-Jewish pogroms forced her to flee to a Carmelite convent in Holland. However, even that did not spare her. In July 1942 the Catholic bishops of Holland issued a pastoral Letter condemning the forced removal of Jews from Catholic schools and the deportation of

Jewish families to Poland. In reprisal, the Nazi authorities ordered the forced deportation of all Catholics of Jewish origin, including members of religious orders. There was the possibility that even at this late stage Edith Stein could have availed of a rescue attempt but in an eloquent testimony to the values that animated her life she is reported as saying that, 'If I cannot share the lot of my brothers and sisters, my life, in a certain sense is destroyed.' On August 2nd Edith Stein and her sister Rosa were arrested and sent to Auschwitz; on August 9th they died in the gas chambers.

So much of Edith Stein's life and death was to highlight the tragedy that befell Europe during the Nazi era. In the last analysis, her search for meaning, for truth and values went hand in hand with the sacrifice of her life, one of countless millions destroyed by the racism and xenophobia that characterised the scourge of Nazism. How distant must the concerns of phenomenology have appeared to one caught up in this tumult; and yet there is a unity to her life that should not be lost to view. From her very earliest philosophical reflections on the theme of empathy she recognised that the world of meaning and values that we seek to constitute is not, and can never be, a world that I constitute as an individual. Rather the world of meaning is given – something received by me as a member of a shared humanity. For Stein, the phenomenological quest led her beyond phenomenology to a search for objective truth – the search for God, under whose shadow all created worlds are called to judgement. It was this search for the truth that was ultimately to lead Stein to the cloistered life of a Carmelite.

From her earliest writings Edith Stein recognised the importance of the state of empathy, that 'in-feeling' which puts me in touch with the experience of others – a world outside of myself. Furthermore, empathy reminds us that our point of contact with the other is not primarily at the level of rational consciousness but rather at the level of feelings. Although one cannot literally feel another's pain or joy, one can nevertheless grasp the pain or the joy of the other empathically – in a sense transferring oneself into it. Finally, in and through the state of empathy I know infallibly that I am not alone – that I do not inhabit a solitary world. If Stein is correct, empathy is both the condition of possible knowledge of the existing outer objective world, and an essential tool to enable me to understand myself. In this context, it is the prior condition of the possibility of the constitution of my world – in particular, the constitution of a world of meaning and values. Above all, empathy reveals the importance of feelings in the quest for meaning and values.

In his homily on the occasion of the canonisation of Edith Stein in 1998, Pope John Paul II reminded his audience that:

> For a long time Edith Stein was a seeker. Her mind never tired of searching and her heart always yearned for hope. She traveled the arduous path of philosophy with passionate enthusiasm. Eventually she was rewarded: she seized the truth. Or better: she was seized by it. Then she discovered that truth had a name: Jesus Christ. From that moment on, the incarnate Word was the One and All. Looking back as a Carmelite on this period of her life, she wrote to a Benedictine nun: 'Whoever seeks the truth is seeking God, whether consciously or unconsciously'.

This is a fitting epitaph to a remarkable woman of the twentieth century, one whose life and writings remind us that the search for meaning and values is not something that ought be undertaken lightly: there is a logic to the search that can lead one in directions that are least expected.

Jean-Luc Marion (1942–)
Born in Paris in the year that Edith Stein died, Jean-Luc Marion is professor of philosophy at the university of Paris. He is a

prolific writer and the author of, among others, *The Idol and Distance* (1977), *Prolegomena to Charity* (1986) and *In Excess* (2001), all translated into English and published by Fordham University Press. Marion represents a current in contemporary French phenomenology that grapples with the possibility of encountering God within a philosophical methodology that by definition 'brackets out' of consideration all consideration of transcendent reality. In *God Without Being* (1982), Marion argues for a God free from all the categories of Being and proposes an alternative location for God in the realm of love or charity. His most recent work published in 2003 entitled *Le Phénomène érotique* (henceforth *PE*) contains his most explicit statement to date about the sheer primacy of love. Specifically, Marion suggests that it is only in the gift of love that one can receive the gift of significance which alone is capable of contesting the ultimate challenge to the search for meaning – namely, the challenge of nihilism contained in questions such as 'what's the use?' or 'to what end?' It is an idea that suggests a link between Marion and Edith Stein: both recognise that the quest for values is intimately linked with the quest to be valued as a person. In his treatment of this theme there are parallels also with the views of Augustine that were addressed above. Taking his theme from the opening lines of Ecclesiastes, 'All is vanity. What does man gain by all the toil at which he toils under the sun?' Marion believes that the ultimate nihilistic challenge posed by the suggestion that 'all is vanity' cannot be sidestepped. Furthermore, it is not one that can be met by anything that I could give to myself because it is only the gift of another's love that offers the type of assurance capable of responding to that challenge.

In a sustained analysis of the challenge posed by 'vanity' Marion scotches the notion that one can confer significance on oneself; and he acknowledges that one's value as a person is critically dependent on being able to offer a positive response to the related questions 'does anyone love me?' and, 'can I in turn be a lover?'

It is not the certainty of my existence that I require, rather the assurance of my significance or my value. It is Marion's contention that it is only in a relationship of love or the promise of this intimacy that one is capable of receiving the assurance of significance that all human beings crave. I can love myself because I receive assurance from somewhere else – I discover myself lovable through the gift or the call of another. In a reflection that reminds one of Levinas, Marion draws the phrase from Isaiah 6:8, 'here I am', to highlight the manner in which significance is mutually given in word or in silence. The only assurance that I want or need is love – the assurance of my dignity as a lover. This assurance is both received and given in the 'here I am' that surges forth as a pledge of eternal love. In and through this pledge or covenant, the 'I' or the ego is actually reborn as lover and beloved. In a manner of speaking, I receive my significance the moment that the other consecrates me as a lover.

The question that this issue brings to the surface is nothing less than that of self-identity – how it is that I perceive myself, what questions define me? It is Marion's contention that the Kantian questions that I can choose, such as, 'who am I? 'what can I know?', 'what ought I do'? or 'what permits me to hope?', will not suffice to penetrate the mystery of self-identity because they do not meet the challenge posed by the question, 'to what end – why bother?' Only a question that is not chosen but rather is experienced at the core of one's being – one that raises issues of meaning and value – only such a question is adequate to sketch the appropriate contours of self-identity. Such a question is 'does anyone love me?' It is Marion's opinion, that only within such a framework that one can legitimately ask 'who am I'? In placing emphasis on the other and indeed the otherness of the other Marion draws attention to the vulnerability that characterises the human situation; self-identity and self-love are received rather than achieved. If Marion is correct, it is not me, but rather the other who is the ultimate guardian of my identity. This 'other' cannot be reduced to me but nevertheless is not a stranger to me.

The significance of Marion's approach is that he situates self-identity under the rubric of love as desire. In a lengthy reflection on the manner in which the gift of intimate love reveals me to myself in my individuality he says:

> I become myself and recognize myself in my singularity when I discover and admit in the end the one that I desire; the one who alone shows me my most secret centre – the one whom I miss and the one who misses me. (*PE*, 172)

Over a long period in and through attending to the desire for the other that is missed I become less and less obscure to myself: 'My desire tells me about myself in showing me that which excites me' (*PE*, 172). All of this reminds one of Augustine who was ever conscious of the manner in which love or desire shapes human nature.

Marion concludes with a brief but convincing reflection on the Christian belief that God is love and on the significance of viewing his incarnate revelation from the perspective of a phenomenology of love. Marion creates an evocative portrait of a God who is both immanent and transcendent, one who is close to us and like us in that he loves like us and a God whose love infinitely transcends our limited capacity. As he says,

> God precedes us and transcends us, but in the first place and above all in that he loves us infinitely more than we love him. God surpasses us in being a better lover. (*PE*, 342)

This reflection on Marion's philosophy allows one to see that contours of the search for meaning and values are inextricably linked to those of love; it is the promise of love that alone can open the door to meaning; it is the gift of love that provides the assurance that there is meaning. Marion's contribution is to have recognised the importance of a gospel of love in meeting the nihilistic challenge that all is vanity. In a Christian schema, one finds such a gospel; God is revealed as the first and definitive other who in loving me enables me in turn to love and in so doing, offers me the assurance that only love can provide.

Notes

1. All translations from the *Crito* are taken from *The Last Days of Socrates*, trans. Hugh Tredennick, London, Penguin Classics, 1954, pp. 79-96.
2. All translations of the *Gorgias* are taken from *Gorgias*, trans. Walter Hamilton, London, Penguin Books, 1960.
3. *Symposium*, 206b-c. All translations of the *Symposium* are taken from *The Symposium*, trans. Walter Hamilton, London, Penguin Books, 1951
4. All translations of the *Metaphysics* are taken from *Aristotle's Metaphysics*, trans. John Warrington, London, J. M. Dent and Sons Ltd, 1954.
4. This is an extract from an unsigned article in the review To-morrow which Richard Ellman has identified as having been written by Yeats. The full quotation reads: 'No man can create as did Shakespeare, Homer, Sophocles, who does not believe with all his blood and nerve, that man's soul is immortal, for the evidence lies plain to all men that where that belief has declined, men have turned from creation to photography.' See Richard Ellman, *The Man and the Masks* (London, 1954), p.250.
5. *Discourse on Method*, 1. All translations from this work and the *Principles of Philosophy* are taken from Rene Descartes, *A Discourse on Method and Other Works*, trans. E. S. Haldane and G.R. Ross, New York, Washington Square Press, 1965.
6. *Critique of Practical Reason*, 166. All translations are taken from Immannuel Kant, *Critique of Practical Reason*, trans. L. W. Beck, New York, Library of Liberal Arts, 1966.
7. All quotations from Heidegger's *Being and Time* are taken from the edition of *Being and Time*, trans. J. McQuarrie and E. Robinson,

Oxford, Basil Blackwell, 1973.
8   M. Heidegger, *An Introduction to Metaphysics*, trans. R. Manheim, New York, Anchor Books, 1961, p. 1.
9   Kearney Richard, *Dialogues with contemporary Continental thinkers* Manchester, Manchester University Press, 1984, p.62
10 *Dialogues*, pp. 45 – 69.

Part Two

THE RESPONSE TO THE QUEST

Introduction

Divided into two parts, the language of symbol and the tradition of response, part two will trace the contours of the search for meaning and values throughout the ages and show the variety of religious and non-religious responses to the great questions of life. It will provide evidence of the search for meaning and values in both ancient and contemporary societies and identify elements of symbolic, mythical and metaphorical thinking in religious and secular traditions.

From the earliest times humans have responded to the quest for meaning in a variety of spiritualities, symbolic languages and meaning systems. The main focus of chapter three is to highlight the manner in which the search for meaning finds expression in the language of symbol and myth, a language that from the earliest recorded civilisations has highlighted a sense of the sacred. An unrivaled resource for this chapter is Mircea Eliade. His writings offer a penetrating analysis of the mythologies that vivify ancient communities and tell us so much about how these myths express insights from these communities on the meaning and destiny of the human species.

Chapter four will trace 'the tradition of response'. It will explore some key myths with a view to analysing the manner in which they offered the ancient civilisations a way of addressing issues that emerge in the course of a quest for meaning. The chapter will then examine the different ways in which both modern and contemporary society have responded to this quest. In this context, chapter four contains an overview of the humanist tradition, including short biographies of key figures in the historical development of humanism. The chapter will conclude with an explanation of some technical terms such as atheism and agnosticism.

3
The Language of Symbol

Forms of symbolic language
All language is symbolic and in that context the language of symbol is etched into the very fabric of what it is to be human, a fact that was to lead the German philosopher Ernst Cassirer (1874–1945) to define humans as symbolic animals. As he correctly observed, humans do not just live life but must give expression to it in symbols. We are quintessentially the creators of symbols. Furthermore, as distinct from signs and signals that are part of the physical world, symbols uniquely belong to human discourse – a world that is constituted by meaning. They are in many ways the building blocks of a world of meaning that encompasses science, religion and art.

Much of the world of symbols is purely conventional with a standard point of reference such as language and mathematics. However, symbols can also act as disclosure models of something that is not fully comprehensible – where language cannot fully capture the reality. Symbols are thus a form of indirect language that point beyond the symbol to a reality that needs to be interpreted. At another level symbols emerge as a means of communicating experiences that disclose a transcendent or depth dimension to reality. Ritual is a particularly potent form of symbolic language that helps to communicate that which at one level is incommunicable. The symbolic language of ritual is also a reminder that the language of symbol is not restricted to or even primarily communicated at the level of rational discourse. The language of symbol is a language of the heart as well as the head. In this context, the emotive character of symbolic language is not something that should be underestimated.

What is often not adverted to is that the language of symbol is not easy to translate. For example, the city of Jerusalem is not just a city but also a potent symbol. However, precisely as a symbol it signifies radically different things to Jews, Muslims and Christians. Similarly, anyone familiar with the symbolic character of gestures, flags, banners and anthems needs to be conscious of the multifaceted nature of these symbols. There is no one meaning that is capable of capturing their symbolic character. Similarly, the care that one must take to ensure that one's gestures are not misinterpreted is a reminder of the way in which symbols can symbolise different things for people from a variety of cultural backgrounds.

One of the most powerful expressions of the language of symbol is the myth. As a form of symbolic language it has a number of particular characteristics that are well summarised by the theologian John McQuarrie.[1] The language is dramatic: it is concrete and particular, the language of action or story; the myth points beyond itself and becomes interpretative for a whole series of incidents and situations; the language is evocative: it is language on several different levels; myth is immediate to those in a mythical culture: the mythical person is immersed in the myth; supernatural agencies play a part in mythic stories; myth is usually characterised by remoteness in time and place, something that gives it a generality and a universal quality; a myth is not a private story, rather its role is to inform or shape the life of a community; the mythic story becomes a model for all humanity and a model for eternity.

The importance of symbols

Symbols emerge in the formulation of responses to questions concerning the meaning of life because of the transcendent dimension of the experiences that give rise to these questions. One of the foremost authorities on comparative religion, Mircea Eliade, has painstakingly shown that from the earliest recorded history societies have had recourse to symbols, many of which are transcultural, both to understand the questions of the meaning of life and to formulate responses to these questions. An example of one of the many symbols explored by Eliade is that of ascension. As he explains it, the motif of ascent symbolises a breakthrough to a different level of existence; rituals of ascension are expressions of the value of 'height'; death is about transcending the human state and passing to the beyond. Typically, the journey to some 'higher sphere' is depicted or understood as an upward journey, a trudge up a mountain path. In Indian myth, Yama, who is the first person to die, leads others through the mountain passes. In Egypt, Ra uses a ladder to climb from earth to heaven. Australian aborigines speak about a great tree which souls climbed to get to heaven. Reaching heaven, then, is an ascent: Jacob's ladder, Mohammad seeing a ladder rising from the temple, St John of the Cross depicting mystical perfection as the ascent of Mount Carmel.

Allied to the symbol of ascension is that of 'flight'. As an instance of the importance of this symbol Eliade points out the many references to 'the symbols of the soul as a bird, of the wings of the soul, etc., and the images which point to the spiritual life as an elevation and the mystical experience as an ascension'.[2] It is a symbol that is to be found in all of the great world religions; one that suggests a universal sense of the desire for, and the possibility of, freedom from the limitations of the material world. Eliade has investigated numerous other such symbols of which one of the most impressive is his treatment of the earth as a woman or mother, a symbol that suggests fertility, and more importantly, the links that exist between human and cosmic creation. As he says, ' the fundamental conception – that a mother is only the representative of the telluric (earth) Great Mother – lies at the origin of customs without number' (Eliade, 167). From almost every corner of the globe there are records of similar birth-rituals, whereby the newborn child was placed on the earth, as if to signify the 'true' mother.

From the earliest times the symbolic importance of numbers has also been recognised, and they have proven to be potent ways of giving expression to the belief in a meaningful universe: one guided by a divine presence or the presence of the Gods. One of the most celebrated examples of the symbolic importance of number is to be seen in the Babylonian construction of the twelve signs of the zodiac through a juxtaposition of the occurrence of twelve full moons within the solar year and the series of constellations of stars in the zodiac band. For the Babylonians the number twelve and specifically the signs of the zodiac became key symbols of cosmic order. Likewise, in the Judaeo-Christian tradition the number twelve is a potent symbol of order. One notes for example the twelve tribes of Israel and, in the New Testament, the choice of twelve apostles.

As might be imagined, two of the principle symbols of cosmic order are time and place. In the earliest mythic cultures the sacred becomes present in time and place. These cultures perceived time as heterogeneous; that is, divided in two: between profane/ordinary time and sacred time. The perennial concern in these cultures is to ensure that there is harmony between these two realms. An example of this concern is to be seen in the care taken in near-eastern societies such as Egypt and Mesopotamia to ensure that important events such as a king's coronation were timed to coincide with a particular point in the cycle of nature.[3] The importance attached to symbols of place can be seen in the importance attached in almost every society to a particular 'mountain or primeval hill', the nearest place to the sky and thus to God. In Greek mythology, Mount Olympus was the dwelling place of the Gods. In ancient mythology, the mountain was a symbol of the centre where heaven and earth meet – the place where life began. It was also seen as a symbol of the transcendent or of the passage to the hereafter. The symbolic significance attached to a 'rock' is similar – a symbol of the centre or a symbol of order. Again in Greek mythology, the stone at Delphi marked the centre of the universe.

Finally, one can point to the universal symbolic power of core elements of the cosmos that from the beginning of recorded history have given expression to foundational beliefs regarding the order and the unity of the cosmos. In many ancient cultures the cosmic symbol of the sun was connected with both sovereignty and fertility. For example, in ancient Egypt the sun symbolised the Supreme Being, Rē. Other core elements of the cosmos such as water, fire, air and light were equally potent symbols. Again in ancient Egypt, the waters of the Nile were perceived to be the creative principle from which all life emerged.

As an example of the symbolic power of this constellation of elements one need look no further than the Judaeo-Christian tradition. The symbolic importance of water is to be seen throughout the Bible and is particularly attested to by its place in the Baptism liturgy. The symbols of air and breath give expression to the divine creative power as in the phrases 'the breath of life' and 'breathing upon the waters'. The symbolic importance of fire can be seen in the place accorded to the Paschal fire in the Easter liturgy. Similarly, the use of both fire and air as symbols of the Holy Spirit is to be seen in the Pentecost liturgy. The symbolic significance of light in the Judaeo-Christian tradition is amply attested to by the frequency with which this symbol is used throughout the Bible as well as the place that it occupies in both Jewish and Christian ritual. In the Johannine tradition, light is a key symbol that is used to describe the person of Jesus Christ. Other Christological symbols in the Johannine tradition include the Vine, the Shepherd, the Lamb and the Bridegroom, the 'bread of life' and the 'fountain of living water'. Finally, there is the symbol of the 'Cross', which is the most potent symbol in the Christian tradition. Both adorned with the figure of Christ or simply as a bare cross, this symbol gives expression to the core Christian belief in the Paschal mystery – the death and resurrection of Christ.

The power of symbolic language
The ability to evoke and to sustain commitment is eloquent testimony of the power of symbolic language. All forms of ritual and symbolic rites of initiation show clear evidence of the ability of symbol to engender commitment and the ritual character of much symbolism is intended to promote a participative engagement with the world of the symbol; ritual does not encourage neutral observers. From another perspective, there are very few Irish people who would be unaware of the power of a popular anthem such as 'The Fields of Athenry' to evoke commitment or to engender a form of group solidarity. Similarly, to anyone remotely familiar with recent Irish history, the symbolic power of flags, drums, flutes, bagpipes, painted wall murals and kerb stones to sustain commitment to a 'cause' is all too obvious. These symbols have not only the power to evoke commitment they also have the power to include or exclude; in many cases they are deliberately invoked for the purpose of exclusion. The concern expressed by many in Northern Ireland to ensure 'neutral' symbols on police uniforms and in public buildings such as courthouses and county offices is a case in point. Although symbols can never be neutral, one can appreciate the desire for inclusive symbols rather than those that are perceived to exclude one section of the population.

The power of symbols is also reflected in their ability to juxtapose or join together two discrete ideas. The world of marketing is adept at using symbols to suggest connections in the mind of the consumer: symbols used to suggest that a particular alcoholic drink is good for one's health or that a particular fashion accessory will make one a more interesting person. The impact of such suggestive use of symbols on individual consumption patterns is easily measurable. Likewise, all societies make use of this ability of symbols to juxtapose different ideas in order to engender or to sustain a particular vision of national identity. Symbols familiar to an Irish audience, such as round towers, shamrocks and groupings of traditional musicians, have been used at one time or another to suggest a particular national or cultural identity. The fading significance of some of these symbols is, however, a reminder of one important caveat to the power of symbols, namely that they have continually to be renewed. They are only powerful so long as they communicate that which they symbolise and with the passage of time even what were once the most powerful of symbols can become empty of any symbolic power.

Alongside symbols, one should not ignore the power of myths to shape communal identity. To those that suggest that we live in a post-mythic age it is well to remember the manner in which two of the great ideologies of the twentieth century, namely communism and Nazism, attained their status within a mythical framework – the eschatological myth of the kingdom of the proletariat and the mythological stories of the Germanic race that sought to give credence to the idea of racial supremacy. Indeed one of the most pervasive ideologies of the last hundred years, namely capitalism, is also not without its mythologies: the consumerist myth that seeks to identify happiness with material prosperity, and the myth of a capitalist society as a 'land of the free', being but two examples. History, even contemporary history, is interpreted in mythical form and the power of these myths to shape the contemporary psyche is appreciable. One only has to advert to the manner by which some versions of history describe an Irish nation that has been re-born phoenix-like from the ashes of 1916 and the manner in which historical figures such as Pearse and Connolly attained archetypal status. Likewise, one can observe the manner in which the events surrounding the siege of Derry and the Battle of the Boyne have been transformed into myths that seek to confirm the status of the Protestant people of Ulster as a 'chosen people' in a manner not totally dissimilar to the self-understanding of the Jews. As with all symbols, the power of myths lies in their ability to be perceived as in some way revelatory of reality. When this no longer occurs the myth becomes obscured and is reduced to the status of a legend or simply a story/fable.

4

The Tradition of Response

Myth and early cosmologies

While acknowledging the fallacy of presuming that contemporary humans live in a post-mythic age, one is conscious nevertheless of the differences that characterise the pre-philosophical world from the one that we inhabit today. In the ancient mythical cultures there did not exist any critical distance between the myth and reality. In relating to the world, the ancients perceived themselves to be part of the world in a manner that precludes the subject/object distinction, one that is key to scientific thought. Furthermore, in looking for a cause of an event the ancients will more often look for a 'who' rather than a 'how'. This is well expressed by Frankfort,

> If the rivers refuse to rise, it is not suggested that the lack of rainfall on distant mountains adequately explains the calamity. When the river does not rise, it has refused to rise. The river, or the Gods, must be angry with the people who depend on the inundation. (*Before Philosophy*, 24)

In these ancient civilisations, the cosmologies symbolised the belief that human beings are in touch with a reality that transcends them and that, in a real sense, human societies participate in the divine order – a participation so intimate that in many of the ancient cultures the earthly society and the cosmos are seen as part of one embracing order.

One of the very oldest cosmic mythical 'texts' from the ancient world that we possess is that which is imprinted in the stone symbolism of the Irish burial site of Newgrange. Covering an area of over one acre, Newgrange is surrounded by ninety-seven kerbstones. Some of these are richly decorated with megalithic art depicting squares, lozenges, triangles, chevrons or zigzag lines and the frequent use of single and multiple circles and arcs. In addition, there are three large stones guarding the entrance to a nineteen-metre-long inner passage that ascends to a cross shaped chamber with a corbelled vault rising vertically above the horizontal cruciform axis. The passage and chamber of Newgrange are illuminated by the winter solstice sunrise; a shaft of sunlight shines through the roof-box over the entrance and penetrates the passage to light up the chamber. Lastly, the exterior of the burial chamber is covered in white quartz stone that is very visibly interspersed with egg-shaped granite stones. All of these construction details would seem to be significant, suggesting the symbolic significance of this site.

Built over five thousand years ago, this stone text provides us with the earliest possible evidence of religious and spiritual behaviour in that key rite of passage, namely the rite of burial. In a valuable commentary on this stone text that draws on a detailed knowledge of comparable sites in other countries, the Irish philosopher Brendan Purcell[4] provides us with convincing evidence that Newgrange can only be understood if one recognises that in its construction one witnesses the reenactment of the central cosmic myth of death and re-birth. The sheer scale of Newgrange suggests the idea of a spiritual centre. The symbolic significance of this site as a sacred site at the centre of the earth is further suggested by the presence of,

(a) three large stones guarding the entrance to the burial chamber, (b) the passage to the centre of the chamber is an ascent and (c) the axis point is located at a fifth point, where the four parts of the cross meet; the number five was widely used in ancient cultures as a symbol of the centre of the earth. The idea of Newgrange as a symbol for the centre of the earth, a place where heaven and earth meet, is further suggested by the grouping together of two sets of symbols, (a) triangles symbolising perhaps the re-ordering power of lunar rebirth and (b) the squares or lozenges that symbolise the earth.

Unquestionably, the most important feature of this burial chamber is the manner in which the sun bursts through the roof-box over the entrance and shines up the passage to the inner chamber at sunrise on the shortest day of the year. The accuracy of this Neolithic astronomic measurement is truly extraordinary, and is undoubtedly the result of much painstaking work. Although one cannot read the minds of those who constructed Newgrange, it is hard to imagine that this work was undertaken on a mere whim. The opposite is clearly the case, a belief reinforced by the symbolic significance attached to the winter solstice, the shortest day of the year. The studies of Mircea Eliade[5] offer ample evidence of the importance of the winter solstice in the ancient world. As he says,

> Throughout the north, the gradual shortening of the days as the winter solstice approaches inspires fear that the sun may die away completely. The falling or darkening of the sun becomes one of the signs of the coming end of the world, of the conclusion that is, of the cosmic cycle, generally to be followed by a new creation and a new human race. *(Patterns in Comparative Religion, 147)*

The juxtaposition of the two classical cosmic symbols of place (the sacred centre) and time (the winter solstice) suggest that for these Neolithic inhabitants of Ireland Newgrange was the location for that all-encompassing mythic cosmic drama of death and re-birth, something further suggested in the proliferation of chevrons as well as the egg-shaped granite stones both of which have been suggested as symbols of rebirth. Brendan Purcell's summary is as follows,

> Here, at the centre of the world where heaven, earth and underworld intersect, the Boyne people expressed their experience of the mysterious answer to their search for participation in everlasting order. Here they deployed all their artistic, technological, astronomic and measuring skills to elevate midwinter sunrise into a cosmic YES between sun and earth at the zero point of their mutual forsakenness. (Purcell, 47-48.)

The existence in Ireland of elaborate burial chambers of the antiquity and scale of Newgrange, Knowth and Dowth is vivid illustration of the extent to which the ancient world would have been conscious of the larger cosmic and transcendent horizon within which meaning is located.

As distinct from stone edifices, the earliest written cosmologies took the form of mythologies, of which the Babylonian creation myths and the Genesis story recounted in the Bible are but two of the most documented. However, every civilisation had its own origin myths, many of which have traits in common. Indeed, it is widely regarded that the Babylonian creation myths are the model for most of the stories in the Biblical account recorded in *Genesis* 1-11. Ancient Egyptian culture had a number of overlapping mythological accounts of creation, one of the most famous of which is to be found in chapter seventeen of the *Book of the Dead*. In the following extract, the author associates himself alongside the creator God (Rē-Atum).

> I am Atum when I was alone in Nūn (the waters of chaos out of which life emerged); I am Rē (the sun God) in his (first) appearances, when he began to rule that which he had made. What does that mean? This 'Rē, when he began to rule that which he had made' means that Rē began to appear as a king, as one who existed before (the air-God) Shū had (even) lifted (heaven from earth), when he (Rē) was on the primeval hillock which was in Hermopolis... I am the great God who came into being by himself. Who is he? The great God who came into being by himself is water; he is Nūn, the father of the Gods. (In another version he is Rē – the sun God.)[6]

In this creation myth, one sees juxtaposed the great Egyptian cosmological symbols of sun and water – creation from the water of chaos reminding one of the phrase from the book of Genesis 'the earth being formless and void, with darkness over the surface of the deep' (Gen. 1.2). One also can observe the importance the Egyptians attached to the idea of the creation hillock – the Egyptian symbol shows a rounded mound with the rays of the sun streaming upward from it. As Frankfort states it, 'the pyramids themselves borrow this idea of a rising hill as a promise to the deceased Egyptian buried within the pyramid that he will emerge again into new being.' (*Before Philosophy*, 60) It has already been observed that the importance of the high place that the pyramid imitates is not confined to ancient Egyptian culture; throughout the ancient world, it symbolises the place of passage to the hereafter, the place where earth and heaven meet.

Evidence of religious and spiritual behaviour in ancient societies

Evidence of religious and spiritual behaviour in ancient societies can be seen in two of the most famous of the 'ancient and near eastern' texts, namely the Babylonian *Epic of*

Gilgamesh and the Egyptian *The Dispute of a Man, Who Contemplates Suicide, with His Soul*. While making no presumption that these are religious texts, both of them show an acute sensitivity to the core questions of meaning that shape religious sensibility.

The *Epic of Gilgamesh*[7] was known throughout the Mesopotamian world and could be dated as early as 1200 BCE. As the celebrated oriental scholar, J. B. Pritchard, describes it, 'the poem deals with such earthy things as man and nature, love and adventure, friendship and combat – all masterfully blended into a background for the stark reality of death.' (Pritchard, 72) The central characters are the young Gilgamesh, the ruler of Uruk in southern Babylonia, and Enkidu, whom the Gods have created to be Gilamesh's friend. Together, they set off on various adventures all of which show the depth of their friendship. And then tragedy strikes. Enkidu offends the God Enlil by slaying the monster Huwawa who guards the forest for Enlil and, for that offence, he is duly condemned to death. Up until that point Gilgamesh had been contemptuous of death. But on the death of his friend Enkidu, recounted at the end of *Tablet VII*, all that is changed, and the stark reality of death faces him. Throughout *Tablets VIII, IX and X* the enormity of the tragedy reveals itself; he even refuses to accept the reality of the death of his friend. This extract from *Tablet X*, addressed possibly to the Goddess Ishtar, reveals his state of mind.

> He who with me has shared all hazards –
> the fate of man has overtaken him.
> All day and night have I wept over him
> and would not have him buried –
> my friend might yet rise up at my (loud) cries,
> for seven days and nights –
> until a maggot dropped from his nose.
> Since he is gone, I can no comfort find,
> keep roaming like a hunter in the plains.

> O ale-wife (the Goddess Ishtar), now that I have seen your face,
> let me not see the death which I ever dread.

As the last lines of this passage suggest, Gilgamesh is not only haunted by the spectre of the death of his friend, but in the midst of this tragedy, he begins to see his own death and also to fear it, raising questions as to whether 'I too like him will lie down not to rise again for ever and ever?' *Tablet X, ii* (Assyrian version). Inflamed by the terrifying reality of death, he sets out in pursuit of the 'holy grail' of eternal life. With the following words in *Tablet X, iii,* the Goddess Ishtar warns him of the folly of pursuing his quest

> Gilgamesh, whither are you wandering?
> Life, which you look for, you will never find.
> For when the Gods created man, they let
> death be his share, and life
> withheld in their own hands.
> Gilgamesh, fill your belly –
> day and night make merry,
> let days be full of joy,
> dance and make music day and night.
> and wear fresh clothes,
> and wash your head and bathe.
> Look at the child that is holding your hand
> and let your wife delight in your embrace.
> These things alone are the concern of men.

He does not listen to her advice and when eventually he succeeds in crossing the waters of death he meets a wise man called Utnapishtim. His initial advice, contained in *Tablet X, vi,* seems to reinforce the perceived wisdom that death cannot be overcome.

> Do we build a house for ever?
> Do we seal (contacts) for ever ...
> The dragon-fly [leaves] its shell
> that its face might but glance at the face of the sun.
> Since the days of yore there has been no [permanence]...

However, at the behest of his wife, Utnapishtim tells Gilgamesh about a secret plant that grows on the bottom of the sea and that has the power to rejuvenate him. After much effort he finds it, and, but for a quirk of fate, everlasting youthful life would have been his. Tired from his exertions, Gilgamesh leaves the plant on the shore while he goes for a swim. While he is in the water a snake sees the plant and eats it. Immediately the serpent gains immortality – the power of sloughing its skin and so renewing its youth.

> Then Gilgamesh sat down and wept
> Tears streaming down his cheeks,
> He took the hand of Urshanab, the boatman.
> For whose sake Urshanab, have I strained my muscles?
> For whose sake has my heart's blood been spent?
> I brought no blessing on myself–
> I did the serpent underground good service.

This concludes the final verses of *Tablet XI*. At one level it is a deeply unsatisfying ending. As Frankfort observes: 'an inner turmoil is left to rage on, a vital question finds no answer.' (Frankfort, 227) And yet, that is not the whole story. For a poem written at the dawn of civilisation – over three thousand years ago, it reveals an extraordinary willingness and ability to reflect on the deepest of human mysteries, namely the mystery of death. Furthermore, it shows clear evidence that the mythic form is capable of sustaining analytic discourse of a most sophisticated kind, and is capable of grappling with questions that go to the heart of religious belief. For example, like

Augustine in his reflections on the death of a friend, the author of Gilgamesh shows an acute awareness that it is in the death of a friend/loved one that the reality of death is revealed in all its starkness. However, the most interesting parallel is with the question that underlies the Biblical book of Job. What is most striking about the epic of Gilgamesh is the manner in which it treats the onset of death as one would treat the question of evil. What has a good man done to deserve death – the ultimate evil? It is an issue that plumbs the depths of religious sensibility and one that raises the most fundamental question concerning the possibility of affirming a world of meaning.

From a very different culture, namely the Egyptian world at the beginning of the Middle Kingdom, approximately 2000 BCE, and considerably earlier than the *Epic of Gilgamesh,* one finds another remarkable text that shows further evidence that the ancients did not lack the ability to reflect on foundational questions concerning human meaning. This is entitled *The Dispute of a Man, Who Contemplates Suicide, with His Soul.*[8] In the course of an excellent short commentary on this text the celebrated philosopher Eric Voegelin[9] summarises the text as follows,

> The man is dejected by the misery of the time and wants to cast off a life that has become senseless. But he hesitates before the irrevocable act; his soul is not in agreement with his resolve. In the dispute between the man and his soul the arguments for and against suicide are presented, until the decision is reached and the soul agrees to go with the man wherever he goes. (Voegelin, 98)

Very early in the dialogue it is obvious that the soul fears for the consequences of this course of action because, in the Egyptian culture of that time, suicide was regarded as immoral, and a person who committed suicide was not permitted to receive a proper burial. The course of action suggested by the soul is to 'pursue the happy day and forget care.' (v. 69) This suggestion is not well received by the man. He expresses his horror in the following rather colourful passage, 'Behold my name will reek through thee more than the stench of crocodiles, more than sitting in the assembly among the crocodiles.' (v. 96–97) As the poem progresses we become more aware of why it is that the man's life seems to be without meaning.

> To whom can I speak today?
> One's fellows are evil;
> the friends of today do not love.
> To whom can I speak today?
> Faces have disappeared:
> every man has a downcast face toward his fellow.
> To whom can I speak today?
> A man should arouse wrath by his evil character,
> but he stirs everyone to laughter, in spite of the wickedness of his sin.
> To whom can I speak today?
> There are no righteous:
> the land is left to those who do wrong.
> To whom can I speak today?
> The sin that afflicts the land,
> it has no end. (Taken from v. 102–130)

In this series of verses, one observes the manner in which the belief in the presence or absence of a world of meaning is linked to the societal absence of or disregard for core values. As the following verses show, death seems to him to be a more desirable option than living in the midst of this ethical wasteland.

> Death is in my sight today
> like the recovery of a sick man.
> Death is in my sight today
> Like the odors of lotus blossoms

> Death is in my sight today
> like the passing away of rain.
> Death is in my sight today
> like an unclouding of the sky,
> like an illumination that leads to what one did not know.
> Death is in my sight today
> like the longing of a man to see his home again,
> after many years held in captivity.

The poem moves towards its conclusion with a strong statement of belief that a final justice awaits all in the next world: 'Why surely, he who is yonder will be a living God, punishing a sin of him who commits it.' (v. 141) The intimacy of the relationship between the man and his soul is revealed in the final passage where his soul promises that whatever the man decides, 'I shall come to rest after you have relaxed (in death). Thus we shall make a home together.' (v. 151)

Whatever the outcome of the dialogue, it does raise fundamental issues. The argument is that the horror of personal self-destruction (suicide) is as nothing compared to the horror of what might be deemed to be moral self-destruction – being forced to live and tacitly accept the values of a society that has morally disintegrated. Four thousand years later, it must have been a dilemma that crossed the minds of many good Germans forced to live under the Nazi tyranny or good Rwandans who lived through the genocide in Rwanda. If nothing else, the dialogue reveals that human sensibility to core issues surrounding the quest for meaning and values is something that transcends historical and cultural boundaries.

The sense of the sacred in contemporary culture

Whatever about the evidence of the sacred in antiquity – and there is abundant proof that it was very evident indeed – the culture that we have inherited today is a world apart. The secular ethos of contemporary culture is perceived to be one that is less hospitable to either the sense of the sacred in life or the recognition of a spiritual core to human nature. Falling attendance at religious services, declining vocations and the decreasing influence of the Churches in the western world are perceived to be illustrative of this phenomenon. However, one must be careful not to presume to draw conclusions based on a single hypothesis, namely, the secularisation of society, as there may be a whole range of other factors at play. Given the vastly increased range of outlets for social exchange, the changed educational and employment environment, these societal changes may have little or nothing to do with a loss of a sense of the sacred or the spiritual.

To what extent is the contemporary world exclusively secular – a culture that asserts itself at the expense of the transcendent, the divine or the sacred? This raises the question as to how one can measure the sense of the sacred or the contours of spirituality in today's world. The task of measuring values and beliefs is difficult but not impossible and we are fortunate to have two series of authoritative surveys that have recently charted Irish belief patterns in the context of international comparisons.[10] Both the 1991 and the 1998 ISSP (International Social Survey Programme) and the 1981, 1990, and the 1999/2000 EVS (European Values Study) surveys have done a remarkable job in tracking the changing pattern of belief, practices and values in the western world – particularly in Europe, over the past twenty years.

Over the past three surveys, the EVS has measured the extent to which the adult population accepts a theistic frame of reference. A summary of the findings is given in *Table 1*.

Table 1: *EVS: Adults who believe in God: Republic of Ireland*

	1981 EVS (All)	1990 EVS (All)	2000 EVS (All)
Belief in God	95%	96%	96%
Belief in a personal God	77%	67%	65%
Belief in some sort of spirit or life force	15%	24%	24%
Don't know	6%	7%	8%
No God or life spirit	2%	1%	3%

These figures reveal a near-universal acceptance of belief in God amongst adults aged eighteen years of age or older. It is a statistic that has remained constant throughout the lifespan of the three surveys. The most recent Northern Ireland figure at 93% is comparable. In fact, as is shown in *Table 2*, there is evidence of a very high acceptance of belief in God throughout the European continent, and that despite the fact that Great Britain, France, the Scandinavian countries and some of the former communist states are widely regarded to be amongst the most secular countries in the world.

In the most recent EVS statistics only two of the countries surveyed show a figure of less than 50% for belief in God. However, as we see in *Table 1,* not all those who believe in God also believe in a personal God. In the 1998 ISSP study, the Republic of Ireland figure of 78% for belief in a personal God who is concerned with every human being was the second highest of all the countries surveyed; only the Philippines (88%) scored higher. The corresponding figure for the USA was 77%, Northern Ireland 66%, Italy 54%, Canada 49%, Spain 46%, Great Britain 37% and France 29%. The lowest percentage at 15% was recorded by the former East Germany.

Table 2.
EVS 1999/2000: Adults who believe in God

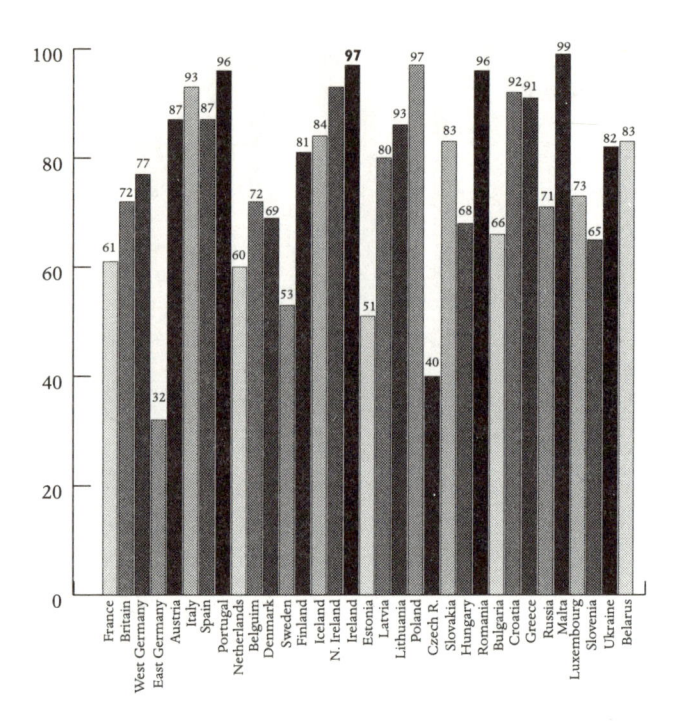

Country	%
France	61
Britain	72
West Germany	77
East Germany	32
Austria	87
Italy	93
Spain	87
Portugal	96
Netherlands	60
Belgium	72
Denmark	69
Sweden	53
Finland	81
Iceland	84
N. Ireland	93
Ireland	97
Estonia	51
Latvia	80
Lithuania	87
Poland	97
Czech R.	40
Slovakia	83
Hungary	68
Romania	96
Bulgaria	66
Croatia	92
Greece	91
Russia	71
Malta	99
Luxembourg	73
Slovenia	65
Ukraine	82
Belarus	83

Although belief in a personal God is low in some of the countries surveyed, nevertheless the findings on the more basic question of belief in God in *Table 1* offer firm evidence of a sense of the sacred in contemporary western society. This viewpoint would seem to be reinforced by the evidence in *Table 3* regarding the extent to which adults define themselves as religious.

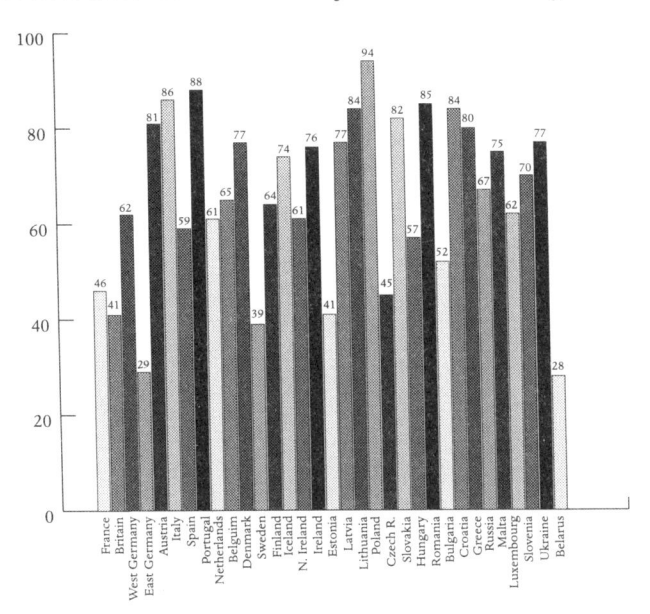

Table 3: *EVS 1999/2000 Adults who define themselves as religious*

[Bar chart showing percentages by country: France 46, Britain 41, West Germany 62, East Germany 29, Italy 86, Austria 81, Spain 88, Portugal 59, Netherlands 61, Belgium 77, Denmark 65, Sweden 39, Finland 64, Iceland 74, Ireland 61, N. Ireland 76, Estonia 41, Latvia 77, Lithuania 84, Poland 94, Czech R. 45, Slovakia 82, Hungary 57, Romania 85, Bulgaria 52, Croatia 84, Greece 80, Russia 67, Malta 75, Luxembourg 62, Slovenia 70, Ukraine 77, Belarus 28]

Table 3 also indicates that in 26 out of the 33 countries surveyed, more than 50% of the adult population defined themselves as religious – a statistic that suggests evidence of an appreciation of the spiritual in human life.

Looking in more detail at some Irish statistics in *Table 4*, there is further evidence of a high level of awareness of the spiritual. Furthermore, it is noticeable that the figures for belief in life after death, which suggest a reluctance to embrace a purely materialist philosophy, have actually increased over the past twenty years.

Table 4: *EVS: Acceptance of core Christian beliefs: Republic of Ireland*

	Belief in God	Belief in life after death	Belief in heaven	Belief in hell	Belief in sin
1981 EVS	95%	76%	83%	54%	85%
1998 ISSP	94%	78%	85%	53%	—
2000 EVS	96%	80%	86%	54%	86%

In addition, these figures suggest a high level of adherence to core religious (Christian) beliefs. Furthermore, it is striking that all of these figures have remained remarkably constant over the twenty years covered by the surveys. However, one must enter a caution; it is evident that these statistics do not tell the whole story because 20% of those surveyed in 2000 also believe in reincarnation – something clearly not found in the Christian panoply of beliefs.

Statistics that measure attendance at religious services have traditionally been used to assess the evidence of religious belief in society. However, it is arguable that people's attachment to personal prayer offers a better way of measuring religious sensibility because it provides evidence as to the extent to which the spiritual dimension of human life is appreciated. Both the 1998 ISSP and the 1999 EVS surveys measured the frequency of prayer in people's lives. As we can see from *Table 5*, the figures recorded by the two surveys were not identical. Looking at the percentage figure for praying several times a week the ISSP figure at 45% is considerably lower than the comparable EVS figure at 60%.

Table 5: *Frequency of Personal Prayer: Republic of Ireland*

	1999 EVS	1998 ISSP
Every day	46%	—
Several times a week	60%	45%
Once a week	70%	70%

In terms of international comparison, the ISSP survey figures place Ireland in the top third of the countries surveyed. However, the Republic of Ireland figure in the ISSP survey at 45% is considerably lower than that recorded by the ISSP in the Philippines (80%) and the USA (60%). It is also marginally lower than that recorded in Northern Ireland (46%). At the other end of the scale, the percentage who said that they never prayed was lowest in the Philippines (0%) followed by the

Republic of Ireland at 5%. The comparison with Ireland's nearest neighbours is as follows: Northern Ireland (17%) and Great Britain (35%).

A more valuable barometer of the importance of prayer in people's lives is to be found in answer to the question as to whether one draws comfort and strength from prayer. The 1981 EVS reported a figure of 80% and the 1990 EVS a figure of 82%; in neither survey did the figure for any age group fall below 64%. In answer to the corresponding question in the 1999 EVS survey as to whether one draws comfort and strength from religion, 76% across all ages said yes with only the 18–26 age group (54%) having a figure of less than 60%. The 1999 EVS figures for Catholics in the Republic and Northern Ireland are: ROI (80%) and NI (85%) respectively. The importance attached to prayer in these statistics would seem to offer clear evidence of the limited appeal of a secularist mindset.

When looking at the overall picture in Europe in *Table 6*, the following profile emerges:

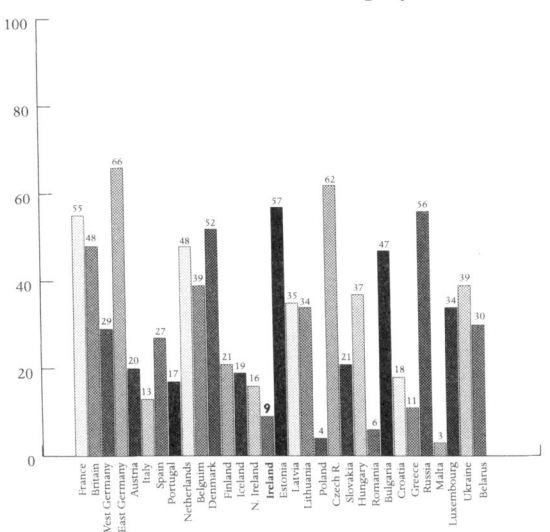

Table 6: EVS 1999/2000: Adults who never pray

This final set of statistics suggests that there persists a strong religious sensibility across all European countries; in only six of the countries surveyed are there more than 50% of the adults who say that they never pray. There is little evidence in these figures to bolster the secularisation thesis; in fact if anything the opposite is the case. What we find in these statistics is a convincing case for the persistence of religion – something that suggests that a sensibility to the sacred is something that transcends both cultural and generational boundaries.

The humanist tradition
From the standpoint of a cultural anthropologist, the persistence of religion is a phenomenon which suggests that key aspects of culture are invariant over time. Nevertheless, one ought to be wary of minimising the truly seismic changes in culture that have occurred in the relatively recent past, in particular, the shift from a cosmo-centric universe to an anthropo-centric world-view that heralded the arrival of modernity. The earliest intimations of this cultural change are to be seen in the emergence, during the Italian Renaissance of the fifteenth and sixteenth centuries, of the humanist tradition. Humanism is a broad church. Founded on the desire to recover the philosophical and cultural treasures of classical antiquity, in the minds of many today it has come to be synonymous with a set of beliefs that is proposed as an alternative to a theistic and specifically Christian world-view. Whether this secular or atheistic humanism is representative of the scientific positivism of Auguste Comte, or the atheistic existentialism of Friedrich Nietzsche and Jean Paul Sartre, it proclaims that humans will achieve their potential only to the extent that they desacralise themselves and their world: they will not be truly free until they have killed the last God.

On a large canvas, humanism is a celebration of human nature – one whose earliest focus was on a recovery of the self-confident artistic portrayal of the human spirit that was characteristic of so much of classical Graeco-Roman sculpture. In poetry, literature, art, music and sculpture, humanism sought to affirm the nobility of the human project – to recapture that insight reflected in the words of the psalmist, 'thou hast made him little less than the angels'. This earliest phase of humanism was also characterised by a desire to return to the classical world of Plato and the Greek city-state as a means of breaking free from the cultural embrace of Scholasticism – a system perceived as stifling the spirit of human enquiry through the subordination of all forms of scientific and philosophical discourse to revelation. One of the most interesting examples of this characteristic of humanism is to be seen in the Florentine foundation of the Platonic Academy by Giovanni della Mirandola. Much of the writings of celebrated humanists such as Petrarch, Erasmus and Flavio Biondi also reflected this focus. Basing his writings on classical literature, Petrarch concerned himself with expounding ideas on the nature of a cultivated and ethical life. Biondi is principally remembered for relegating the earlier cultural synthesis of Scholasticism (1200–1450) to the status of a 'middle' age between the world of antiquity and the 'modern' humanist world of Renaissance Europe. This curious use of the term 'Middle Ages' continues today.

In the world of the eighteenth-century European Enlightenment, the humanist tradition found expression in a celebration of the human spirit of scientific enquiry that gave rise to the phrase 'the age of reason'. Some of the most renowned humanists of this period included Goethe, Kant, Voltaire and Rousseau. What characterised their humanism was an emerging sense of human autonomy, one that was secured through the critical power of human reason: these humanists were first and foremost rationalists. They were also increasingly attracted to the political ideals of classical antiquity and in particular to the ideals of the Roman Republic reflected in the writings of Cicero. The stoic ideals of equality and universal fraternity – the ideal of universal citizenship – became synonymous with the ideals of political liberation that found expression in the French revolution. In the post-enlightenment period, the political philosophy of Karl Marx was to give a different slant to the classical ideals of equality and universal fraternity by proclaiming that the realisation of these ideals will only be achieved through the historical struggle to overcome class divisions. In their confident assertion of the progress of civilisation, the writings of Karl Marx captured the classical humanist spirit. However, his lasting contribution to the humanist tradition is undoubtedly his recognition of the historical character of human nature. In and through his searing critique of what he perceived to be the inner logic of both capitalism and Christianity, Marx would give to humanism an atheistic and socialistic character that in many respects survives to the present.

The twentieth century gave rise to an altogether different form of humanism, one that is loosely described as an existentialist humanism. Personages most closely associated with this development of humanism include the existentialist philosophers Heidegger, Sartre and Camus. This expression of humanism lacks both the self-confident belief in the power of reason or the confident belief in human progress associated with forms of Marxist philosophy. However, it does reflect the humanist desire to celebrate human autonomy – in this case the autonomy of one freed from the illusion of religious belief, a freedom born through the embrace of nihilism or a philosophy of the absurd. This proclamation or celebration of individual freedom that so marked the existentialist writings in the twentieth century is one that carries echoes of the humanist spirit throughout the ages, even if its unsentimental acknowledgement of an absurd universe is not one that many would find a cause for celebration. In what follows we will briefly look at the following key figures in the humanist tradition: Erasmus, Karl Marx, Albert Camus and Hannah Arendt.

Erasmus (c.1466–1536)
Born in Rotterdam, Erasmus is the most well-known of the Renaissance humanists. An eclectic writer and many-sided character, he travelled widely and operated at the intellectual heart of early sixteenth-century Europe. He was a lifelong friend of Thomas More, the celebrated English Chancellor and author of *Utopia*, who was subsequently executed by Henry VIII. Erasmus was also a counsellor to the future Emperor Charles V, and although he sympathised with the ideals of the Reformation he strenuously defended the importance of the freedom of the will against the views of Martin Luther. Among his many notable achievements was the production of a critical Greek edition of the New Testament – a prodigious endeavour that was, unfortunately, not well-received by the Church authorities, perhaps because it was seen to challenge the status of the Latin *Vulgate* edition. One of his lasting contributions to the humanist spirit was his belief in the importance of education – the human capacity for self-improvement through education. He wrote widely on educational topics and was very conscious of the importance of education in training the mind, facilitating moral and spiritual development and promoting civic virtues. The many references to Erasmus in the writings of the earliest Jesuits testify to the influence of his theory of education – his belief in the importance of the teacher, teaching methodology and the innate perfectibility of human nature. Incidentally, he was one of the first to campaign vigorously against corporal punishment.

Erasmus could deservedly be regarded as a Christian humanist as he steadfastly promoted the figure of Christ as the model for his vision of the human person. However, his Christian humanism was not always to find ready acceptance from either the Catholic or the Reformed wings of the Church – something not helped by the sharply satirical tone of some of Erasmus' more celebrated works. In *Praise of Folly*, a work regarded as one of the satirical classics of the Renaissance,

Erasmus reserves some of his most caustic comments for both scholastic theologians and the prelates of the Church – comments which were to lead to the books being condemned at the Council of Trent and placed on the index of banned books. Incidentally, in *Praise of Folly* he does not spare teachers or philosophers either, describing the latter as exhibiting a pleasant form of madness by their insistence 'that they alone have wisdom and all other mortals are but fleeting shadows.'[11]

Erasmus' problems were not confined to his relationship with the Catholic Church. Even though critical of the excesses of the Church which led to the Reformation and sympathetic to the desire to return to the biblical roots of the faith, Erasmus nevertheless found himself in conflict with the Reform movement and, in particular, Martin Luther. The focus of their disagreement was the crucial issue of the freedom of the will and the perfectibility of human nature through dedication to a moral life. Erasmus shared the Renaissance humanists' love for the world of Platonism and Neo-Platonism and one of the hallmarks of this tradition is a belief in the power of self-determination. In Luther's opinion, the position of Erasmus seemed to endorse Pelagianism, a heresy to which he was fiercely opposed. To Luther and the other leaders of the Reformation, anything that was perceived to minimise or qualify in any way the centrality of grace in the economy of salvation was impossible; this was the issue upon which there would be no retreat. Clearly, this dispute was not one that Erasmus was capable of resolving and, at a deeper level, it was one of the issues that signaled the more general decline of this phase of the humanist movement. The confrontational nature of the world of post-Reformation Europe would have little time for the eclectic and more tolerant ethos of Renaissance humanism.

Karl Marx (1818–1883)
In the revival of the humanist tradition of the Enlightenment there were many writers, artists and philosophers who

contributed to the celebration of human nature that is reflected in the phrase, 'the age of reason'. However, it is at least arguable that it is in the political philosophy of Karl Marx that the humanist legacy of the Enlightenment is most clearly to be seen. Born in the German town of Trier, Marx was a convinced atheist but was conversant with the Jewish faith from his earliest childhood – his grandfather had been a rabbi and his father had only converted to Protestantism because of the anti-Semitic prejudices of that society. Despite the avowed atheism of his philosophy, the writings of Marx are deeply influenced by a Judaism that interprets history in messianic categories. The vision of an eschatological goal of human liberation was to become the lynchpin of his humanist philosophy.

In his earliest years as a university student Marx became interested in Hegel's philosophy of history, particularly the revolutionary possibilities that it seemed to offer. In 1843 he published *Towards a critique of Hegel's philosophy*. In this work are to be found the key features of his criticism of religion as 'the opium of the people'. Following his acquaintance with his friend and benefactor Friedrich Engels, the focus of Marx's philosophy shifted from the critique of religion to the critique of capitalism. In a series of articles and pamphlets Marx dedicated himself to exposing the excesses of nineteenth-century capitalism and the barbarous nature of colonial exploitation. Because of his revolutionary ideas, which challenged the existing economic order of nineteenth century capitalism, Marx was forced to move with his family to Brussels where he wrote a number of works on dialectical materialism and scientific communism. In one of these papers there is to be found the phrase that encapsulates the revolutionary character of his thought. 'Philosophers have merely interpreted the world in various ways: the point however is to change it.' (*Thesis on Feuerbach,* 11) During his time in Brussels he founded the Communist league, and in 1848 he published the *Manifesto of the Communist party*. Forced to leave Brussels, Marx moved to

Paris and then to London. While in London he successfully completed his last major publication entitled *Das Kapital* (*On Capital*, 1867). Marx spent the remainder of his life in London where he directed the activities of the *International Workingmen's Association*, which among other things, campaigned for the transfer of land into common ownership, a shorter working day and Irish Home Rule.

Many would interpret Marx's philosophy exclusively in terms of his materialism and the revolutionary character of the class struggle that he proposes – a vision that can be summed up in the description 'Dialectical Materialism'. What is not often acknowledged is the humanist character of his philosophy – the celebration of the dignity of human nature and the desire to provide a pathway for the liberation of humanity from its state of alienation. Marx was imbued with a passionate desire to unmask the causes of oppression and his writings contain some of the most memorable critiques of industrial and colonial oppression ever written. Given his belief that human nature can be explained in material and economic terms it is hardly surprising that he would look in the economic structures of society for both the causes and the resolution of human alienation. Marx advocated the revolutionary overthrow of capitalism as the only possible way of ensuring the liberation of humankind from the source of all alienation, namely the bondage of economic slavery.

Although many commentators have seen in Marx's philosophy a 'Gospel' of social liberation that has much in common with the ideals of early Christianity, there is no doubt but that from his perspective the humanist goal of social liberation and Christianity were fundamentally at odds. Marx never deviated from the opinion expressed in an 1843 publication that, 'the criticism of religion is the presupposition of all criticism.' (*Towards a critique of Hegel's philosophy*, Introduction) What he meant by this phrase was that the overthrow of religion is the essential first step in the revolutionary process. At first sight this would seem to be a paradoxical position to take considering that Marx was of the opinion that religion was invented as a means of coping with alienation. In a memorable passage Marx expresses this viewpoint:

> Religious misery is in one way the expression of real misery, and in another a protest against real misery. Religion is the sigh of the afflicted creature, the soul of a heartless world, as it is also the spirit of spiritless conditions. It is the opium of the people. (*Towards a critique of Hegel's philosophy*, 287)[12]

Marx accepted the thesis of Feuerbach that 'man makes religion, religion does not make man'. He would have readily understood the place of a phrase such as 'blessed are the poor' in a system that he believed to have been invented to alieviate alienation and to enable the 'working classes' cope with economic oppression. The problem with this coping mechanism is that it does not work. As is the case with all drugs, the effect of religion is merely to dull the pain or to provide temporary relief in an imaginary/hallucinatory world. Far from assisting the emancipation of the oppressed workers, the effect of religion is to reinforce that oppression. In dulling the pain of servitude, by offering the illusory promise of eternal happiness in an afterworld, it effectively minimises the possibility of armed revolution and thus serves the interests of the capitalist classes. Therefore, according to Marx, religion must be exposed if the true character of capitalist oppression is to be unmasked. As he says;

> The abolition of religion as the illusory happiness of the people is the demand for their real happiness. The demand to abandon the illusions about their condition is the demand to give up a condition that requires illusions. Hence criticism of religion is in embryo a criticism of

> this vale or tears whose halo is religion ... The criticism of religion disillusions man so that he thinks, acts, and shapes his reality like a disillusioned man who has come to his senses, so that he revolves around himself and thereby around his real sun. (*Towards a critique of Hegel's philosophy*, 287)

Thus, it is the humanist strain in Marx's thought that demands that religion be rejected. There are those who would argue that Marx both underestimates the complexity of human nature and the nature of religious belief. However, the challenge facing those who wish to dispute Marx's thesis is to articulate a vision of religion that carries within it the possibility of truly liberating humans from all forms of alienation.

Albert Camus (1913–1960)
Twentieth-century existentialist humanism is in many respects a far cry from the utopian vision of Karl Marx. As a philosophy that emerged amid the carnage of two world wars, it gives expression to the conviction that the belief in the progress of civilisation that marked the Enlightenment was misplaced. In contrast to this world of reason, existentialist humanism introduces the spectre of an absurd world – the collapse in the belief that meaning can be found or indeed that there is meaning to be found. It shows its humanist character in its heroic affirmation of humanity in the face of an absurd world. In this, it has more in common with the tragic condition of the Greek mythological figures of Prometheus and Sisyphus than with any of the more confident portraits of humanity that has been celebrated hitherto in the humanist tradition. One of the most interesting exponents of this strand of humanism is the French philosopher Albert Camus.

Born in Algeria in poor circumstances, Camus had to overcome many obstacles to receive an education. Following his philosophical studies, he entered on the path of a journalistic career and began to publish short stories and plays. During the Nazi occupation of France Camus edited the French Resistance newspaper, *Combat*. In 1942 he published his first major philosophic essay, *The Myth of Sisyphus*. This was followed in the same year by the publication of his first novel entitled *The Outsider*. Both of these works grappled with the reality of an absurd world and proclaimed a philosophy of defiance or 'revolt against the Gods' – a celebration of absolute freedom that placed Camus firmly within the philosophical milieu of Existentialism. There followed a series of novels of which the most famous are *The Plague* (1947) and *The Fall* (1956). Although these novels continued to reflect the broad lines of existentialist thought, Camus increasingly distanced himself from the philosophy of absolute freedom that was espoused by his colleague Jean Paul Sartre. In his second philosophical treatise entitled *The Rebel* that was published in 1951, one sees evidence of a desire to stress alternative ideals, namely the classical humanist ideals of justice and human solidarity. As he says,

> When the throne of God is overthrown, the rebel realizes that it is now his own responsibility to create the justice, order, and unity that he sought in vain within his own condition and, in this way, to justify the fall of God.[13]

During this time Camus further estranged himself from the intellectual circle of French existentialism by his criticism of the French Communist party. His philosophy became progressively more in tune with the ancient Greek culture that inspired the humanist tradition. In 1957 he was awarded the Nobel Prize for literature. He died in a car accident in 1960.

In his earliest philosophical work, *The Myth of Sisyphus*, Camus' humanism finds expression in an embrace of the mythical Greek tragic hero Sisyphus who had challenged the Gods and as punishment had been condemned to ceaselessly rolling a rock to the top of a mountain, whence the stone would fall back of its own weight. With a gesture in the direction of the plight of labourers in the mass production systems of capitalist economies, Camus remarks,

> They [the Gods] had thought with some reason that there is no more dreadful punishment than futile and hopeless labour.[14]

For Camus, the fate of Sisyphus mirrors that of all human beings – destined to the futile task of seeking meaning in an absurd world. Unlike those who sleep-walk in this world, Sisyphus is a truly tragic hero because at every step of the way he is conscious of his wretched condition, a consciousness that paradoxically enables him to pour scorn on his fate and to celebrate the absurdity – a stance that frees him and indeed has the potential to free us from the ultimate drudgery of a life of pretence or self-absorption. In quoting the immortal words of the blinded Oedipus, 'that all is well', Camus celebrates the liberating thought that fate is henceforth a human matter that both can and must be settled amongst ourselves. It is in this spirit that Camus believes that,

> Sisyphus also concludes that all is well. This universe henceforth without a master seems to him neither sterile or futile. (*Sisyphus*, 111)

It is, however, a sobering conclusion that leaves us with Sisyphus at the foot of the mountain eternally to 'find one's burden again'.

This philosophy of revolt, freedom and passion is articulated in a series of deeply evocative novels that captured the spirit of the age, none more so than *The Outsider* and *The Plague*. The former can be read as a reflection on the precarious and ultimately doomed status of a French Algerian. However, at another level, it gives expression to the outsider status of one who refuses to take refuge in religion – refuses to pretend that there is meaning. The book traces the contours of the outsider status of the central character Meursault. The book is framed by the death of this man's mother, and it is death that reveals in all its starkness the absurdity of the world. Living out her last years in a home for the aged his mother had both refused to take refuge in religion and had audaciously struck up a relationship with another resident. In a moment of inner conversion to the heroic character of her atheism, the book concludes with the following celebrated proclamation of Camus' philosophy:

> And now, it seemed to me, I understood why at her life's end she had taken on a fiance; why she'd played at making a fresh start. There, too, in that Home where lives were flickering out, the dusk came as a mournful solace. With death so near, Mother must have felt like someone on the brink of freedom, ready to start life all over again. No one, no one in the world had any right to weep for her. And I, too, felt ready to start life over again. It was as if that great rush of anger had washed me clean, emptied me of hope, and, gazing up at the dark sky spangled with its signs and stars, for the first time, the first, I laid my heart open to the benign indifference of the universe. To feel it so like myself, indeed so brotherly, made me realize that I'd been happy, and that I was happy still.[15]

In the ironical use of the symbolism of baptism, Camus is both able to suggest a newness of perspective and the radical nature of the conversion that is entailed in and through embracing a philosophy of absolute freedom. Camus would be one with Sartre in acknowledging that in this world one is condemned to choose without hope. It is a world in which we are left alone and without excuse. And yet, unlike Sartre, he refuses to admit that it is a world in which one cannot be happy. Rather in this stance Camus is at one with the nineteenth-century German philosopher Nietzsche's adoption of the tragic ethic of the Greek God Dionysus – the God of intoxication, passion and ecstasy. As Nietzsche put it:

> The crown of the laughter, the rose-wreath crown: to you my brothers, I throw this crown. Laughter I have pronounced holy: you higher men ... learn to laugh. (*Thus Spoke Zarathustra*, Part IV, 20)[16]

In the face of impending death, the Camus of *The Outsider*, like Nietzsche before him, wished to highlight the contrast between the creative employment of the passions – the affirmation of life that embraces a Dionysian ethic – and what he perceived to be the Christian negation of life and denial of the passions.

If in *The Outsider* it is death that reveals the absurdity of the world, in *The Plague* it is innocent suffering, in particular the suffering of innocent children. For theists and particularly those of a Christian persuasion there is no more difficult issue. How does one square the circle created by the reality of the suffering of children and the belief in a loving and all-powerful God – 'the creator of heaven and earth'? There are few novels which can rival *The Plague* in their presentation of the problem as can be seen from this memorable extract from a dialogue between the priest (Fr Paneloux) and the humanist doctor (Dr Rieux) following the death of the only child of a mutual friend.

> [Rieux] 'Ah! That child, anyhow, was innocent – and you know it as well as I do!'
> ... 'there are times when the only feeling I have is one of mad revolt'.

> 'I understand', Paneloux said in a low voice. 'That sort of thing is revolting because it passes our human understanding. But perhaps we should love what we cannot understand.'
> ...[Rieux] 'No, Father. I've a very different idea of love. And until my dying day I shall refuse to love a scheme of things in which children are put to torture.'[17]

The reference to the theme of revolt in the interjection of Rieux tells us that this person represents Camus. And yet, unlike Meursault in *The Outsider,* the person represented by Rieux is not simply determined to be angry or even to 'be happy'. In and through the character of a doctor, Camus testifies to a very different response to this manifestation of the absurd, one that does not so much pit him against the organs of religion as represented by the priest (Paneloux), but rather incongruously places him at his side. This is illustrated in the following passage, which commences with an interjection from Dr Rieux on the subject of religious faith,

> [Rieux] 'It's something I haven't got; that I know. But I'd rather not discuss that with you. We're working side by side for something that unites us – beyond blasphemy and payers. And it's the only thing that matters'. (*The Plague*, 178)

The ideal is the classical humanist ideal of human solidarity, and as the book unfolds, one is increasingly conscious that, despite their differences, Camus believes that there is a bond that unites the Humanist and the Christian, one that is founded on a genuine solidarity in the face of the struggle against all forms of evil or suffering. The book concludes with a reminder of 'the never ending fight against terror and its relentless onslaughts ... by all who, while unable to be saints but refusing to bow down to pestilences, strive their utmost to be healers.' (*The Plague*, 250–251)

In *The Plague* Camus poses the question, 'Can one be a saint without God?' In the figure of Dr Rieux he offers us the picture of a secular or humanist saint. This is a far cry from the not-so-splendid isolation of the characters that are portrayed in Sartre's many novels – characters that give substance to his belief that 'hell is other people'. The desire to create a world marked by the humanist concerns of justice and solidarity is further developed in Camus' second major philosophical work entitled *The Rebel* (1951), which expresses the imperative to rebel against all forms of oppression, including belief in a God who limits or denies human freedom. In a re-working of Descartes, 'I think, therefore I exist', Camus asserts, 'I rebel – therefore we exist' (*The Rebel*, 28). However, even as he penned that defiant manifesto, Camus is increasingly conscious of the complexity of the relationship between atheistic humanism and theism. As he says,

> And so the history of metaphysical revolt cannot be confused with that of atheism. From one angle, it is even identified with the contemporary history of religious sentiment. The rebel defies more than he denies. (*The Rebel*, 30–31)

By the time that Camus came to write *The Fall* (1956), much of the confident optimism of *The Outsider* and the idealism of *The Plague* had dissipated. In this the last of his novels, one is faced with the most difficult face of an absurd world, namely one in which it is not possible to find forgiveness. As the title suggests, Camus is reflecting upon the theme of human fallibility or sinfulness. The humanist sinner (Jean-Baptiste Clemence) of *The Fall* replaces the humanist saint (Dr Rieux) in *The Plague*. The name Jean-Baptiste is meant to remind us that the true outsider is a John the Baptist figure crying in the wilderness a message of repentance for the forgiveness of sins. In *The Fall*, repentance is in vain because there is no forgiveness. In an ironic twist to the classical view that belief in God constrains human flourishing, Camus in the person of Jean-Baptiste comments:

> God is not needed to create guilt or to punish. Our fellow men suffice, aided by ourselves. You were speaking of the Last Judgement. Allow me to laugh respectfully, I shall wait for it resolutely, for I have known what is worse, the judgement of men. For them, no extenuating circumstances; even the good intention is accounted a crime. Have you at least heard of the spitting cell? ... Well, that *mon cher*, is a human invention. They didn't need God for that little masterpiece. ... I'll tell you a big secret, *mon cher*. Don't wait for the Last Judgement. It takes place every day.[18]

The humanism depicted by Camus in *The Fall* is a sobering reflection on the inhumanity that is all too present in every person. The struggle against evil remains constant but the face of evil is now the face in the mirror. In this context, there is no salvation, no possibility of even a temporary victory over evil because, as the biblical resonance of title suggests, we are all implicated in evil. We live in a very unforgiving world. In this deeply pessimistic assessment of human nature, one is more conscious of a longing for a God who will bring forgiveness than any rejection of God as an outdated hypothesis.

Hannah Arendt (1906–1975)
In the twentieth century, the outlines of humanist thought largely mirrored the contours of Existentialism. However, the political and moral catastrophes of this century also provoked a much greater re-engagement with political discourse than anything proposed by Existentialism. The attempt to recover the true political character of the human spirit in the face of twentieth-century totalitarianism is one that has in no small measure shaped the philosophical output of Hannah Arendt.

Whether or not she would be comfortable with the designation of 'humanist', no writer has devoted more effort to a study of the totalitarianism associated with both Nazism and Stalinism. In *The Origins of Totalitarianism* (1951) and *The Human Condition* (1958) she observes that totalitarian regimes are united in their refusal to share the world with entire races and classes of human beings – a refusal to acknowledge a common world that both allows human beings to be distinct and yet relates them to each other. In this refusal of 'plurality' or individual diversity, totalitarianism, whether of the 'right' or the 'left' variety, denies that human beings can transcend the collective embrace of an animal species governed by laws of nature or history – a law of nature that some races are unfit to live (Nazism) and a law of history that certain classes are on their way to extinction (Marxism). Much of the philosophical output of Hannah Arendt was devoted to countering this thesis.

Born in Hanover, Germany, of Jewish parents, Hannah Arendt studied under both Heidegger and Karl Jaspers. In 1929 she published her doctoral thesis entitled *Love and St. Augustine*. Involved in political agitation on behalf of the Jews against Nazism, she fled to Paris in 1933. Following the fall of France she was interned in unoccupied Vichy from where she escaped in 1941, eventually making her way to the USA. She subsequently became an American citizen and dedicated much of the remaining years of her life to a study of the individual's relationship to the human community, an indispensable project in the quest to understand the moral and political context for the rise of totalitarianism.

In her critique of the dangers of an atomised and de-politicised culture of modernity her writings have a particular contemporary relevance. While acknowledging that modernisation has turned out to be extraordinarily good in promoting production and consumption for an expanding population, she is all too conscious that a society that is too absorbed in consumption – a consumer society of 'atomized, isolated individuals' – is easy prey to the re-emergence of totalitarianism. In the course of an excellent commentary on the philosophy of Hannah Arendt,[19] the Irish philosopher Dermot Moran remarks,

> The issues of alienation, homelessness, and isolation of modern humanity are central to her analysis. Arendt's treatment of the global nature of totalitarianism is Heideggerian in manner: totalitarianism aims at 'total conquest and total domination' (*The Origins of Totalitarianism*, xxx)[20].
>
> Totalitarianism is only possible in specifically modern society where everything – including our sense of reality – is managed. People are deracinated and endlessly manipulated. In particular totalitarianism feeds on the isolation of modern humanity and its sense of homelessness. (Moran, 299)

In the words of Arendt:

> What prepares men for totalitarian domination in the non-totalitarian world is the fact that loneliness, once a borderline experience usually suffered in certain marginal social conditions like old age, has become an everyday experience of the ever-growing masses of our century. (*The Origins of Totalitarianism*, 478)

Despite the devastation wrought by the totalitarian regimes and the ever-present possibility of its being repeated, Hannah Arendt's philosophy never succumbed to the temptation of despair or even extreme pessimism. That this is the case is undoubtedly due to a remarkable insight that characterised her philosophy, namely the recognition of the power of new beginnings. Just as the motif of death was to define the world of her one-time mentor Heidegger, so that of birth, the continual possibility of new beginnings, was to define hers. As she says,

> The miracle that saves the world, the realm of human affairs, from its normal, 'natural' ruin is ultimately the fact of natality ... the birth of new men and the new beginning, the action they are capable of by virtue of being born. Only the full experience of this capacity can bestow upon human affairs faith and hope.[21]

For an explanation of the origin of this insight one need look no further than her reading of St Augustine. She frequently quotes a passage from *The City of God, X11. 24* that reads: 'And so to provide that beginning, a man was created, before whom no man ever existed.'[22] In this celebration of the newness of the human spirit in every individual creation is to be found the most obvious contribution of Arendt to the humanist tradition. Although the unpredictability of that which is new is not without its dangers, nevertheless, it does serve to undermine the basis of totalitarian regimes. At the very least, it makes it difficult to believe in any ideology that proposes itself as an explanatory hypothesis for the entire course of human affairs.

The dialogue between religion and science[23]
The belief that the world is created is fundamental to most major religions and in particular, Judaism, Islam and Christianity. It expresses the belief that the world is ordered/purposeful and that the principle of this order is not to be found in the world but in God. In other words, to accept a theory of creation is to acknowledge that the world is the object of the creative act of God: it is not sufficient in itself.

The major point of conflict between the scientific and religious world-views of creation was the controversy over evolution that dominated the science/religion dialogue in the late nineteenth and early part of the twentieth century. This controversy arose largely because of the failure on the part of the Christian Churches to keep in mind the crucial distinction between the conviction that the world is created and any particular theory as to how the world has come to be as it is. In its concern to uphold the truth of the Bible, the Churches felt obliged to argue for the literal truth of the first three chapters of the book of Genesis. In the light of our understanding today of the different literary genres in the Bible we can see that the creation accounts in these chapters of Genesis were not meant to be scientific accounts of how the world was created. Similarly, while acknowledging that some proponents of the theory of evolution have argued and continue to do so from an atheistic standpoint, no theory as to how the world evolved can be intrinsically atheistic because science cannot prove whether the world was created or not, any more than it can prove the existence or non-existence of God. A belief in creation does not commit one to any particular theory as to how the world was created. The answer to the question as to how the world has evolved is one that falls within the domain of science and science alone.

In contemporary scientific discourse there are two contrasting cosmologies that are called respectively, the big bang theory and the steady state theory. The former is by far the more accepted of the two cosmologies, and its origins go back to Einstein and his theory of general relativity. Although Einstein accepted the common scientific view of the time that the cosmos was eternal and static it was not long until scientists perceived that his theory of relativity was impossible to reconcile with the idea of a static universe. As the theory of relativity shows, if the universe were eternal and static the various masses would by now, under the force of gravity, have collapsed upon one another. An alternative was proposed, namely, that the universe is expanding. In the early 1920s, through an examination of light waves, the American astronomer Edwin Hubble made a startling discovery that showed the correctness of Einstein's equations, which implied that the universe was in fact expanding. Not only is the universe expanding but his examination of light waves also allowed him to observe that the expansion rate is slowing. If this theory is correct it follows that its beginnings can only be explained by positing an initial explosion or big bang that marks the beginning of both space and time. The point from which the present universe expanded out in a colossal explosion of energy and heat is termed a 'space-time singularity'.

The British astronomer Fred Hoyle put forward an alternative theory to explain the expansion of the universe. In opposition to the big bang theory, he proposed that the universe is infinitely old and has neither evolved nor changed through time. The belief is that the expansion of the universe is constant – as the universe expands, new matter is created so that its density remains constant. By avoiding the notion of a beginning by putting forward an infinite time-span, this model was perceived by some to be at odds with a theory of creation. However, this issue is no longer relevant because the steady state theory is increasingly perceived to be an inferior cosmological model to that of the big bang.

One of the factors in persuading scientists in favour of the big bang theory was the discovery of the existence of background radiation in 1965 by two American astronomers, Robert Wilson and Arno Penzias. This discovery offers clear evidence that the universe must have had a beginning in a singular cosmic event – an initial explosion. The best estimate for the date of this event is fifteen billion years ago.

Whatever scientific theory concerning the origins of the universe finds acceptance does not negate the fact that both scientists and theists share a common horizon. In their struggle to unlock the secrets of the universe scientists offer eloquent testimony to the intuition that the universe which we inhabit is intelligible, a stance that is framed by the rejection of both nihilism and scepticism. In opposition to the claims of nihilism science rests upon the trust that the universe is ordered; in contrast to the claims of scepticism science rests upon the belief that these laws are accessible to human reason and that scientific experimentation is capable of uncovering the complex matrix of laws that govern the universe. In the last analysis, science like religion rests upon the shared belief that the universe in which we live is both ordered and intelligible. It is precisely this conviction that is reflected in the Christian doctrine of creation.

Non-religious responses to the questions of life

The secular humanist tradition
Humanism is any philosophical system that situates the focus of its enquiry on the human subject, celebrates the dignity of the person and explores the question as to how one envisages human fulfilment. It first emerged as a deliberate attempt to justify the Renaissance and has continued in various forms ever since. Its development is closely associated with the development of the empirical sciences in the seventeenth and eighteenth centuries and the subsequent emergence of a positivist culture that denies the existence of anything that cannot be fitted within the boundaries of scientific measurement. Some of the more celebrated expressions of this theme are atheistic, such as Scientific Positivism, Marxist Humanism and Existentialist Humanism. All of these philosophical traditions, in different ways, see as their task the removal of the dehumanising factors in society that cause alienation, and in this list they include religion.

Atheism
Atheism is the denial of the existence of God. Atheism can take a number of forms:

- Theoretical atheism: a denial of God's existence. Reasons given for theoretical atheism include (a) the belief that science and religion are incompatible, and (b) the impossibility of reconciling a belief in God with the existence of evil.
- Practical atheism or religious indifference: a denial of God's existence based upon the belief that the question of God's existence is of no consequence.
- Militant atheism: a denial of God's existence based upon the belief that religious belief is a harmful aberration that retards human progress.

Agnosticism

Scepticism either denies (a) that the human person is capable of knowing the truth, or that (b) there is such a thing as objective truth. Agnosticism is a form of scepticism that expresses the belief that the human mind is incapable of knowing whether or not God exists. For the most part, agnosticism is based upon the view that we can have no knowledge of that which goes beyond the limits of the material, scientific world.

Reductionism

Reductionism is the name given to any form of belief that arbitrarily restricts the boundaries of what can be known or what exists in order to render credible an atheistic viewpoint, one that proclaims that religious belief lacks any basis in fact. The most common form of reductionism is Scientific Positivism. Originally this was a theory of knowledge, which proclaimed that nothing can be known that is outside the boundaries of scientific measurement. In more recent times, Positivism has come to represent the atheistic ideology that affirms (a) that nothing can be known outside the material world because nothing exists outside of its boundaries, or (b) that religion is an outmoded and superstitious form of belief that will be superseded by a scientific/positivist world-view.

Notes

1. John McQuarrie, *God Talk*, London, SCM Press, 1967, pp.171-179.
2. Mircea Eliade, *Myths, Dreams and Mysteries*, trans. P. Mairet, London, Collins, 1960, 5th Impression, 1976.
3. See Henri Frankfort et al., *Before Philosophy: The Intellectual Adventure of Ancient Man*, Maryland, Penguin Books, 1949, p.35
4. Purcell, Brendan, 'In Search of Newgrange: Long Night's Journey into Day', in Kearney, R. (ed.), *The Irish Mind*, Dublin: Wolfhound Press 1985, pp.39-55 and pp.319-323. In what follows, I would like to ackowledge my indebtedness for the insights contained in Brendan Purcell's article.
5. Eliade, Mircea, *Patterns in Comparative Religion*, London, Sheed and Ward, 1969.
6. See James B. Pritchard, ed., *Ancient Near Eastern Texts*, New Jersey, Princeton University Press, 1955, pp.3-4.
7. All quotations from the *Epic of Gilgamesh* are taken from *Ancient Near Eastern Texts*, pp.72-97.
8. All quotations from the *The Dispute of a Man, Who Contemplates Suicide, with His Soul* are taken from James Pritchard, *Ancient Near Eastern Texts*.
9. Eric Voeglin, *Order and History (vol. 1): Israel and Revelation*, Louisiana, Louisiana State University Press, 1956, pp.98-101.
10. I wish to acknowledge the assistance of Tony Fahey of the ESRI. A more detailed treatment of this theme is to be found in Eoin G. Cassidy, ed., *Measuring Ireland: Discerning Values and Beliefs* (Dublin, Veritas, 2002), pp.17-93.
11. Erasmus, *Praise of Folly*, trans. Betty Radice, (London, Penguin Classics, 1971, p.151
12. 'Towards a critique of Hegel's philosophy', in *Karl Marx: The Essential Writings*, ed. R. Bender, Harper and Row, New York, 1972.
13. Albert Camus, *The Rebel*, trans. Antony Bower, London, Penguin Books, 1965, p.31.
14. Albert Camus, *The Myth of Sisyphus*, trans. Justin O'Brien, London, Penguin Books, 1975, p.107
15. Albert Camus, *The Outsider*, trans. Stuart Gilbert, London, Penguin Books, 1961, p.120.
16. Quoted from, Friedrich Nietzsche, *The Birth of Tragedy*, trans. Walter Kaufmann, Vintage Books, New York, 1967, p.27.
17. Albert Camus, *The Plague,* trans. Stuart Gilbert (London, Penguin Books, 1960), pp.177-178.
18. Albert Camus, *The Fall*, trans. Justin O'Brien, London, Penguin Books, 1963, pp.81-82
19. Dermot Moran, *Introduction to Phenomenology* London, Routledge,

2000, pp.287- 319.
20. Hannah Arendt, *The Origins of Totalitarianism*, London, Allen and Unwin, revised edition, 1967.
21. Hannah Arendt, *The Human Condition*, Chicago, University of Chicago Press, 1998, p.247
22. See Hannah Arendt, *Love and Saint Augustine*, Chicago, University of Chicago Press, 1996, 53, pp.129-134.
23. See Fachtna McCarthy and Joseph McCann, *Religion and Science* Dublin, Veritas, 2003, pp.133-143

Part Three

CONCEPTS OF GOD

Introduction

The purpose of part three is to reflect on the way in which the concept of God is bound up with the search for meaning and values. The conviction upon which this study is based is that: (i) the manner in which quest for meaning is revealed will influence the way in which God or the Gods are portrayed, and (ii) the way in which God or the Gods are revealed will in turn shape the parameters within which this search for meaning is experienced. Divided into three chapters (the Gods of the ancients; the concept of revelation; and naming God, past and present), it will reflect on the wide variety of the ways that God or Gods have been described. In part three we also pay attention to the manner in which God can be known, either through the acceptance of faith in divine revelation and/or through converging arguments based on human reason.

At the outset of a chapter that seeks to explore connections between the search for human identity and the experience of religion one must be alert to the dangers of a functionalist approach to religion. Much of what constitutes the sociology of religion is based on the conviction that it is possible to give a 'social' or societal explanation for the existence of religious belief and the contours of religious practice. If taken to extremes, this approach either avoids or dismisses the foundational question as to the substance of religion, or reinterprets it in terms of the societal needs of the time. Consider the Israelites' original experience of Yahweh: a concern for justice was fundamental to this experience. A functional approach might suggest that the 'revelation' of Yahweh as a just God is not to be seen as a truth claim about God and the covenant relationship, but rather as a function of the pragmatic concerns of the Israelite community to find some effective way to shore up privately intuited moral principles.

Another example of this functional approach in sociological explanation would be to see religion as an important institutional outlet for the articulation of the grievances and aspirations of certain social groups. In this regard, Karl Marx saw Christianity as the religion of the oppressed lower orders in the Roman Empire; the nineteenth-century German philosopher Friedrich Nietzsche saw it as an expression of the resentment of the powerless and excluded; and the nineteenth-century sociologist Max Weber saw Christianity as a 'salvation religion' of the urban middle classes, displaced and individualist. There is, in fact, very little historical evidence to support any of these claims, but even if there was, it misses the point that it is the substance of religion that should determine its function rather than the other way around.

Much of the contemporary writing in the sociology of religion presumes that there is a privileged, secular vantage point from which to view religion. This position has its origins in the atheistic positivism of the founder of sociology, Auguste Comte (1798–1857), a philosophical position which suggested that the phenomenon of religion could be explained in the context of an early stage in the evolution of the human species. The overt atheism of Comte may not be representative of the sociology of religion, nevertheless a functional approach to religion adopted by sociologists and some theologians and philosophers is not without its dangers. An excessive concern with the question of the relevance of religion to the needs of society can inadvertently neglect foundational questions as to the truth of religion. To suppose that the function of religion is determined by societal concerns rather than by the truth of God's existence is either to misunderstand or misrepresent the defining characteristic of what it is to be a religious believer.

5

Gods of the Ancients

Descriptions of the Gods in ancient myths
To what extent are the portraits of the Gods expressive of the quest for meaning? What do the descriptions of the Gods in ancient society tell us about human existence – the fears, hopes, anxieties and beliefs that shape our lives? The painstaking work of Mircea Eliade that is published in *Patterns in Comparative Religion*[1] offers an unrivalled insight into the Gods of the ancient world and shows clear evidence of a link between the quest for meaning in that ancient world and the manner in which the Gods were portrayed. One of his discoveries is that many of the most important divine symbols in the ancient world transcend cultural and religious boundaries. This suggests that, at some level, the descriptions of the Gods in ancient myths arise out of experiences that are shared by people from very different cultural backgrounds.

The first 'portrait of the Gods' that Eliade explores is one that is influenced by the cosmic symbolism of the sky, and reflected in the belief in the existence of sky Gods or a great sky God. The importance of this cosmic symbolism can also be seen in the references in the ancient world to the Gods of thunder, lightning or rain, all of which are important fertility symbols, and also to the images of sun and moon Gods, images that highlight issues of life, death, and the expectation of rebirth. Given the sense of the transcendent that is expressed by the image of the sky, it is hardly surprising that the sky is one of the commonest symbols for the divine in ancient mythological stories. For example, the aboriginal culture of Australia abounds in images of the divine beings that are linked to the sky and the world of stars and meteors, one of which is Baiame. As Eliade explains it:

> Baiame, the supreme divinity among the tribes of South-East Australia, dwells in the sky, beside a great stream of water (the Milky Way), and receives the souls of the innocent. He sits on a crystal throne; the sun and moon are his 'sons', his messengers to the earth. Thunder is his voice; he causes the rain to fall, making the whole earth green and fertile; in this sense too he is creator. For Baiame is self created and has created everything from nothing. Like the other sky Gods, Baiame sees and hears everything. (Eliade, 41)

It is interesting to observe the constellation of so many different sky symbols contained in the description of the God Baiame. In this one figure there coexists the characteristics of a creator and a fertility God, one who is both omnipotent, omniscient and who ensures life and fertility. He is also an ethical God – a judge who rewards the innocent. To a contemporary observer, it is remarkable how so many of the key themes that shape human meaning are explored in this Australian aboriginal portrayal of a sky God. Examples of similar beliefs abound in ancient societies, one example of which is to be seen in a belief in the 'Dweller in the Sky' that is to be found among the Selk'nam nomad hunters of Tierra del Fuego – the southern tip of the South American continent. According to Eliade (44), this God is not only the omniscient creator but also the author of the moral law, the judge and the master of all destinies. In Mesopotamian culture, the key Babylonian God Anu means 'the sky'. 'He is the supreme ruler, and the symbols of his kingship are used by all kings as source and justification for their authority; symbolically, the king gets his power directly from Anu.' (Eliade, 65) Throughout the known world, these images are replicated in a manner that stresses the mysterious and transcendent nature of God: the image evoked by the sky as the divine sphere is that of inaccessibility rather than something that is close to human beings. Exceptions to this rule include the Greek God Zeus and the Roman God Jupiter, both of whom have more dynamic and concrete functions.

One of the most interesting constellation of images highlighted by Eliade is that reflected in the close association of the word for a God and that for a day (Latin, *Deus* and *Dies*) evoked by the God Dieus, which as he says is the hypothetical God of the light sky, common to all Aryan tribes.

> Certain it is that the Indian Dyaus, the Roman Jupiter, the Greek Zeus and the Germanic God Tyr-Zio, are forms evolved in the course of history from that primeval sky divinity, and that their very names reveal the original twofold meaning of 'light (day)' and 'sacred' (cf. the Sanskrit *div*, 'shine', 'day', *dyaus*, 'sky', 'day'; *dios, dies; deivos, divus*). (Eliade, 66)

Unlike the more remote Vedic/Hindu God Dyaus, the Gods Zeus, Jupiter and Tyr-Zio (Thor and Odin – Mercury and Mars) were much more active in the world. In the religions of Greece and Rome respectively, Zeus and Jupiter are symbolised by the image of a thunderbolt, evidence of their power and connection with storms and rain – the harbingers of fertility. Zeus and Jupiter were the sovereign Gods, and they punished with thunderbolts of lightning all those who transgressed moral or social boundaries. Similarly, the Germanic divinities,

Thor and Odin were Gods of tempest and combat who ruled the world through their power.

The notion of sky Gods manifesting themselves in storms is common throughout the ancient world. It is an idea that links the idea of a creator God with the symbol of fertility. As an example of this phenomenon, Eliade (82) points to the Celtic belief in Taranis (from the Celtic root Taran, to thunder, cf. the Irish *torann*, 'thunder'). This link between a creator sky God and a fertility God is most clearly to be seen in the earliest Hindu description of the sky God Indra that is contained in the earliest Vedic literature (approx. 1500 BCE). As Eliade says:

> Storms are the supreme unleashings of creative force; Indra pours down the rain and governs moisture of every kind, so that he is both God of fertility and the archetype of the forces that originate life. ... He makes fields, animals and women fruitful; he is invoked at weddings that the bride may bear ten sons, and innumerable invocations refer to his inexhaustible power of generating life. (Eliade, 85)

What is interesting is that in this portrait it is fertility rather than creation that is emphasised: his physical power, symbolised in the weapon of the thunderbolt, is designed to promote fertility. The symbol of the bull used to depict the God Indra strengthens the symbolic connection between the creative and the procreative functions. It is not the only example of a sky God symbolised by the figure of a bull. Among the many examples of this phenomenon mentioned by Eliade is that of the Greek God Zeus. As he observes: 'It was as a bull that Zeus carried off Europa (epiphany of the Great Mother), had his liaison with Antiope and attempted to violate her sister Demeter'. (91) Eliade is convinced that the link between these symbols and that of the Great Goddess or the great Earth mother is no accident. Rather, it suggests that the ancients were keen to place emphasis on the Earth mother and the role of the Gods in cooperating with this Goddess to ensure fertility. As he says:

> That they [the sky Gods] are sacred is due to their sacred marriage with the great Earth Mother. Their celestial nature is considered of value for its life-bringing functions. The sky is primarily the place where thunder 'bellows', where the clouds gather, and where the fertility of the fields is determined; the place, in fact, which ensures the continuance of life on earth. (Eliade, 91–92)

The evidence of a gradual metamorphosis in the ancient world of the impersonal creator sky Gods into the more dynamic fertility Gods is not without its significance. It reflects an increasing concern with fertility in the ancient civilisations as they gradually abandoned a nomadic lifestyle in favour of one based on the domestication of animals and the cultivation of crops. In this changed cultural climate, created by the development of an agricultural economy, the dependency on the cycles of nature is obvious: there is an ever-present need to be assured that there is an order to the cosmos, and it was primarily to this end they had recourse to the fertility Gods. In many of the ancient cultures this shift of emphasis is to be seen in the replacement of the symbol of the sky with that of the sun – one of the most important symbols of fertility, which attained a particular prominence in the religion of the Egyptian pharaohs.

Alongside the image of the sun must be placed that of the moon.[2] The regularity of the lunar cycles ensured that it is this symbol, above all, that would be used to express the cyclical character of nature – fertility, regeneration and inexhaustible life; in ancient mythologies the great Goddesses of universal fertility share as much in the sacred nature of the moon as in that of the earth. In some civilisations, such as the Pygmy culture of Africa, the moon is depicted as the mother of all living things. In other civilisations, the link between the cyclical character of the moon and the menstrual cycle gave rise to the idea of the moon as woman's consort; in the traditional Eskimo culture, unmarried girls would not look at the moon for fear of becoming pregnant. (Eliade, 155)

Polytheism and the emergence of monotheism

The wide range of Gods that were accepted in the ancient world, and the diverse functions that they served, testifies to the complexity of the world in which the ancients lived and their vulnerability in the face of many uncontrollable forces. It suggests also a need to be reassured about the purpose and the fruitfulness of the world in the face of a precarious existence. Alongside the wide range of Gods in the ancient world, one can also observe the closeness of their Gods to the world of nature. This feature of ancient religions suggests a divinisation of the natural world, or at least, a sensitivity to a divine presence in all forms of nature. In both of these respects, the world-view of the ancients is far removed from the secular ethos of contemporary society.

In the religions of the ancient cultures, the existence of a wide range of Gods suggests that polytheism – the belief in more than one God – was an unquestioned assumption. However, although the evidence points to a widespread acceptance of polytheism in the ancient world, it cannot be said that this practice admitted of no exceptions. Apart from the rejection of polytheism that shaped the history of Judaism, some of the other major world religions that appear to be polytheistic may not in fact be so described: a case in point is the Hindu religion. There are few religions that can lay claim either to a greater antiquity than Hinduism – four thousand years of unbroken tradition, or to a belief system that contains more Gods; most Indian villages have their own God whom they venerate. As a consequence, the study of Hinduism offers an unrivalled opportunity to reflect on the issues that gave rise to polytheism or fostered the emergence of monotheism.

Unlike the great monotheistic religions, Hinduism has neither a founder nor a prophet, nor has it any ecclesiastical/institutional structure nor even a set creed. Some Hindus worship Shiva, others Vishnu or his incarnations, most notably Krishna or Rama and, others again, one of the thousands of Gods that populate the Indian villages.

Hinduism as we know it today emerged in the middle of the second millennium BCE in the wake of the Ayran invasion of northern India. From the Ayrans came the Vedas, the oldest of the Hindu sacred texts. All the subsequent strands in Hinduism are linked more or less clearly to this Vedic tradition. Agni, Indra and Varuna are the earliest Hindu Gods of the Vedic period. Agni is the God of fire and sacrifice, the one who restores life to all beings. He is also the one who unites earth, heaven and the atmosphere in between. Indra is the sky-God and God of war. He is both the dynamic God of fertility and the archetype of the forces that originate life. The dynamic force of fruitfulness is omnipresent – he has inexhaustible reservoir of vitality: he makes fields, animals and women fruitful; he is invoked at weddings so that the bride may bear ten sons. Varuna is also a sky God. In Vedic literature it is his majesty as a universal sovereign that is stressed; he is the upholder of cosmic order with power to punish and reward.

In this earliest period of the Vedic scriptures the stature of these Gods suggests an acceptance of a polytheistic stance. However, with the advent of the Upanishad writings of the later Vedic period (800 – 400 BCE) the picture changes. Taken as a whole, these writing show a movement away from a primitive polytheism and its mythologies towards a more unified and inward understanding of reality: they often conclude that everything is ultimately one, thus adopting a form of monism. In these later Vedas, the ultimate or absolute is Brahman, and the world is generally conceived of as coming into being through emanation; as necessarily evolving, rather than by a definite act of creation in time, or by a decisive choice of Brahman who is the source of all that is. In this vision, the world of immediate experience is seen as continuous with its source; something of the Source has flowed down to us. Brahman is other than the world we experience but not wholly other: at the deepest level all is one.

In sharp contrast to the earlier Hindu Gods, Brahman is an extremely abstract concept of God, one that is completely devoid of anthropomorphic images. The following verse from the Rigveda scriptures anticipates this vision.

> Then neither Being nor Not-being was, nor atmosphere, nor firmament, nor what is beyond. What did it encompass? Where? In whose protection? What was water, the deep, unfathomable? (Rigveda, 10, 129)

Brahman is the origin, the cause and the basis of all existence, and yet this one who is the One is neither God nor Goddess, without attributes, without form, without task – omnipresent and yet imperceptible.

Ever since the time of the Upanishads, Hindus have accepted the all-encompassing Brahman to be the final reality, nevertheless this belief has remained bound up with an abundance of anthropomorphic, personalistic Gods that are more accessible – Gods with whom it is possible to have a devotional relationship. An instance of this is the reemergence in the late Vedic period of the devotion to the Gods of Shiva: the source of both good and evil; the destroyer of life but also the one who re-creates new life, and Vishnu: the controller of human fate who works always for the good of the entire world, the salvation of its cosmic and moral order, and the redemption of all humanity. According to the Hindu tradition, the work of Vishnu is carried out by means of his incarnations. Two of the more famous of Vishnu's incarnations are the Gods Krishna and Rama. In the Hinduism of today, it is these two Gods that inspire the greatest popular devotion. The God Krishna is the hero of many myths, most notably the Bhagavad Gita, he is depicted as a lover, a warrior and a king. Rama is a noble hero who combated the evil in the world. He is the symbol of virtue or integrity.

The remarkable feature of Hinduism is its ability to combine in one religious system two very different ways of understanding God or the Gods. What it suggests is that the polytheistic appearance of Hinduism masks an altogether different vision, where the Gods and indeed all earthly realities are but manifestations of the One or tend towards the One. This monistic or pantheistic view of reality is neither polytheism nor monotheism. The unity of all reality runs contrary to polytheism; the lack of any distinction between creator and creature or the divine and human – the idea that everything that exists is an expression of the divine, runs contrary to classical monotheism. It is a belief system that proclaims creation as a free act of God rather than a necessary emanation or outpouring from the One.

What the Hindu portrayal of God or Gods reveals about the search for meaning is the all-encompassing character of that quest. What is equally important is that Hinduism also testifies to its complexity – the need to embrace contradictions. It is not often enough acknowledged that each of the Hindu Gods is to a greater or lesser extent a unity of opposites. Firstly, each of the Gods has a consort who is also a God and whose qualities either complement or contrast those of his/her divine partner. For example, Kali or Durga is the consort of the God Shiva. In contrast to Shiva the destroyer, Kali is perceived as the 'great mother', one who is both gentle and benevolent. Secondly, not only is there a contrasting set of qualities between these two Gods, but also there are internal contrasts within the portrayal of each of them. Shiva is the destroyer but he is also the one who re-creates new life. Kali is the benevolent mother but she is also perceived to be the God of judgment and death and is portrayed wearing a necklace of human skulls. This internal contrasting set of qualities is replicated in the portrayal of the 'trinitarian' set of Gods represented by Brahman, Vishnu and Shiva: Vishnu is the preserver, Shiva the destroyer and both are manifestations of Brahman – the One. Finally, one sees evidence of internal contrasts in the classical Vedic Gods. Agni the God who restores life to all human beings is also portrayed as a demon (an asura) and sometimes depicted as a coiled snake. The God Varuna who upholds cosmic order is also depicted as the God of the ocean where serpents dwell, and even sometimes depicted as a serpent.

This unity of opposites is one of the most primitive ways of expressing the paradox of divine reality: the reconciliation or rather the transcendence of all contraries. What needs to be added is that this feature of Hindu religious speculation provides valuable lessons not only for those that seek to comprehend the nature of the divine but also for those who seek to understand what it is to be human. Who cannot be aware of the conflicting tendencies that can shape the path of human progress?

If Hinduism shows the difficulty of categorising the precise nature of a religious belief in God or Gods, nevertheless, the development of monotheism as distinct from polytheism or any form of monism is inextricably linked to the history of Judaism. The other two monotheistic world religions outside of Judaism, namely Christianity and Islam, owe their origins in one form or another to their links with the faith of the Israelites

In any historical survey of religions in the ancient world one issue stands out: the tenacious struggle by the Israelites to hold fast to a belief in one God, a monotheistic stance that was made all the more remarkable by the fact that this was a major departure from the cult patterns of the ancient Semitic world; in the ancient Near East the existence of divine beings was universally accepted. Although the earliest documentary evidence by the Israelites of their monotheism is the sixth century BCE, there is little doubt but that it marked their faith from the very beginning. The covenant relationship between Yahweh and the Jews is inexplicable outside of a strict adherence to monotheism; the most striking demand of the covenant is that Israel shall worship no God but Yahweh. The monotheistic character of the Israelites faith is reinforced by the prohibition of images. In the whole panoply of Near Eastern religions there is no other example of this prohibition. All of the ancient Gods were symbolised by means of images – mostly anthropomorphic.

The concept of God in key monotheistic traditions

A study of the concept of God in Judaism, Christianity and Islam offers us an opportunity to examine to what extent a shift from a polytheistic to a monotheistic faith perspective is reflected in values that might be constitutive of a search for meaning.

Judaism
The prohibition of images in Judaism is a reminder of their belief in the transcendent God; it is a belief that is far removed from any suggestion of monism or pantheism. From a Jewish perspective, Yahweh is unlike any created being and therefore is not capable of being described. As against that, the Old Testament never speaks of Yahweh without attributing human traits to him. What is stressed is the personal benevolence of Yahweh expressed in the formation of a people – the covenant relationship. His relation to his people has been described as that of a father to a child or husband to a wife: personal communication is possible. Unlike most of the ancient religions, Judaism emphasises the personal and not just a cultic relationship with God. Furthermore, God is never seen as an abstraction or an impersonal force. One of the most distinctive

characteristics of their God in comparison with the idols of the surrounding nations was their belief in a God who speaks and acts. The Genesis account of the origin and fall of Adam and Eve, which is unique to the tradition of Judaism, reflects this perspective; it also gives recognition to moral responsibility – the ethical character of human nature.

The Israelites used a range of names to describe God, such as 'El' or 'Elohim' and 'Shaddai'. The former is a word for God that is common to all of the Semitic cultures. For the Israelites it signifies the 'Holy One' as in 'the wholly other' – a title that lays stress on the transcendence of God. The latter was a word used in the early Patriarchal literature and probably signifies 'The Almighty'. The name that is most characteristic of the Israelites faith is Yahweh. Its meaning is uncertain, but it closely mirrors the verb to be – 'I am who am'. It suggests also the idea of a creator: he who brings into being whatever comes into being.

Christianity
Christianity shares a common history with Judaism, and the concept of God revealed in the Old Testament holds equally for Christianity as it does for Judaism. What is unique to Christianity is the belief that in the person of Jesus one witnesses the fullness of God's self-revelation. In that context, the challenge to understand the Christian concept of God can only be met through a study of the New Testament portrayal of Jesus.

The first thing that strikes the reader is the range of title or names that are used in the New Testament to describe Jesus. The most common of these is the title of Jesus as Kyrios or 'Lord'. It is the title that replaced the Jewish usage of Yahweh, and it is one that lays stress on the authority of Jesus as universal Lord. Jesus is also described as the Messiah, originally a Jewish title to describe the anointed king who would establish in the world the definitive reign of Yahweh; in the Jewish faith, the expectation of the Messiah embodied one of the principal hopes for Yahweh's intervention to save his people. Jesus named as the Messiah is frequently linked with other salvific figures such as the Suffering Servant, or the Son of Man, the lowly messenger of the powerful kingdom of God, or the son of man delivered into the hands of sinners. The title of Jesus as Prophet – an eschatological prophet – also carries consequences for his possible fate; in ascribing this title to Jesus, his disciples would have been all too conscious of prophets who were killed. Linked to the belief in Jesus as the Messiah, is the title of Jesus as High priest, a name that expresses the core Christian belief in the 'paschal mystery', the sacrifice for sins accomplished on the Cross: the priesthood of Christ that supersedes the Levitical priesthood; a new covenant has come into the world with a new priesthood. Jesus' eternal priesthood and eternal sacrifice also reflects his compassionate nature, his ability and willingness to sympathise with sinners. Other New Testament titles include 'Bread of life' and 'Shepherd': the former draws attention to the Eucharistic character of the ministry of Jesus, the latter to the pastoral nature of the ministry of Jesus. The manner in which Jesus reveals the nature of God can also be seen through an exploration of core teachings in the New Testament such as the Beatitudes. These teachings reveal God to be a merciful and compassionate God; one who is closest to those who are poor, as well as those that are persecuted in the name of righteousness.

The most distinctive feature of the Christian concept of God is its Trinitarian character. This remarkable portrait of God as a communion of love between the Father, Son and Holy Spirit is one that is revealed in the 'paschal mystery' of Jesus' death and resurrection. In this revelation, God is shown as a communion of tri-personal love; an inclusive and forgiving love that extends even to enemies. In the early Christian writings there are many examples of attempts to disclose the mystery of the Trinity but unquestionably the most detailed and systematic exploration was that provided by Augustine of Hippo. In the course of this study he pursued the possibility of understanding this mystery in terms of the dynamics of love; one that proposed the Father as the One who loves, the Son as the One who is loved, and the Holy Spirit as love itself. Although, Augustine would have been all too conscious that God is at some level unknowable, nevertheless his tentative portrait of the Trinity offers an image of an inclusive or generous portrait of love that not only illuminates the mystery of God as love, but also offers a privileged point of entry into the mystery that is human existence. In a reflection upon human existence under the rubric of love in the fourth book of the *Confessions*, he contrasts a love between two people that is exclusive or obsessive and a love that is inclusive or generous: one that includes a third, which is none other than the love of love itself or the Holy Spirit who is love. In this vision, one is offered a portrait of human nature that finds fulfilment in giving expression to a love that extends to all whom God loves even one's enemies. In the context of a reflection on the search for meaning, it is a perspective that offers some valuable lessons.

Islam
For a Muslim, the only source of knowledge of God is God himself, and God has revealed himself in the Qur'an – a book that is literally God's word. Based upon the Qur'an, Muslims attribute ninety-nine names to God or Allah, but by far the most important is his status as God alone. The creed taken from the first line of the Qur'an, and recited by Muslims five times daily, is a simple statement of this monotheism:

> 'There is no God but Allah and Muhammad is his prophet'. Islam was founded on Muhammad's struggle against the polytheism of the Arabian tribal religions in the culture in which he lived and thus a strict

monotheism is the touchstone of their faith. Not only is Islam founded on a monotheistic base but also Muslims believe that it is this adherence to monotheism that divides Islam from Christianity. In a criticism of what Muslims perceive to be the Christian doctrine of the Trinity, the Qur'an states: 'They misbelieve who say, "Verily God is the third of three."' (Sura, 5:77)

One of the most striking aspects of Islam is the manner in which it draws out the practical implications of monotheism for social life. Muhammad linked his monotheism to a humanist philosophy that connected faith in the one God with a belief in the fundamental equality of all human beings before God, and a consequent demand for social justice. The Qur'an has many references to the fate that awaits those who do not heed this teaching.

Alongside the oneness of God, Muslims lay stress on his transcendence: Allah is the creator and there is an unbridgeable gulf between Allah and all other creatures. As in Judaism, the cardinal sin in the religion of Islam is that of associating any other God or being with the true God; this sin is called the sin of *shirk*. The very word Islam means 'submission to God', and all aspects of human life are lived under his command. Muslims regard their adherence to a belief in God's transcendence as incompatible with another key Christian article of faith, namely the Incarnation and in an obvious criticism of this Christian doctrine the Qur'an states,

> He is God alone, God the Undivided.
> He does not beget and he is not begotten.
> There is none coequal with him. (Surah, 112)

From a Muslim perspective, the Christian belief in the Incarnation compromises a belief in the absolute otherness of God. However, although Allah is a transcendent God, this does not prevent Muslims laying emphasis on God's engagement with the world. In particular, they place great importance on their belief in the merciful nature of Allah as well as his creative power in the universe; in the Qur'an, all the Suras (chapters) start with the words, 'In the name of God the Merciful, the Compassionate'. Muslims also lay emphasis on the judgment of God at the end of time and, above all, God's lordship over the origin, nature and destiny of man. As it states in the Qur'an,

> He is Allah, besides whom there is no other God.
> He is the Sovereign Lord, the Holy One, the giver of Peace, the Keeper of Faith; the Guardian, the Mighty One, the All-powerful, the Most High!
> Exalted be He above their idols!
> He is Allah, the Creator, the Originator, the Artist.
> (Sura, 59: 23)

As these quotations illustrate, it is the sovereignty of God that is uppermost in the minds of Muslims: an authority that is unquestioned, and one that, from the very beginning of Muhammad's preaching, has shaped the religious character of the Islamic faith.

6

The Concept of Revelation

Divine revelation: God as known through self-revelation
In responding to the series of questions that shape human existence many people are led to the acceptance of a theistic world-view; they are drawn to a belief in the existence of a God who provides the assurance that, despite the vicissitudes of life, there is nevertheless meaning – a coherence to the world in which we live. The question then arises as to who is this God. Can one ever know the mind of God, and if so, how? The classical response to this question is that God can be known through the use of human reason and revelation. The extent to which the power of reason is capable of penetrating the mind of God is an issue that is the subject of much controversy; what is not in doubt is the importance of revelation, something that stems from an acceptance of the transcendence of God in some form or other; revelation is part of the self-understanding of all religions.

The acceptance of revelation in all religions does not mean that its meaning is incontrovertible. Across the main world religions, there are some marked divergences concerning the extent and manner of God's self-revelation. For instance, unlike the Judaeo-Christian perspective, the Islamic faith does not contain a promise of God's self-revelation; what is revealed in creation and above all, in the Qur'an is the inscrutable will of God. An examination of the method of God's revelation shows evidence of similar divergences. For example, Islam places a unique emphasis on scripture as the means of God's revelation, and indeed views Judaism and Christianity alongside Islam as the three great 'religions of the book'. However, in the sense that Muslims understand it, Judaism and Christianity are not religions of the book. Unlike Muslims who believe that the Qur'an was actually dictated word for word by God, neither Jews nor Christians believe that a heavenly author has actually written the Bible; the Bible is the inspired word of God, but it is through the many different human authors of the Bible that we find the one Word of God. In addition, Jews and Christians would be slow to accept the Muslim designation as religions of the book because it might be seen to neglect their belief that God reveals himself primarily in and through history. Not only is this a core tenet of the Judaeo-Christian view of revelation but also it is not to be found in any of the other great world religions.

The significance of revelation in different religious traditions

The conviction that God (Yahweh) is a God of revelation is fundamental to Jewish belief because the Bible teaches that human beings of themselves cannot know God; only when He lets Himself be known, when He decides to reveal himself, can He be known. What is of the utmost importance for the Jews is the belief that God's self-revelation occurs through the successive periods of Israelite history in a manner that transforms history into salvation history. The word of God working in history demonstrates that history is promise, and it creates in history what is all-important for the Old Testament, the link between promise and fulfilment.

In Jewish history, the prophets played a crucial role in facilitating the revelation of God. The witness of their lives and their role as the conscience of Israel was always understood as a manifestation of God's will. The other great medium of God's self-revelation was and remains today the institutions of Israel: as the creator of the Jews as the chosen people, God is perceived to have revealed himself in the institutions of Israel. The inherited tradition of Israel is also seen as an expression of his voice and hence the rabbis have a special role of interpreting his will in the Torah.

In common with Judaism, Christianity holds that God's revelation takes place in history, and that the history of God's relations with his people is both the object and the means of his revelation. The portrait of God and the promise of God as revealed in the Old Testament is also to be found in the New Testament. What marks off Christianity from Judaism however, is the belief that Jesus Christ is the fullness of revelation or the self-communication of God. Christ as the Son of the Father is himself the utterance of God. In addition, the contrast in the New Testament between law and spirit draws attention to the Christian emphasis on revelation as a personal encounter rather than a collection of doctrines or legal principles.

What distinguishes the Christian from the Muslim view of revelation is also this trusting commitment to Jesus as the ultimate standard of the Christian concept of God and humans. The part that the Qur'an plays for Muslims is played for Christians not by the Bible, but by Christ – God's word made manifest in human form. Furthermore, in placing emphasis on the self-revelation of God in Christ, Christians are conscious of the Trinitarian character of the God that is revealed. The Father reveals himself through the Son and through him reaches humans in the Holy Spirit. Seen from a Trinitarian perspective, Christians also acknowledge the role of the Holy Spirit in God's continuing self-revelation in and through the Church as the Body of Christ. Where the culmination and final form of God's self-communication and revelation in Christ is present explicitly and in a socially constituted form, we have what is called the Church. In Islam, one does not find anything resembling this vision.

In Islam the author or revelation is the personal God (Allah), and the content of revelation is his will, whose decree governs all the realities of the world and displays itself as commandments. There is, however, no promise of a self-revelation of God and a participation in the divine life that would form the basis of a history of salvation. As in Judaism, Muslims believe that God reveals himself through the prophets, although unlike Judaism, the prophets are literally the mouthpieces through whom God himself speaks. Muslims differentiate clearly between the messenger and the message. Unlike in Christianity, there is no promise of a self-revelation of God and no acceptance of divinity of Jesus, which to their eyes shows a failure to respect the difference between the messenger and the message.

For the Muslims, scripture is the essential thing: God reveals himself in a book. The Qur'an not only interprets what God has said, but actually contains God's own words. This is the reason why Muslims believe that the Qur'an is fundamentally untranslatable. In his Word, the Qur'an, the Muslim comes closer to God than anywhere else. In this respect, Islam takes the scripturalisation of religion to the limits. Furthermore, since the revelation of the Qur'an God has ceased to speak to man; unlike Christianity, there is no Holy Spirit who continues to work in the life of the community or Church. For Muslims, the Qur'an as the source of revelation is all-important. Not only has it molded the Islamic law, supplying quite specific doctrines and moral principles: human responsibility before God, social justice, and Muslim solidarity, but it has also shaped Islamic art and literature, in short, the whole Islamic mentality.

The Hindu religion of India is also a religion of revelation. In the Vedas, an uncreated word is uttered which finds an echo in the world of human discourse. In this revelation, the word becomes the sacred law governing worship and the social order. The notion has been kept that the Vedas were eternal revelations, with no beginning, not even fashioned by the Gods, and only passed along by the seers. For a Hindu, contact with the holy word is like contact with the Gods.

All the great Hindu religions, including those that came into existence later, are revealed religions, and are connected more or less clearly to a Vedic tradition. That is why the more than ten thousand verses of the *Rig-Veda*, the oldest of the four Vedas, (1000 BCE at the latest) were preserved even when people no longer really knew what to make of their contents. Great care has been taken to transmit the verses orally to this day. In the ancient Vedantic religion there are four great collections of Scriptures: *Rig-Veda*, *Sama-Veda*, *Yajur-Veda* and *Atharva-Veda*. In the four great collections, each of which was closely connected with a particular priestly function, religious knowledge of an early period was codified once and for all.

The meaning of the transcendent in some religious traditions

When one comes to the end of the search for meaning what will one have found? What is clear is that one will not have found some-thing, because meaning is not something that can be grasped as one might grasp an object. The inappropriateness of any type of language that suggests a purely material horizon for the quest for meaning becomes obvious when one reflects upon a reality such as beauty. In seeking to explain the beauty of a piece of music one can suggest that the composition is pleasing to the ear or that it possesses a creative or an imaginative quality. However, no matter how painstaking the search, it is never possible to grasp fully the essence of its beauty. This is because realities such as beauty, love, goodness and truth are not graspable as one might an object. In the experience of a truthful person or the interior beauty of someone kindly or the goodness of a friend or the love of a mother, one is confronted by something truly divine: a dimension of reality that transcends the boundaries of a world of objects; in short, one is exposed to the spiritual.

Since the beginning of time religions have attempted to portray their understanding of God in a manner that gives expression to this transcendent or spiritual dimension of reality. Christians believe that it is by reflecting on the mystery of truth, goodness, beauty and love that one can begin to explore the mystery of God and the manner in which God is revealed in the world. These privileged dimensions of creation and, in particular, human existence can be described as the four footprints of God in the world. As present in human experience they reflect the immanence of God in creation; as realities that are essentially mysterious, they reflect the transcendence of God – the fact that, at some level, God is unknowable. From another perspective, these realities also offer Christians a way of understanding the quest for self-identity and the search for fulfilment. The belief is that attention to the mystery of truth, beauty, goodness and the unity that is love ennobles a person and opens up four privileged pathways to God.

Although the three classical monotheistic religions, Judaism, Christianity and Islam, strongly uphold a shared belief in the transcendence of God, nevertheless they offer some contrasting views of this theme. In particular, one does not find in the Islamic faith the same emphasis on the 'Transcendentals' or the footprints of God as one does in Christianity. This is hardly surprising given the overriding concern in Islam to stress the absolute transcendence of God.

The theme of the transcendent in the different religious traditions offers a unique vantage point on which to study contrasting images of God among the world religions, because the two great oriental religions, Hinduism and Buddhism, do not place anything like the same emphasis on the transcendent as do the classical monotheistic religions of Judaism, Christianity and Islam. As we have observed earlier, Hinduism offers a set of internal contrasts that to an outsider must seem baffling. At one level, there is an infinite set of deities that are the object of devotion at a communal level. On the other hand, there is an overarching belief in Brahman, the origin, the cause and the basis of all existence. In effect, what is proposed in Hinduism is monism: a system that seeks to transcend all divisions even that between immanence and transcendence. For a Hindu, every particle of matter and human gesture is divine because there is no other reality. At one level, there can be no concept of the transcendent as understood in the Judaeo-Christian tradition, because all reality is one. And yet, at another level, the transcendent is omni-present, because in each gesture one can see a spark of the divine. The rich tapestry that is Hinduism offers a perspective in which all life, even the most insignificant, deserves to be treated with reverence.

Buddhism shares many of its central ideas with Hinduism, in particular, the doctrine of reincarnation and the law of Karma. According to Buddhists, however, every part of the universe is subject to change and decay. Furthermore, although the Mahayana Buddhism tradition, centered in China, Japan and Korea shares the Hindu vision of a mystical union with the one supreme spirit, this is not representative of Buddhist teaching. The strict Buddhism of the Theravada school, centered in Sri Lanka and South East Asia rejects the Hindu belief in the unity of the individual soul (*atman*) with God or Brahman. Not only is the idea of a God in the sense of a higher or transcendent being not accepted but also there is no universal acceptance of the existence of an enduring individual soul. Happiness or human fulfilment (*nirvana*) is rather little more than a transformed mode of human consciousness. In this sense, Buddhism supports a monistic view of the world that is characteristic of Hinduism – a type of Pantheism. Unlike Hinduism however, there is no universally accepted acknowledgment of a divine source of life or goal to human striving.

What is clear is that Buddhist thinking does not centre on the veneration of one person, human or divine. The only true source of meaning and values that has any transcendent character is the teaching of Dharma; this teaching is timeless and neither linked to history nor subject to change. Furthermore, Buddha is neither a God nor a God-sent mediator; he cannot act as a saviour or redeemer for others. Technically, a Buddha is anyone who has reached enlightenment; there are many Buddhas in the pantheon of Buddhist veneration. One interesting feature of the more liberal Mahayana teaching as distinct from the stricter Theravada school is its doctrine of Bodhisattva – one who is destined for enlightenment. In this tradition, the sacrificial love of the Bodhisattva is so great that he completely denies himself the promised entry into *nirvana* in order to continue indefinitely to work for the good of others. Thus the Bodhisattva is more than a teacher; the witness of his life is more akin to that of a saviour or redeemer – the helper of the needy in every situation. Mahayana Buddhism has thus some features in common with Christianity. For some, Bodhisattva is even conceived of as a type of Christ figure.

7

Naming God: Past and Present

Images of God in traditional and contemporary cultures

As has been observed already, the images of God in the ancient world mirrored the concerns, the desires and the hopes of the peoples of the earliest civilisations. The sky images that included those of storms and thunder focused attention upon the need to affirm a cosmic order; the numerous fertility images such as the earth mother or symbols such as the earth or the moon suggest the importance that has to be attached to this issue in the struggle for survival, often in a hostile environment. The symbolic representation of God in the ancient world lays emphasis on the power to create or to ensure the successful procreation of the species. In this context, God is an omnipotent God: a creator who is frequently endowed with magical powers; in some cases, the power of the creator God is called upon to ensure victory over enemies.

With the notable exception of the ancient Egyptian civilisation, almost all of the earliest cultures had recourse to anthropomorphic images such as that of a father or a mother; images that introduce a familial and/or caring dimension to the idea of a creator and/or fertility God. Interestingly, in some traditional African societies the image of God as father or mother depended upon whether the society was patriarchal or matriarchal, and this was often decided by the simple tribal tradition as to whether a newly wedded bride or her husband would leave their own family unit to live with the family of their spouse. In the societies where tradition dictated that the bride would live in the family unit of her husband, the images for God are almost universally male; in the other case, the images for God are almost universally female.

In the earliest expressions of both the Judaeo and the Christian traditions, the image of God as a father was perceived to express the idea of a creator and a sustainer of cosmic order, but even more importantly, it portrayed an image of a God who creates and sustains a community. From the very beginning, the idea of a covenant relationship that God has created between Himself and 'the people of God' is one that is central to both Judaism and Christianity. It evokes the image of a caring and a faithful God, one whose relationship with 'his people' is characterised by fidelity to the relationship and a love that extends the bounds of forgiveness beyond anything comparable in the ancient world.

In the contemporary world, the experiences of the divine presence and the concerns/hopes that shaped the lives of ancient society remain for the most part undiminished. Concerns about the fragility of human life or the difficulty of finding anyone in whom one can place one's trust shape the horizons of meaning today just as much as in an earlier age. Nevertheless, there are differences.

Unlike the cultures of the ancient world that depended so much on the vagaries of the natural order, today's world is one in which people have unprecedented power over their environment; people have the power to shape or misshape the natural world in a way that would have been inconceivable to the ancient civilisations. Unfortunately, the human propensity to abuse power can be seen in the onset of global warming and the increasing pace of the destruction of the bio-diversity that constitutes life on this planet. In such a cultural climate, there has been a re-discovery of the image of a God of creation, less the omnipotent God who controls the world, but rather the One who cherishes the diversity and beauty of creation. It is an image of a God who works in collaboration with us – his co-creators – so that together in partnership, a reverence for the gift of creation may be re-kindled in society.

In the world of today, there is an all-pervasive sense of a shrinking world or a global village. One of the consequences of this culture of instant communication is that people can no longer claim to be ignorant of instances of injustice that are all too evident in the world. However, it is not just the advances in communication technology that interconnect people, the multi-national character of contemporary business leaves no corner of the planet untouched. Unfortunately, the effect of their influence on the poorer has not always been positive; there is an increasing awareness of the existence of structural injustice in the world that needs to be addressed. In such a cultural climate it is hardly surprising that one of the most persuasive images of God is that of a God of liberation – One who is in solidarity with those on the margins of society and whose ministry on earth was to challenge instances of injustice wherever they were to be found.

The emergence of a new recognition of the dignity of women and their contribution to society is one of the more striking aspects of the contemporary culture. Equally important, however, has been a renewed cultural sensitivity to the feminine dimension of existence, a consciousness that is contributing to an enriched understanding of nature and culture. This cultural movement is one that has given rise to a parallel awakening to the feminine in God, a recognition that has exposed the inadequacies of the traditionally male images of God that were, until recently, a feature of the cultural landscape of the western world.

Religious and spiritual interpretations of experience

As the Second Vatican Council came to the end of its deliberations, the focus shifted to a reflection on the relations of the Catholic Church to non-Christian religions. In October 1965 under the title *Nostra Aetate* (*In Our Time*), a short declaration on this subject was published. In its appreciation and respect for the variety of religious responses to the great questions of life, it was to have a major influence in shaping an interfaith dialogue between the world religions. The declaration correctly perceived that the basis for interfaith dialogue is the existence of a universal community founded on a common belief in a shared status as creatures whose origins and destiny is in a relationship to God. Religious believers become conscious of this shared humanity as they recognise the universality of the questions that define human beings – questions that can loosely be categorised under the heading of the search for meaning and values. This vision is well articulated in the following passage from *Nostra Aetate*:

> Human Beings look to their different religions for an answer to the unsolved riddles of human existence. The problems that weigh heavily on the hearts of human beings are the same today as in the ages past. What is the person? What is the meaning and purpose of life? What is upright behaviour, and what is sinful? Where does suffering originated, and what end does it serve? How can genuine happiness be found? What happens at death? What is judgment? What reward follows death? And finally, what is the ultimate mystery, beyond human explanation, which embraces our entire existence, from which we take our origin and towards which we tend? (*Nostra Aetate* 1.3)

It is questions such as these that awaken the religious impulse that is at the heart of human nature. That they do is partly due to the manner in which they define human existence, but even more so, because they reveal a dimension to human existence that is essentially mysterious or transcendent. As archeological research shows, the question as to what happens at death is one that played no small part in the life and customs of peoples across all cultural boundaries. Indeed, from the earliest recorded history and in every known civilisation the burial of human beings was invested with a ceremonialism that can only be explained with reference to a universal sense of the sacred and a belief in some form of immortality. The mysterious or transcendent dimension of human experience is further underlined by the manner in which religion acknowledges the holy or the sacred: there are very few cultures that don't value the ideal of holiness or saintliness, and where a holy or saintly person is not revered. It is an ideal that encompasses the ethical character of human nature, but one that is not confined to the ethical. Rather, it gives expression to a religious conception of human nature that acknowledges the ultimate mystery beyond human explanation referred to in the above quotation.

Where does suffering originate and what end does it serve? What happens at death? What is judgment? What reward follows death? Drawn from universal human experiences, these two sets of questions alluded to in *Nostra Aetate* provide a valuable point of entry into an interfaith dialogue that fosters an appreciation of the variety of religious responses to the great questions of life.

In the Judaeo-Christian tradition, suffering is never something that is willed by God, rather it is linked to that of evil or sinfulness, which has its origin in the misuse of human freedom. Jews and Christians alike have traditionally put forward the existence of a misplaced pride or the failure to acknowledge one's status as a creature as the cause of this suffering. From their faith perspective, human beings are created in the image and likeness of God and human fulfilment is attained in the free acceptance of this gift. However, the desire to be like God is not the same as the desire to be God, a distinction that is not always acknowledged, and it is this refusal to admit this difference between a creator and a creature that is the root cause of the sin of pride. As Augustine puts it: 'Pride is a perverted imitation of God. For pride hates a fellowship of equality under God and seeks to impose its own dominion on fellow men, in place of God's rule.' (*City of God*, 19:12) On another level altogether, the mystery of suffering is perceived to be a part of the human condition; illness of whatever kind is a sobering reminder of the transitory nature of human existence as it is lived in this world. In that perspective, suffering can be seen as a way of directing our attention from this earthly city to an eternal city, where again, in the words of Augustine, 'There will be true peace, where none will suffer attack from within himself/herself nor from any foe outside.' (*City of God*, 22:30)

Although Muslims neither believe in the Christian doctrine of original sin nor the sacrificial death of Christ in atonement for sins, they nevertheless share much in common with the Judaeo-Christian viewpoint. In the Islamic tradition, disobedience to the will of God is the root cause of all sin, and also the cause of suffering in the world. Muslims believe that those who refuse to accept the will of God will experience no peace in this world or indeed in the life that follows death.

On the issue of the origin and purpose of suffering, the Hindu and Buddhist traditions are closely aligned. In both of these religious traditions, suffering is identified with ignorance, the cause of which is desire. In the Hindu tradition, desire is the cause of suffering because it draws us to cling to what is illusory and therefore unfulfilling: it prevents us from recognising our true destiny in the unity of Being or Brahman. Although Buddhism does not accept the Hindu view of human fulfilment, nevertheless the whole thrust of Buddhist teaching is to alert one to the dangers of unfettered desire and also to devise methods to overcome it. The state of *nirvana* or peace that attends enlightenment is one free from all desire, and thus impervious to the vicissitudes of life.

In answer to the related questions as to: what happens at death? what is judgment? and what reward follows death? there are widely different viewpoints, even within religious traditions that are closely allied. In the Christian tradition, the notions of death, judgment and immortality are all intimately linked within the context of the belief in God's forgiving love and the belief in human freedom. Christians accept that the quality of one's life as lived on this earth does influence the quality of the 'life to come'. The belief in judgment reflects the viewpoint that there is a fundamental option to be chosen, and that the consequences of this fundamental option will be respected.

Judaism shares a similar perspective to that of Christianity. However, the concept of personal salvation is not central to contemporary Judaism, and many Jews are agnostic about the existence of an after-life. Orthodox Jews believe in an after-life where God's company can be enjoyed more intimately than was the case in this life, yet Judaism has rarely concerned itself with speculations about the nature of heaven or hell.

In contrast to Judaism, the belief in a last judgment alongside the belief in life after death is revered as one of the core beliefs in Islam. According to Muslims, angels visit the dead in their graves and question them on the principles by which they have lived and acted; the good are allowed to enter into Paradise and the evil ones are consigned to Hell. Some Muslims believe that all those who practise Islam, however falteringly, will gain paradise. The majority of Muslims, however, believe that only those whose good deeds outnumber their evil deeds will gain their eternal reward.

In contrast to the monotheistic religions of Judaism, Christianity and Islam, Hindus do not believe in a last judgment or an eternal life as classically described by the idea of heaven or paradise. Rather, it is the belief in reincarnation that is the core tenet of the Hindu faith; after death, one is reborn again into this earthly world. In the sense that Hindus believe in karma – that the quality of one's life will influence how one will be reincarnated, one could say that Hindus believe in a type of judgment. However, it is far removed from that as classically understood in the Judaeo-Christian or Muslim traditions. Finally, *Moksha* or salvation is essentially union with God or Brahman: absorption and loss of identity in the One, rather than life in the eternal love of God that is characteristic of Christianity.

As is the case in the treatment of other core religious themes, the position adopted by Buddhism on this issue is similar to that of Hinduism. Both Hindus and Buddhists believe in reincarnation; Buddhists commonly hold that there are as many as six realms into which one may be reborn. However, this acceptance of reincarnation must be qualified by the acknowledgement that, in the Theravada school of Buddhism, widely regarded as the most representative school of Buddhism, there is no agreement concerning the existence of an eternal soul that is passed on through successive rebirths. The fact also that, in this school of Buddhism, there is very little evidence of any belief in divine source of life, means that the idea of a judgment is one that has little significance.

The variety of religious interpretations of human experience is not confined to the area of doctrine; rather it is only in the arena of religious practice that the diversity of religious responses can truly be appreciated. It must not be forgotten that, just as human experience provides an interpretative framework for assessing religion, so also, religious practice provides a privileged vantage point for the interpretation of human experience. In this context, anyone presuming to sketch the contours of the search for meaning in human experience would do well to study the spiritual dimension of human living that embraces the mystical, holy, prophetic, poetic and aesthetic forms of religious practice as they offer an unrivalled source of information on how humans interpret their own experience.

Common to all world religions is an acknowledgment of the holy: a Hindu who devotes his/her life to meditation, a Buddhist life that is lived in accordance with dharma (the teachings of Buddha), a Muslim whose life is lived in fidelity to the five pillars of Islam, a Jew whose life is shaped by the Torah, or a Christian whose life is lived in the light of the two-fold commandment of love. Examples of the poetic and the aesthetic dimensions of religious experience would include the experience of transcendence that is engendered through an engagement with literature, music and art. Examples of the mystical could include reference to the importance attached to the practice of meditation in both Hindu and Buddhist traditions. Also the popularity of the writings of Thomas Merton illustrates the importance that is attached to the mystical interpretation of experience in contemporary Christian spirituality. Finally, the manner in which the life and work of Mother Teresa of Calcutta has struck a chord in the conscience of the world is a reminder that the prophetic dimension of religious experience is never far removed from contemporary consciousness.

Establishing the credibility of religious belief
Over the course of this chapter we have drawn attention to the fact that, at some level of our experience, each person is touched by the desire for truth and beauty and a sense of moral goodness, by the freedom and voice of conscience and by a longing for happiness. In these experiences religious believers discern signs of the seed of eternity that they believe to be present in each person and which have their origin in God. Whether or not they are correct in their assumptions, the importance of the issue is not in doubt. If there is no link between reason and revelation there is no possibility of recognising God and, furthermore, no reason to receive God's revelation. To be taken seriously in a secular world, those who accept a theistic world-view have to show that the truth of

God's revelation can be recognised, either because it meets our deepest needs, confirms our highest aspirations, or concurs with the way in which we experience the world.

In responding to this concern to offer a credible account of what motivates a person to believe in God one ought to avoid the temptation to seek to prove God's existence as one would the existence of any other object in the world. Whether or not one can 'prove' God's existence in a manner that is acceptable to scientific scrutiny is open to debate, but even if one could, what purpose would it serve? And what exactly would it prove? Will it solve the problem of God as one would solve a mathematical problem? And when we have solved that problem, what next? Is it little more than an intellectual puzzle? These questions are listed to highlight the truth of the statement that, 'the existence of God is not a problem to be solved, but a mystery to be lived.' With these words, the French existentialist philosopher **Gabriel Marcel (1889–1973)** wished to alert his readers to the manner in which an over-preoccupation with scientific proofs can impoverish the search for a reason to believe. Who is the God in which one wishes to believe? Is he or she simply a superior clockmaker – someone capable of engineering the 'big bang' that set the cosmos in motion, or is this being a God of love, one in who is present in the way that a loved one is present to me? What is clear is that one cannot prove the existence of love, or of the presence before me of someone who loves me as one would prove the existence of an object, and neither would one want to.

It is quite legitimate to seek to demonstrate rational grounds for the existence of a God who is the creator of the world as long as one does not presume that this is the only, or indeed the most important question to be asked of God. From a Christian perspective, God is love, and the path to the knowledge of God is inseparable from that which one travels in search of knowledge about a person who loves us. It is a path that has very little to do with scientific 'proof' because it is a journey that one makes with one's heart as much as with one's head. As the French philosopher **Blaise Pascal (1623–1662)** put it, 'the heart has its reasons of which reason knows nothing.' This has nothing to do with blind sentimentalism but is a simple acknowledgement of the fact that in the interior of each person the presence of God can be recognised, albeit that it is in mystery and obscurity.

In acknowledging the validity of the heart as a starting point in the journey to find reasons to believe in a God who loves us, one is drawn inevitably to that memorable passage from the opening lines of Augustine's *Confessions* 'You have made us for yourself, O Lord, and our hearts are restless until they rest in you'. In this passage, Augustine reminds us of his conviction that as God comes to meet us he does not appear as a stranger, because the desire for God is written in our hearts. He also alerts us to the yearning in our hearts to know the truth about ourselves and about the world in which we live, one that in every generation and in every culture has found expression in the search for God. This insight is expressed in a poem by George Herbert entitled 'The Pully'[3]. In the poem, God reflects on all the gifts that he has given to human beings. For fear that they might forget his love for them and their love for Him, he decides to hold back just one gift: that of being totally at home or satisfied in the world. This reflection is beautifully expressed in the final verse:

> Yet let him keep the rest,
> But keep them with repining restlessness:
> Let him be rich and weary, that at least,
> If goodness lead him not, yet weariness
> May toss him to my breast.

In a commentary on this poem, Michael Paul Gallagher perceptively remarks, 'the absence of a lasting rest even in a "rich" existence often serves as a starting point for a journey towards faith.' (Gallagher, 66)

To complete this brief journey along the 'interior' paths to God, there are three others that need to be mentioned: (i) 'the calls of conscience', (ii) 'the experience of personal existence', and (iii) 'the experience of spirit'. The direction of both of these 'proofs' is not out into the world, but like Augustine, they are paths that direct us to the interior of the person – to the heart; the conviction is that it is here that God is to be found. In the words of Augustine, 'You are closer to me than I am to myself.'

The former approach is associated with the nineteenth-century English theologian, **John Henry Newman**. In pursuing this path, Newman asks us to discover the drama that is our own conscience, a drama that can be all too easily smothered in a self-centered world. As he understood it, conscience is a great interior guide to God simply because it is the voice of God. As Michael Paul Gallagher acknowledges, this call of conscience is not without its moments of pain, and there is the danger that one will seek to foreshorten the search because of an unwillingness to accept this pain:

> To stay faithful to that experience of struggle is hard. It means encountering demons in various forms. There is the demon of despair born from the sheer enormity of the world's pain. There is the demon of guilt born from the constant failure of the self to live one's own hopes. At these points of impotence the need for some 'salvation' is experienced. And in this way God can come into view on the road of conscience – to some people as a voice of judgement and call, to others as the source of a desire to live a more generous life, and to others again as the saviour needed if I am to keep going along any road of steady loving. (Gallagher, 76)

It is an insight well expressed in the following perceptive comment by Albert Camus: 'In the time of innocence I did not know that morality existed. I know it now'.

The existentialist philosopher Gabriel Marcel took a similar approach when he spoke of the importance of the experience of the 'broken world' (*le monde cassé*).[4] As he puts it:

> Don't you feel sometimes that we are living ... if you can call it living... in a broken world? Yes, broken like a broken watch. The mainspring has stopped working. Just to look at it, nothing has changed. Everything is in place. But put the watch to your ear, and you don't hear any ticking. You know what I'm talking about, the world, what we call the world, the world of human creatures... it seems to me it must have had a heart at one time, but today you would say the heart had stopped beating. (Marcel, 21–22)

How to explain this experience of a world that is broken? It is the only world that I have ever experienced, therefore how do I know that it is broken? And yet Marcel was only echoing a universal experience that the world is not as it should be. This draws Marcel to acknowledge that in the heart of everyone is an intuition of a different world, one in which one can find beauty, harmony and peace; not only an intuition but also a longing for this alternative world.

From where do we obtain this intuition of a harmonious world and what prompts us to desire beauty? The experience of restlessness or homelessness suggested by the phrase 'a broken world' raises in no uncertain terms the question of whether or not there exists a transcendent dimension to life. Are we to say that the intuition of beauty and the desire for a world touched by beauty is simply an illusory human projection or an ideological construct? Is beauty to be explained in terms of an elaborate attempt to cloak the absurdity of the world with a veneer of meaning – a type of patchwork quilt which warms and protects us from the chill winds of reality? One could equally argue that the reverse is true and that those who would deny the existence of a spiritual and transcendent dimension to life are arbitrarily refusing to acknowledge the implications of the experience of homelessness or exile in a world from which beauty is absent.

Marcel speaks of each person as a pilgrim person (*Homo Viator*), one who is drawn to the experience of the need for transcendence by the God given intuition of a better world; one who is drawn to make the journey that will lead to the acknowledgement of the existence of a God in whose presence beauty and peace will be found.

The second approach is also one that is characteristic of Marcel's philosophy. Born in Paris, he became an accomplished musician as well as a philosopher. Through his love of music and his reflections on philosophy he rediscovered his Catholic faith. Marcel vehemently rejected the idea that philosophy could be perceived as a series of abstract theories. Rather he believed that the philosopher must be *engagé* (involved), and that philosophy is nothing more than personal reflection on the concrete human situation. For Marcel, this life of personal involvement is one that always embraces 'the other'. He never ceased to believe that human existence finds its fulfilment in a loving relationship – in a God-centered communion of persons that is characterised by mutual fidelity and hope.

All of his approaches to God are based upon a deep reflection on the mystery of personal existence – the discovery of the 'self' and the discovery of others. At the heart of his philosophy is the recognition that to live a truly personal existence is to take the risk to trust others, to hope in others – a hope that 'our love will never die', and to love – to live in communion with others. One can believe that this view of life is a fool's paradise – that there is little or no evidence to support a life marked by these virtues: little reason to adopt a life marked by faith/faithfulness, hope or love. However, as Marcel perceptively recognised, this does not fully account for the fact that people in all cultures and across all generations have opted for a life marked by these virtues – and found their lives ennobled by this choice; they cannot all be classified as misguided. How to explain this refusal not to have faith or to hope or to love – that is, unless there is a God who is faithful, who provides the reassurance for the hope that proclaims that 'our love will never die' and who not only loves us as individuals but creates the conditions within which one can experience community.

The third path entitled 'the experience of spirit' is the path of religious experience or, more simply, the path of prayer. As the great theologian Karl Rahner said, 'I continue to believe in God because I pray every day.' This approach is indelibly associated with the contemplative spiritual journey of Teresa of Avila, and beautifully expressed in her own words:

> Sometimes even when reading, I would unexpectedly experience a consciousness of the presence of God, of such a kind I could never doubt that he was within me or that I was completely engulfed in Him... The soul seems to be completely outside itself. The will loves. The memory I think is almost lost; while the understanding does not work to reason, it is amazed at the extent of all it can understand. (Quoted by Gallagher, 81)

The desire for God may be written in the hearts of all people in every generation, but the question remains: does anything correspond to this desire? Is it just wishful thinking, a continuation of every child's dream for a father or mother figure? Perhaps God is a phantasm that we invent to dull the pain of human deprivation or to mitigate the many disappointments that accompany human life.

Over the centuries, many religious believers have attempted to address these issues by pointing to another series of converging and convincing arguments that would allow an unbiased observer to acknowledge the credibility of a theistic world-view. These approaches can be grouped under two headings based upon two different starting points, (i) the one that begins with the world of the human subject, and (ii) the one that begins with the world outside the human subject. The former reflects upon the inner dynamics of human rationality; its most celebrated expression is to be found in the 'Ontological argument'. The latter approach that was adopted by Aquinas reflects upon the fact that, despite the transient character of this earthly existence, we encounter a world that is intelligible and purposeful, and that the world does not contain within its own resources an explanation either for its intelligibility or its purposefulness.

From the starting point that is the human subject, but nevertheless very different to the approach taken by Augustine – an argument based upon pure reason rather than human experience – one of the most celebrated arguments for the existence of God is to be found in the writings of **Anselm (1033–1109),** abbot of Bec in Normandy and Archbishop of Canterbury. Anselm's conception of a rational basis of faith led him to wonder how he might give intellectual support to his belief in God. In his famous treatise, the *Proslogion,* he developed what has come to be known as the 'Ontological Argument'. Over the course of the centuries, this argument has been subject to a searching examination. It has had numerous critics, most notably from philosophers of the standing of Aquinas and Kant. Variations of this argument have also had their staunch defenders, most notably the philosophers Descartes and Leibnitz. Whatever one's assessment of the logical character of the argument, the fact alone that it is still the subject of debate, a thousand years after it was proposed, is testimony to the enduring worth of this reflection. It retains a fascination even today because of the confidence that it exhibits in the ability of the human mind to reach knowledge of God in this life.

The argument is given in its most extensive form in the following passage from the second chapter of the *Proslogion.*

> And so, O Lord, since you give understanding to faith, give me to understand – as far as you know it to be good for me – that you exist, as we believe, and that you are what we believe you to be. Now we believe that you are a being than which none greater can be thought. Or can it be that there is no such being, since 'the fool had said in his heart, "There is no God"? But when this same fool hears what I am saying – 'A being than which none greater can be thought' – he understands what he hears, and what he understands is in his understanding, even if he does not understand that it exists. ... But clearly that than which a greater cannot be thought cannot exist in the understanding alone. For if it is actually in the understanding alone, it can be thought of as existing also in reality, and this is greater. Therefore, if that than which a greater cannot be thought is in the understanding alone, this same thing than which a greater cannot be thought is that than which a greater can be thought. But obviously this is impossible. Without doubt, therefore, there exists, both in the understanding and in reality, something than which a greater cannot be thought. (*Proslogion*, 2)

Traditionally, Anselm's argument has been perceived to hinge upon the idea that existence is a perfection and that therefore God as 'something than which nothing greater can be thought' must exist in reality, because the fact of existing makes something 'greater' than something else that exists in thought only – all that is in reality is greater than what is only in the mind. This idea that existence or even necessary existence – as might be suggested by *Proslogion 3* – is a perfection of being is a thesis that Aquinas would not countenance. He makes this abundantly clear in the following passage from the *Summa Theologiae*:

> Even if the word God were generally recognized to have that meaning ('that than which nothing greater can be thought'), nothing thus defined would thereby be granted existence in the world of fact, but merely as thought about. Unless one is given that something in fact exists than which nothing greater can be thought – and this nobody denying God's existence would grant – the conclusion that God in fact exists does not follow. (*S.T.* 1.1. 2)

Recent research into Anselm's argument suggests that both his traditional defenders and detractors have misinterpreted the purpose of the *Proslogion* and the structure of the argument; Anselm is not engaged in any attempt to suggest that existence is a perfection/predicate of being and that the proposition that God exists is a logically necessary truth.

Whatever the truth about Anselm's intentions, Descartes, some four centuries later, seized upon this interpretation in his formulation of the Ontological Argument. The most detailed account of his argument is to be found in the fifth *Meditation*. The following is a passage from this work:

> I clearly see that existence can no more be separated from the essence of God than can its having its three angles equal to two right angles be separated from the essence of a rectilinear triangle, or the idea of a mountain from the idea of a valley; and so there is not any less repugnance to our conceiving a God (that is a Being supremely perfect) to whom existence is lacking (that is, to say, to whom a certain perfection is lacking), than to conceive of a mountain which has no valley. (*Meditation 5*)

The most celebrated critique of Descartes Ontological Argument is to be found in Kant's *Critique of Pure Reason*. He makes the point that existence is not a logical predicate, and that furthermore, there is already a contradiction in introducing the concept of existence – no matter under what title it may be disguised – into the concept of a thing that we profess to be thinking solely in reference to its possibility. As with Aquinas, the idea that a theoretical concept of an absolutely necessary being implies that it exists in the real world is not one that was ever likely to be acceptable to a critical thinker such as Kant.

In contrast with the Ontological Argument, whose starting point is human reason rather than human experience, the celebrated five ways of **Aquinas** take as their starting point the cosmos – the world outside of the human subject. They are entitled the 'Cosmological Arguments'.

Aristotle was the first to recognise that the intelligibility of the universe hinges upon being able to find a first cause that is capable of explaining both the origin and the purpose of all movement. This insight was rediscovered in the world of thirteenth century Scholasticism and became the corner stone of the philosophy of Thomas Aquinas; it was to shape the subsequent development of scholastic philosophy. However, the importance of Aquinas is to be seen in his ability to recognise that what applies to movement equally applies to existence. It is not just movement that needs to be explained; questions surrounding the possibility of movement are but an instance of a larger series of questions which draw attention to the deceptively simple fact that the world does not explain itself.

In the philosophy of Aquinas it is the existential question (why is there something rather than nothing?) that has priority. No longer is philosophy primarily concerned with what a thing is, i.e. a being that is subject to movement: growth and decay; rather the focus is on a question that is prior, namely, one which points to the existential fact 'that it is' – the fact that something is rather than nothing. As Aquinas recognised, it is one thing to understand how the world works but it is quite a different thing to stand back and enquire as to why the world exists in the first place. In drawing attention in the 'Third Way' to the contingent or accidental character of the world, Aquinas realised that the existence of a being that necessarily exists is an inevitable consequence, if the intelligibility of human experience is to be respected. This being, God, whose very essence is to exist, is the creator: the one who explains the beginnings and the purpose of creation. Thus each of the five 'proofs' begins with the recognition of experiences that draw attention to the contingent or accidental nature of existence as it is experienced.

The 'First Way' closely resembles Aristotle's argument for the existence of God as 'unmoved mover'. It is a proof that is based on the universal experience of movement among all material beings, and looks to the existence of God as the cause and origin of all movement. Based on the more general observation that every effect must have a cause, the 'Second Way' looks to God as the first cause of all being. The 'Third Way' argues from the fact that nothing in this world exists as of necessity, to the existence of God as a necessary being, who is both the creator and sustainer of all beings. This proof is the most original of Aquinas' five ways and his approach is well expressed in the following passage from the *Summa Theologiae*:

> Some of the things we come across can be but need not be, for we find them springing up and dying away, thus sometimes in being and sometimes not. Now everything cannot be like this, for a thing that need not be, once was not; and if everything need not be, once upon a time there was nothing. But if that were true there would be nothing even now, because something that does not exist can only be brought into being by something already existing.... One is forced to suppose something which must be, and owes this to nothing outside itself; indeed it itself is the cause that other things must be. (*S.T.* 1.1. 3)

The argument is one from the existence of contingent beings, namely those that don't possess the reason for their existence within themselves, to the existence of a necessary being, one that is the cause of its own existence: whose essence is existence, a definition reflected in the biblical phrase, 'I am who am'.

The 'Fourth Way' is based on the gradation that is observed in things. As Aquinas puts it:

> Some things are better, truer, more excellent than others. Such comparative terms describe varying degrees of approximation to a superlative; for example, things are hotter and hotter the nearer they approach what is hottest. Something therefore is the truest and best and most excellent of things, and hence the most fully in being.... And this is what we all God. (*S.T.* 1.1. 3)

As a proof, its structure is similar to what we observed earlier, namely that the recognition of various degrees of beauty, truth and goodness causes us to acknowledge the existence of one who is both the fullness of Truth, Goodness and Beauty and the cause or creator of these perfections in the world; such a person is God. A version of this proof is to be found also in the writings of Augustine. He was not slow to acknowledge that in the desire for beauty we receive a glimpse of a world that is not subject to decay; in the experience of beauty we receive a trace or a footprint of the One who is Beauty itself, namely God. Just as art draws us to praise the artist, so, likewise, the recognition of beauty draws us to praise the creator of beauty.

The 'Fifth Way' reflects upon the experience of the world as intelligible. As Aquinas correctly observed, we encounter the world as intelligible, ordered and purposeful and yet the world does not possess within itself an explanation either for its intelligibility or purposefulness. The reasoning of this proof is well expressed in the following:

> Goal-directed behaviour is observed in all bodies obeying natural laws, even when they lack awareness. ... But

> nothing lacking awareness can tend to a goal except it be directed by someone with awareness and understanding; the arrow, for example, requires an archer. Everything in nature, therefore, is directed to its goal by someone with understanding, and this we call God. (*S.T.* 1. 1. 3)

As Aquinas perceptively observed, an outcome that is intelligible and purposeful cannot be caused by chance happenings because only a random or chance outcome will emerge from a chance beginning. The experience of purposefulness at all levels of existence therefore points us inexorably towards the acceptance of an intelligent being who is the creator of the world and the goal to whom all things tend; such a person is God.

The 'cosmological' approach adopted by Aquinas is one that places him in dialogue with the world of science. Prompted by the desire to know and by the refusal to accept either that the universe is absurd or that its laws are inaccessible to human reason, scientists in all ages have given expression to the human impulse to understand the world in which they live. In their struggle to unlock the secrets of the universe they offer eloquent testimony to the intuition that the universe which we inhabit is intelligible, a stance that is framed by the rejection of both nihilism and scepticism. In opposition to the claims of nihilism science rests upon the trust that the universe is ordered; in contrast to the claims of scepticism science rests upon the belief that these laws are accessible to human reason and that scientific experimentation is capable of uncovering the complex matrix of laws that govern the universe. In this context, the Five Ways can be seen as a series of reflections on science's foundational assumptions – the conditions for the very possibility of science.

Developments in the world of contemporary physics draw attention to a similar approach to God in what is called the anthropic principle. This principle argues for the reasonableness of a theistic world-view from the fact that a delicate balance seems necessary in the universe's character, similar to that actually found if it is to prove capable of evolving systems of a complexity sufficient to sustain conscious life. As the contemporary English physicist John Polkinghorne observes, 'fine-tuning of the cosmic knobs is necessary to make men'.[5] Just how fine the tuning needs out to be is graphically revealed in his following comment:

> We know that there has to have been a very close balance between the competing effects of explosive expansion and gravitational contraction which, at the very earliest epoch about which we can even pretend to speak (called the Planck time, 10^{-43} sec. after the big bang), would have corresponded to the incredible degree of accuracy represented by a deviation in their ratio from unity by only one part in 1060. Had that balance tilted a little more in the direction of expansion, then matter would have flown apart so fast that a world would have resulted too dilute for anything interesting to happen in it. On the other hand, had the balance tilted a little more in the direction of contraction then the world would have collapsed in again upon itself before we had time to appear upon its scene. (Polkinghorne, 22-23)

This is clearly a non-trivial fact that calls for some explanation other than sheer luck or blind chance. The anthropic principle may not provide mathematical certainty that God exists; however, the implausibility of any other explanation does lend credence to the reasonableness of a hypothesis that proposes a theistic world-view.

To conclude, the variety of paths to God outlined above, testify to the spirit of wonder that animates the search for meaning; the unquenchable thirst to understand oneself and the world in which one lives. The belief is that one will only do justice to the nobility of the quest for meaning if one is attentive to the restless heart, the majesty of the name of God, the mystery of the world's existence, the call of conscience, and the experience of God.

Notes

1   Mircea, Eliade, *Patterns in Comparative Religion*, London, Sheed and Ward, 1958.
2   For a detailed treatment of this theme, see Mircea Eliade, *Patterns in Comparative Religion,* pp.155-187.
3   I am indebted to Michael Paul Gallagher for drawing my attention to this poem. For an excellent and very accessible treatment of the various approaches to establishing the reasonableness of faith see his book entitled *Free to Believe*, London, Darton Longman and Todd, 1987, pp.60-86.
4   See Gabriel Marcel, *Mystery of Being, Vol. 1* (South Bend, Indiana, Gateway, 1950, pp.18-39. For an excellent article on Marcel, see the article by Gerard Hanratty, 'The Theistic Philosophy of Gabriel Marcel', in Gerald Hanratty, *Studies in Gnosticism and in the Philosophy of Religion,* Four Courts Press, Dublin, 1997, pp.160-173.
5   John Polkinghorne, *Science and Creation*, London, SPCK, 1988, p.22. For an excellent summary of the anthropic principle see the volume in this series by Fachtna McCarthy and Joseph McCann, entitled *Religion and Science*, pp.118-125.

Part Four

RELIGION AND THE EMERGENCE OF VALUES

Introduction

From the beginning of time, foundational questions have found expression in the sets of dialogues that constitute the great religions of the world. Religion could indeed be described as a locus for remembering, reflecting and celebrating the core human experiences that give rise to questions, such as: what is the meaning and purpose of life? How can happiness be found? In this scenario, the history of religions is nothing less than a series of road maps that have charted the manner in which human beings have grappled with these core issues.

In part three, we observed the close relationship between the search for meaning and values and the concept of God. Part four continues this theme, but alerts us to the two-fold nature of this relationship. The aim of chapter eight is to alert us to the importance of theological anthropology – the manner in which the understanding of God in the main world religions has contributed to the self-understanding of the adherents of these different religions. The conviction underlying this study is that a religion's portrayal of God and its understanding of the divine/human relationship has ethical implications that shape the manner in which the search for meaning and values is conceived.

It should be acknowledged that a study of this topic is not without its difficulties. Firstly, it is difficult to assess with any degree of certainty the extent to which the concept of God in the different world religions has influenced the concept of the person and the contours of the search for meaning among the adherents of these religions. Clearly, there are those who would wish to suggest that there is a God whose self-revelation shapes the self-understanding of the members of the faith community; however, the opposite viewpoint would be expressed by those who argue from the perspective of a functionalist view of religion. From this standpoint, it might be suggested that it is not God's revelation which shapes the self-understanding but rather the other way around; it is the existence of a diversity of socio-economic, geographical and cultural backgrounds – divergent human experiences – which account for the different concepts of God that constitute the world religions. On the assumption that there is a God, the truth probably lies somewhere in the interrelatedness of these two perspectives.

Secondly, even if one grants the eminently plausible thesis that there is a relationship between the concept of God and the concept of the person, one must acknowledge that the specifics of this influence may be difficult to pin down with any degree of accuracy. Unquestionably, one can observe common characteristics between the concept of God and the person, but it is something else to prove that there is a causal relationship between the two. Therefore, while not denying the importance of this approach, it is important to acknowledge the tentative nature of any conclusions that might be drawn.

Chapter nine offers a sustained reflection on non-religious responses to the great questions of life, with a view to showing attempts to derive communal values from sources other than religion. In the course of this chapter we explore key moments in the emergence of a secular value system and a culture that espouses liberal values; both of these non-religious sources of communal values have exercised a not-insignificant influence on the shape of liberal democracy in the western world and the widespread societal acceptance of this form of social organisation in the last hundred years. The chapter concludes with a brief description of the different types of relationships that exist between religions and the secular world: from those that advocate a theocracy to those that seek to foster a complete separation of Church and state.

8

Religion as a Source of Communal Values

The relationship between the concept of God and the person
Given that all people share a common human nature, it would be surprising if investigations were to uncover widely divergent views on the concept of the person across the different religious traditions. In fact, one is struck by just how many of the core beliefs about the person remain constant throughout all the main world religions. For example, all of these religions accept that the concept of the person is to be understood in the context of a relationship with a divine source of meaning; all recognise that humans are social beings; all acknowledge an ethical dimension to human nature; to a greater or lesser extent, all profess a belief in the existence of a spiritual substance or a soul, a core dimension of the person that transcends the boundaries of the material world; and to a greater or lesser extent, all accept that as creatures, human beings have a responsibility to care for the habitat and the diversity of life in the world.

However, even in this summary checklist of some characteristics of human nature that the world religions share, one can detect a difference of emphasis. For example, Buddhists are by no means united in accepting the existence of a soul or principle of identity that 'survives' death. Similarly, whereas Hinduism and Buddhism have consistently placed a high premium on a reverential or respectful attitude to the diversity of life in the world, the same cannot be said of the practices that have informed the three monotheistic religions. While all these religions acknowledge that the non-human world is part of God's creation and therefore deserving of respect, nevertheless, in the case of Christianity, the historical focus on the spiritual 'soul' has, in some cases, diverted attention away from the recognition of the interrelatedness of all species and the consequent need to show due reverence for all forms of life on this planet. A more detailed study of the concept of the person in the different religions will reveal further examples of differing emphases.

In the case of the Judaeo-Christian tradition, the understanding of the person is bound up with the belief that humans are created in the image and likeness of God. This belief suggests a close interrelationship between the concept of God and the concept of the person. Flowing from the idea of a creator God who respects his creation, and of a just God who creates all equally, it offers the rationale for a theological statement on the dignity of human nature that affirms the equality of all human beings in the sight of God. Even if the course of history is littered with examples of how little attention was paid to this belief, nevertheless, it does provide a benchmark for a Christian view of society. This Christian theological statement about equality is not one that is shared in like manner across all religious boundaries. For example, for some traditional Hindu writers, the person is defined by his/her membership of a caste; Hindus trace the origins of the different castes to the different parts of the body of the first man. This theological basis for the belief in the caste system may provide Hindus with a strong sense of community identity, but it makes it extremely difficult for them to either acknowledge or to affirm in practice the equality of all persons.

One of the more interesting themes worth exploring is the relation between the concept of the person and the idea of transcendence. The monotheistic character of Judaism, Christianity and Islam provides strong support for an understanding of human nature that is defined in terms of a personal relationship with God. This is indeed the case. In the Judaeo-Christian tradition, the experience of a personal relationship with God is etched into the very fabric of the belief system. It is a relationship that comes from membership of a community sustained by the covenant. A consequence of this covenant character of the divine/human relationship is that the concept of the person in both Judaism and Christianity contains a strong emphasis on the social identity of the person as a member of a community. An obligation to promote social justice at all levels of society is consequently at the heart of the Judaeo-Christian vision of the person; it is an ethos that is increasingly at odds with the individualist character of contemporary western society.

While all three religions accept the possibility of a personal relationship with God, the nature of this relationship varies among the different religions. For example, while the virtue of obedience to God's law is strongly imprinted in the self-understanding of the adherents of all three religions, it finds its strongest emphasis among Muslims, where the virtue of obedience is literally inserted into the very title of their religion: the word Islam means submission to God. From another perspective, while the possibility of a loving relationship with God is to a greater or lesser extent acknowledged in these three religions, it is among Christians that it receives by far the most emphasis; the biblical stress on the importance of obedience to the law of God, as enshrined in the 'Ten Commandments', is transformed into the two-fold commandment of love. Interestingly, the intimacy of the divine/human relationship that so characterises the self-understanding of Christians has no parallel among Muslims. In fact, apart from the Sufi tradition, the idea of a personal relationship with God is not something that is stressed. The singular importance that Muslims attach to the transcendence or the 'otherness' of God, and the lack of anything comparable to the Judaeo-Christian belief in God's self-revelation in history, may account for this difference of emphasis.

A concept of the person that is shaped by a belief in a personal relationship with God will inevitably bring to the surface the theological issue of grace: God's loving action in the world. More than any other topic, the stance that one adopts regarding the need for grace will shape the contours of one's concept of the person. A theology of grace is central to the broad spectrum that is the Judaeo-Christian tradition, because both the Old Testament and New Testament covenant relationships are founded on God's initiative. In this regard, the contrasts with the other main world religions are striking. In Islam, there is no such emphasis on grace, and likewise, in Hinduism and Buddhism there are very few, if any, parallels with this aspect of the Judaeo-Christian belief system.

The issue can be addressed in more detail by reflecting on how the different religions describe the way that happiness is to be found. In Judaism, the belief is that happiness is to be found in a life lived in faithfulness to the covenant relationship with God; this faithfulness finds its expression in obedience to God's law as written in the Torah and the Talmud. At different stages in the course of Jewish history, the covenant relationship was perceived as an expression of God's saving love and/or his forgiving love and mercy for his people. Not surprisingly, the Christian tradition is faithful to this understanding of the action of God's love in the world. However, the significance attached to the 'Christ-event' alters the nature and significance of the covenant relationship. In the new covenant established by Christ, the graced nature of the relationship between God and his people stands for the whole salvation freely bestowed by God in Christ. Although, with some variation in emphasis, all

Christians believe that the path to happiness lies in the free acceptance of the gift of love (grace) that is reflected in a life of faithfulness to the two-fold commandment of love, nevertheless, they would all accept that happiness is something received rather than achieved. This shared belief is reflected in the following passage from the First Epistle of John: 'This is what love is: it is not that we have loved God, but that he loved us and sent his Son to be the means by which our sins are forgiven.'(1 Jn 4:10).

In the context of a focus on grace, the concept of the person it brings to mind is one where the stress falls on the motif of love in all its manifestations. However, in the light of the centrality of the paschal mystery in shaping the Christian understanding of grace, one must acknowledge the centrality of the characteristic of love that finds expression in the motif of forgiveness; the emphasis that Christ places on the importance of forgiveness has no parallel. At one level, the stress on forgiveness suggests a rather sobering assessment of the frailty of human nature; at another level, however, it suggests a portrait of human nature that accepts no boundaries to love; in this vision of the inclusiveness of a forgiving love, one comes face to face with a vision of human nature that is deeply ennobling.

In Islam, there is no comparable emphasis on grace. This belief system offers a view of human nature which emphasises that human happiness is to be found in a life of obedience to God, as it is revealed in the Qur'an.[1] Individuals have the freedom to serve God or to disobey Him. Each person chooses for himself/herself and is responsible for their choice. Those who submit to the teachings of God will attain peace; those who refuse to so submit will be condemned. Although Muslims place emphasis on the mercy of God, there is no belief in Islam that is comparable to the Christian belief in the paschal mystery – the forgiving grace of Christ as manifested in and through His death and Resurrection.

In Hinduism, happiness or salvation is described by the word *moksha,* meaning liberation. In essence *moksha* is perceived in two ways: firstly as deliverance from the predetermined and endless cycle of successive rebirths, symbolised by the wheel of *samsara,* and secondly, as deliverance from a world of illusion that is caused by unbridled desire. Thus far the concept of *moksha* is clear. However, Hinduism is far from clear as to the true nature of human destiny. In popular Hinduism, it is perceived as a personal union with one's chosen God, whereas in the classical understanding of Hinduism, human destiny is perceived more as unity or absorption in the impersonal One or Brahman; the image is of the water of a river merging and losing its separate identity in the water of the great Ocean. As distinct from popular Hinduism, in this latter belief system the concept of grace has little or no significance because the monist or pantheist worldview does not admit of a personal relationship with God upon which to base such a theory; the path or paths to human fulfilment are therefore those that are trodden by human beings alone.

Traditionally, Hindus describe three paths to happiness, liberation or enlightenment. *Jnana-Marga* is the way of knowledge, and the focus is on intense study, ascetic discipline including the renunciation of material possessions and, above all, the practice of meditation. The path of *Karma-Marga* is the way of action, and the emphasis is on fulfilling the duties associated with one's state of life, determined by age and marriage. The third path is called *Bhakti-Marga,* the way of divine love. In this path, the emphasis is on worship and devotion. It is the path that places emphasis on the fulfilment of one's duties and responsibilities as a member of a caste. However, the focus is very much on the devotional practices that are associated with worship of the personal God of the particular family or village. In the popular expression of *Bhakti,* these Gods are seen as both personal and gracious, and the means of achieving fulfilment or liberation is ultimately God's grace. In its acceptance of the idea of personal Gods who will intercede on our behalf, it is a vision far removed from the monism or pantheism of classical Hinduism.

In many respects, Buddhism is more akin to classical Hinduism than is the popular devotional expression. Like Hinduism, Buddhism regards salvation as the overcoming of *samsara* through a life lived in accordance with dharma – the teachings of the Buddha. Main-stream Buddhism of the Theravada school has no parallels to the worship of personal Gods in popular Hinduism, and it does not have any particular focus on the veneration of any person, either human or divine; a theory of grace that would describe the action of a loving God in the world is one that would be totally foreign to the school of Theravada Buddhism. In its various forms, Buddhism testifies to the essential inadequacy of this changing world, and to a vision of the person as one marked by suffering and pain that is caused by human desire. The doctrine of each individual's total responsibility for his own fate, strikes some critics as bleak and inhuman, and although Hinduism is also conscious of the destructive potential of desire, the concept of the person that is proposed in Buddhism is of an altogether starker character than anything that is to be found in Hinduism. The core teachings of dharma – 'The Four Noble Truths' – begin with a lengthy litany of the sufferings that are the lot of human nature and conclude with a sustained reflection on a radical system of self-deliverance through the suppression all forms of desire. Nirvana, a state of perfect liberation from the realm of suffering and pain can be attained, but only by a supreme effort which involves a thorough self-mastery through a life devoted to meditation, the moral life and the pursuit of wisdom.

Does the shared acknowledgement of the transcendence of God that characterises the three classical monotheistic religions similarly leave its mark on the concept of the person in their respective communities of faith? With the emphasis today in western societies on issues that touch upon core human rights – the freedom and equality of all people irrespective of gender, race or social background – there is a growing interest in exploring the origins of the concept of the person as free and equal. One of the most interesting avenues of enquiry has been to examine to what extent this development can be traced to the largely Christian heritage of the western world. If it proves to be the case that there is a link between the legacy of a Christian understanding of the divine/human relationship and the widespread acceptance of a human rights culture, this would be further evidence of the value of this topic.

As suggested above, the equality of all human beings does indeed find strong support in the Judaeo-Christian theological statement that 'all are created in the image and likeness of God'. It is also arguable that the strong sense of human freedom and personal responsibility that permeates these classical monotheistic religions is related to their shared belief in the transcendence of God; that it is precisely the existence of a clear distinction between creator and creature in these religions that provides the necessary space for the belief in individual freedom. Interestingly, even the Protestant/Puritan acceptance of some form of predestination does not prevent the acceptance of a strong belief in an ethic of personal responsibility that is shared across all Christian denominations. Whether or not one accepts this linkage between a belief in individual freedom and a concept of the transcendence of God, it is interesting to observe that one finds neither the same emphasis on the transcendence of God nor the same emphasis on human freedom in either Hinduism or Buddhism that one finds in the Christian tradition, and in particular the Catholic denomination. At the core of both the Hindu and Buddhist belief systems is the law of *samsara,* that endless cycle of rebirths that is symbolised by the cosmic wheel to which everyone is tied. The Hindu belief in the importance of *karma* (good works) testifies to the view that the cycle is not totally predetermined or outside the control of human intervention; Buddhists likewise believe that, in and through attendance to the law of dharma, one can break the endless cycle of rebirth. Nevertheless, there is a strong sense of the inexorable hand of fate in both of these belief systems.

9
Secular Sources of Communal Values

The emergence of a secular world with its own value system
In the history of European culture, the emergence of a secular world with its own value system and norms of behaviour must be seen in the context of a desire to cut the link between values and religious belief. It was a development that happened gradually over a period of over three hundred years, beginning with the rise of modern science in the sixteenth and early seventeenth century and culminating in the more recent adoption of a liberal culture. The shape of the emerging secular world-view varied greatly as between different cultural and philosophical traditions. Two examples of this diversity can be seen in the philosophical tradition of empiricism that emerged in the cultural milieu of Anglo-Saxon philosophy, and the rise of existentialism that is largely associated with modern continental philosophy. Over the course of a brief analysis of these two philosophical traditions one will observe a number of key moments in the development of a secular world.

The Enlightenment
The emergence of an independent secular world is linked to that stage in European culture called the Enlightenment, which roughly corresponds to the period between the English

Revolution of 1688 and the French Revolution of 1789. Alternatively described as the Age of Reason, it took as its motto the celebrated saying of Immanuel Kant, *'Sapere aude* – 'Dare to know'. The Enlightenment was marked by a belief in the freedom to make use of one's reason in all fields of discourse. This found expression in the rejection of all traditional forms of authority, the drawing up of the foundations of a secular morality, and the conviction that scientific development would bring human progress. All of these views found their clearest articulation in the cultural milieu of the world of philosophy. As the well-known historian of the Enlightenment, Peter Gay, observed of these *'philosophes'*,

> They used their classical learning to free themselves from their Christian heritage, and then, having done with the ancients, turned their face toward a modern world-view. The Enlightenment was a volatile mixture of classicism, impiety, and science; the *philosophes*, in a phrase, were modern pagans.[2]

One of the most significant of the cultural developments of this period was the emergence of the philosophical tradition of empiricism whose founder is the English philosopher John Locke.

John Locke (1632–1704)
The most influential of all English philosophers, John Locke is widely regarded as having been the source and inspiration of the development of the Anglo-Saxon tradition in philosophy, namely, empiricism in the domain of epistemology, and liberalism in the domain of political theory. His *Essay Concerning Human Understanding* is widely regarded as the most important document in the early development of an empiricist philosophical culture just as the second of his *Two Treatises of*

Civil Government is unquestionably one of the most important treatises in the history of the development of a liberal culture. Furthermore, Locke's influence on the shape of the Enlightenment is unrivalled; he not only provided a philosophical basis for the development of a materialistic or mechanistic world-view but also provided the core ingredients which shaped the political institutions that emerged in the wake of the French and American revolutions.

Born in Bristol, John Locke studied both philosophy and medicine at Christ College Oxford and later became a lecturer in philosophy at the same college. In 1667 he entered the service of the Earl of Shaftesbury and rose to a high position in the public service. However, the prospect of civil war in England forced Locke to flee to Holland in 1683, from which he returned only after the successful installation of William of Orange upon the English throne. He spent the remainder of his life in retirement in Essex.

Locke belonged to the new rational, scientific age in his strong belief in reason and the empirical approach to knowledge. His approach has its origins in the empirical methodology of the English philosopher **Francis Bacon (1561–1626)** whose writings personified the new spirit of scientific enquiry that characterised the world of the late Renaissance and early modernity. Bacon was the earliest advocate of the extension of the inductive method to philosophy, and much of his work was devoted to pointing out the futility of theory that is unrelated to observed fact: 'cease to persuade and begin to demonstrate; cease to believe and begin to know'. Another influence on Locke's empiricism was the Irish scientist Robert Boyle. A close personal friend, Boyle is reputed to have first suggested the idea of the world as a machine like a complex clock and God as the cosmic clockmaker, the one who sets the world in motion and then withdraws from the world. This remote 'deist' view of God was one that would closely resonate with Locke's own views

Locke saw himself as an *underlabourer* – one whose task is to eliminate useless accretions which are an obstacle to the acquisition of genuine knowledge. This standpoint is reflected in the introduction to the *Essay Concerning Human Understanding*, which endeavours in a common sense manner 'to inquire into the original [sources], certainty, and extent of human knowledge, together with the grounds and degrees of belief, opinion and assent.' (*Essay*, 1, Intr., 2, 26) In sharp contrast to a theory of innate ideas that suggests the existence of a God who implants ideas in our mind, Locke proposes a theory of knowledge that takes its inspiration from the new scientific methodology. He adopts the view that the mind is a *tabula rasa* – a blank sheet that is filled by sense perception. For him, the world of human understanding is composed of simple and complex ideas (mental images) of sense perception and reflection: this in essence is what is meant by empiricism.

There are very few today who would accept a theory of innate ideas. Nevertheless, some have argued that Locke's polemic against this theory was motivated as much by the desire to subordinate religion to the methodology of empiricism as to provide a new foundation of knowledge based on scientific foundations. Locke was no lover of tradition and some of his most critical comments are reserved for the philosophical and theological traditions associated with the world of classical Greek philosophy and the Christian Scholastic tradition. Although he did not quite reject metaphysics (for example, the idea that one can have knowledge of God), nevertheless it is only retained at the cost of a breach with empiricist principles that Locke's successor David Hume would expose.

The *Essay* became hugely influential in the world of the eighteenth-century French Enlightenment. It was perceived to give philosophical credibility to an emerging materialist worldview that affirms that the human mind or consciousness is simply a collection of ideas that are reducible to the impressions of sense, a viewpoint that impinges on one's understanding of ethics as well as knowledge. In the absence of a clear indication that the mind can go beyond the world of sense perception to grasp a concept such as 'the Good', Locke bases his idea of ethics upon the link between good/evil and pleasure/pain; goodness procures pleasure and evil procures pain. It is a view of ethics that bears little or no resemblance to anything found in the classical or Christian tradition.

Locke's views had considerable influence on the moral nihilism of an eighteenth-century materialist French philosopher, Helvétius, who proclaimed that man is nothing more than the *sensibilité physique* that functions according to the law of pleasure and pain. In the course of a valuable commentary on the legacy of Locke's philosophy, the Irish philosopher Gerald Hanratty observes,

> In the works of Helvétius, the most radical consequences have been drawn from Locke's thought. On Lockean foundations, Helvétius erected a rigidly materialistic, deterministic, hedonistic and even nihilistic system in which there is little trace of the classical and Christian traditions of European thought.[3]

Although Locke did not himself espouse a materialistic or mechanistic philosophy, nevertheless he did adopt a rationalist/deist concept of God: a picture of an impersonal God who has withdrawn from the world to leave it to run according to its own laws. God as a cosmic clockmaker replaces a belief in a personal God who continues to reveal himself in and through the community of believers.

Locke's most lasting contribution to a modern secular value system is his political theory, which had a significant influence on the shape of liberalism or liberal democracy. Arguably no other philosopher other than Immanuel Kant has been more influential in this regard. The starting point of Locke's political theory is the idea of the state of nature. His view is that human beings are naturally in that state until they freely choose to make themselves members of a society. In this state of nature human beings are naturally rational, free and equal, and they possess inalienable human rights independently of the political recognition granted them by the state. Locke argued that natural rights flowed from natural law, and natural law came from God. For Locke, the God-given duty to preserve one's life entails the necessary existence of basic natural rights to life, liberty, and property.

Locke's proclamation of what is in effect a theory of human rights is a remarkable achievement, and one that was to become the cornerstone of the emerging democracies in post-revolutionary America and France at the close of the eighteenth century. Equally important for the subsequent development of a liberal culture is his view that human beings are first and foremost individuals. For the first time in the history of civilisation human beings no longer see themselves primarily as social beings who belong in a community but rather as individuals. The state only emerges as a product of a social contract between free and equal individuals in order to enjoy the fruits of mutually beneficial cooperation and to protect individual human rights. As he says:

> Men being, as has been said, by nature, all free, equal and independent, no one can be put out of this estate, and subjected to the political power of another, without his own consent. The only way whereby anyone divests himself of his natural liberty, and puts on the bonds of civil society is by agreeing with other men to join and unite into a community, for their comfortable, safe, and peaceable living one amongst another, in a secure enjoyment of their properties, and a greater security against any that are not of it. (*Treatise* II, 8: 95)

As the above quotation makes clear, one of the motivating factors behind the establishment of the state is the need to secure one's private property against hostile forces. It should be noted that Locke provided an important argument in defence of private property, one that would have important consequences for the subsequent shape of a liberal culture. Another major contribution to the subsequent development of the secular values, reflected in the idea of a liberal democracy, is his belief in the importance of a separation of powers between what he calls the executive, the legislative and the federative. Both the importance that Locke attached to the separation of powers and his threefold distinction was a major influence on the distinction between the legislature, executive and judiciary that is the cornerstone of contemporary liberal democracies.

David Hume (1711–1776)

One of the greatest thinkers of the Enlightenment, Hume was born and educated in Edinburgh. His most famous publication is *A Treatise of Human Nature* (1739). Over the course of his life divided up between Edinburgh, London and Paris, Hume devoted himself to a life of writing. He enjoyed a wide circle of friends that included the economist Adam Smith. At an early age, dissatisfied with the Scottish Presbyterianism of his youth, he devoted himself to philosophy and in the process adopted a sceptical or agnostic stance with respect to the existence of God.

Hume dedicated himself to pursuing to the utmost the logic of the empiricist principles enunciated by Locke. As he says in the introduction to book one of *A Treatise of Human Nature*,

> And though we must endeavour to render all our principles as universal as possible, by tracing up our experiments to the utmost, and explaining all effects from the simplest and fewest causes, it is still certain we cannot go beyond experience; and any hypothesis, that

> pretends to discover the ultimate original qualities of human nature, ought at first to be rejected as presumptuous and chimerical. (*Treatise*, 1, Intro.)[4]

Following Locke's empiricist principles Hume insisted that one cannot go beyond experience and that all attempts to go beyond sense experience are futile, and thus all pretence to have knowledge of meta-physical realities such as the existence of God or even the existence of the 'self' (personal identity) or substance is just that, a pretence. All knowledge consists of perceptions that are either impressions (the immediate sensation of external reality) or ideas (the recollection of these impressions). As he says;

> Did our perceptions either inhere in something simple and individual, or did the mind perceive some real connection among them, there would be no difficulty in the case. For my part, I must plead the privilege of a sceptic, and confess that this difficulty is too hard for my understanding. (*Treatise*, 1, Appendix)[5]

In his radical adoption of empiricism even the possibility of science itself is undermined because Hume effectively denies the concept of causality. From an empiricist standpoint there cannot be any knowledge of the laws of nature or cause and effect; all one perceives is one thing following after another, but this is no proof that one is the cause of the other. In the reluctant acceptance of scepticism one comes full circle. Hume's stance is in effect the polar opposite of the confident belief in reason to attain a meaningful interpretation of existence in philosophy or religion that characterised the Greek classical and Christian traditions. As Hanratty observes,

> Throughout his works Hume repeatedly emphasised the fallibility and impotence of human reason. Relentlessly

and ingeniously he employed reason only to denigrate reason's attempts to achieve coherent answers to its questions concerning the origin, order and end of existence. (Hanratty, 45)

The perceptiveness of Hanratty's comments are to be seen in Hume's views on the credibility of a theistic world-view that are outlined in the conclusion to *An Enquiry Concerning Human Understanding* (1748),

> Upon the whole, we may conclude, that the Christian Religion not only was at first attended with miracles, but even at this day cannot be believed by any reasonable person without one. (*An Enquiry Concerning Human Understanding*, X, 2,)[6]

The legacy of Hume's empiricism is profound. It has made a significant contribution to the creation of a liberal culture that is agnostic in terms of religious belief, and sceptical about the possibility of finding answers to questions of meaning and purpose.

In the twentieth century the emergence of a secular world with its own value system and norms of behaviour was taken a stage further in an avowedly atheistic philosophical system, logical positivism, which takes its inspiration from Hume's empiricist theory of knowledge. Separating the world of sense from that of non-sense, logical positivism sought to draw clear boundaries around the world of meaningful discourse in a manner that designates religious belief as nonsense. The logical positivist philosopher A. J. Ayer argued that to affirm a reality that goes beyond the boundaries of the scientific discourse/sense perception is literally nonsense. The debate surrounding this claim is well summarised in the final pages of the *Tractatus Logico-Philosophicus* written by the Austrian-born and Cambridge-based philosopher **Ludwig Wittgenstein**

(1889–1951). The internal dialogue within these pages oscillates between an apparent espousal of logical positivism and the recognition that a world bounded by sense simply does not accord with the way in which the world is experienced. What follows are a few of the more memorable passages from this work:

> 6.41 The sense of the world must lie outside the world. In the world everything is as it is, and everything happens as it does happen: in it no value exists – and if it did exist, it would have no value. If there is any value that does have value, it must lie outside the whole sphere of what happens and is the case. For all that happens and is the case is accidental. What makes it non-accidental cannot lie within the world, since if it did, it would itself be accidental. It must lie outside the world.
> 6.42 So too it is impossible for there to be propositions of ethics. Propositions can express nothing that is higher.
> 6.421 It is clear that ethics cannot be put into words. Ethics is transcendental.
> (Ethics and aesthetics are one and the same.)[7]

As Wittgenstein recognised, a world composed purely of scientific facts does not allow space for one that wishes to include moral obligation – a world that wishes to include the word 'ought' alongside the word 'is'. The logical positivist rejection of metaphysics reflects a viewpoint that finds no space for such key dimensions of human experience as aesthetics and ethics: the love of beauty and of the good, not to mention the love of God. It is not a viewpoint that is sustainable outside of the narrow boundaries of some form of behaviourism or biological determinism, where ethics is reduced to little more than an expression of a survival mechanism. In the following passages, Wittgenstein offers the reader an insight into the rationale underpinning of the pursuit of metaphysical truths:

> 6.43 The facts all contribute only to setting the problem, not to its solution.
> 6.44 It is not how things are in the world that is mystical, but that it exists.
> 6.45 To view the world *sub specie aeterni* is to view it as a whole – a limited whole.
> Feeling the world as a limited whole – it is this that is mystical.[8]

The *Tractatus* is widely regarded as one of the philosophical classics of the twentieth century. In a few phrases at the end of the treatise Wittgenstein shows an extraordinary ability to retrace and indeed recover the paths of metaphysical questioning. As he perceptively recognised, the attempt to categorise ethics, aesthetics and religious belief as nonsense is one that bears little relation to the complexity and richness of reality as it is experienced.

Alongside his theory of knowledge, Hume made an important contribution to the development of an exclusively secular system of values. In keeping with his empiricist principles, he believed that moral judgements could have no metaphysical or religious presuppositions such as the idea of the Good or God, and that reason could never provide any insight into the distinction between good and evil. The core of Hume's moral philosophy consisted, therefore, in the abandonment of the idea of an objective moral order that could be apprehended by reason, and in its place an exaltation of the passions over reason. This conviction is succinctly expressed in the following celebrated passage,

> Reason is and ought only to be the slave of the passions, and can never pretend to any other office than to serve and obey them. (*Treatise*, II, 3, iii)

As we saw above, Locke had elaborated a moral philosophy that was based on a psychology of human passion – the desire for pleasure and the avoidance of pain. Hume's ethical philosophy continues along this path. Classical Greek and Christian moral philosophy had taken reason to be the specifically human capacity that discerned man's final end or supreme good and, as a consequence, the right order of human action. In contrast to both these traditions, Hume did not believe that there could be any appeal to a final end or supreme Good. Virtue is redefined as that which 'is distinguished by the pleasure, and vice by the pain that any action, sentiment or character gives us' (*Treatise*, III, 1, ii).

From the point of view of the development of an independent secular value system, one of the most important legacies of Hume's ethical philosophy was the link that he made between the experience of pleasure and an awareness of the utility of a course of action. In this respect, Hume's philosophy anticipated the theory of utilitarianism of **Jeremy Bentham (1748–1832)** which advocated 'the greatest happiness of the greatest number.' Utilitarianism regards an action as right if it produces just as great or a greater increase in utility and happiness for all concerned than any other action, and regards it as bad if it does not do so. In this system the common good is defined in terms of a goal such as utility or pleasure. The widespread influence of utilitarianism is to be seen in the popularity of these views as expressed by contemporary neo-classical business theorists such as Milton Friedman.

As an independent secular value system, utilitarianism emerged in the wake of a loss of a shared belief in the objectivity of the Good or God. In a utilitarian ethic the good is therefore both redefined in terms of the more measurable goals of pleasure and utility. While not disputing the importance of both pleasure and utility in judging the value of an action, neither of them provides an adequate foundation for ethical behaviour. As anyone engaged in public life could testify, the practice of virtues such as truthfulness, fairness or a respect for the privacy of the individual could hardly be justified solely on the basis of either pleasure or utility. The practice of these virtues is guaranteed to facilitate the pursuit of neither fame nor fortune. Utilitarianism differs from the classical understanding of ethics in at least one respect: for the utilitarian an action is good because it is useful: in the Classical Greek and Christian Scholastic traditions of philosophers such as Aristotle and Aquinas, an action is deemed useful because it is good. The difference is crucial because it touches on the core issue of why one ought to be moral.

Contemporary neo-classical business theorists argue for the importance of observing quite a detailed set of ethical guidelines. But the question is why? With practically no exceptions they argue that given the importance of the relationship of trust between producers and consumers it makes good business sense to conduct one's business in an ethical manner. That is classical utilitarian reasoning which has little to do with ethics and all too much to do with shrewdness. It is a type of reasoning that is concerned with promoting the pragmatic ideal of efficiency rather than the ethical ideal of excellence. From a neo-classical point of view it is simply more efficient for a business to behave ethically than to behave unethically. The key difference between Aristotelianism and Utilitarianism can be summed up in the answer to the following question: is an action efficient because it is excellent or is it excellent because it is efficient? Is a school excellent becauses it is efficient, namely producing high academic achievers, or does it produce high academic achievers because it is excellent? Or again, in deciding upon a course of action, which should we pursue, excellence or efficiency: the good school or one that produces high academic achievers? Any system of ethics that resonates with Aristotelianism would stress the former, whereas any form of Utilitarianism such as that espoused by neo-classical business theorists would choose the latter. In the last analysis, the only answer to the question 'why be moral?' which respects the ethical character of the question is to say, 'we ought to be moral because that is what it is to be a human being.' The absence of a belief in any objective theory of the good robs liberal individualism today, just as it did Hume and Bentham, of any foundation upon which to rationally justify ethical behaviour other than the pragmatic considerations of usefulness or pleasure.

Existentialism
Nothing was more guaranteed to shatter the cultural optimism of the Enlightenment and of modernity in general than the savagery of the trench warfare in the war of 1914–1918. The generation that emerged from that conflict embraced the philosophical ideas of existentialism, a far more bleak vision of a secular world than the empiricist tradition would allow. The existentialist quest for the meaning of human existence shorn of any societal supports may have had its origins in the nineteenth-century writings of the Danish philosopher Søren Kierkegaard and the German philosopher Friedrich Nietzsche, but it was the barbaric political landscape of Europe in the first half of the twentieth century that ensured its mass appeal. Some existentialists such as Kierkegaard, Gabriel Marcel and Karl Jaspers were Christian. However, for the most part, existentialism was marked by the rejection of any theistic source of meaning and values. As the name suggests, existentialism is a philosophical system whose focus is on the meaning of existence or more precisely, the question as to whether human existence has any distinctive meaning. From the perspective of an exploration of the search for meaning and values it is a question that cannot be avoided.

Friedrich Nietzsche (1844–1900)

In the story of existentialism, Nietzsche occupies a central place and his influence upon the writings of Heidegger, Sartre and Camus was considerable. One of the harshest critics of traditional philosophy, Nietzsche was born the son of a Lutheran pastor in Röcken, Germany. He initially pursued a course of studies in theology but these were quickly abandoned in favour of a study of classical literature. At the age of twenty-four he became professor of philology at the university of Basel in Switzerland. For the next twenty years his output was prodigious. Amongst his most famous publications are *The Birth of Tragedy* (1872), *Thus Spoke Zarathustra* (1883), *Beyond Good and Evil* (1886), *On the Genealogy of Morals* (1887) and *Twilight of the Idols* (1889). Unfortunately, the last ten years of his life were marked by deterioration in his mental health. He died in Weimar, Germany.

There are few philosophers who have provided a more searing critique of Christianity and religion in general than Nietzsche. He is most famously remembered for his statement that 'God is dead'. Through this proclamation, Nietzsche signals not only the death of God, but also more importantly, the birth of a culture that can no longer live as if 'God' existed. In acknowledging that God is dead, one must accept the senselessness of any search for meaning and values because in the nihilism of Nietzsche's philosophy there is neither meaning nor value to existence. Furthermore, the 'death of God' signals nothing less than the death of all morality because, in the absence of any objective source of meaning to human existence, all attempts to provide a rational justification for ethics are doomed to failure. In his opinion, the attempt to construct an ethic on any basis other than arbitrary choice is simply a pretence that is designed to obscure the harsh truth that there is only one imperative, namely, the will to power, and only one ethic, 'might is right'.

Christianity is the focus of Nietzsche's harshest criticism because it opposes his guiding principle, namely that God is dead. In particular, Nietzsche is aware that the Christian ethic is totally at odds with the 'master morality' that he proposes for a world free of the illusion of religious belief. Christian values such as love, humility and obedience are an aspect of a 'slave morality', that is to say, a decadent and life-denying culture as distinct from the life-affirming and egotistical natural instincts of individuals who have embraced the 'will to power'.

What is not often enough emphasised is that Nietzsche's uncompromising critique of Christianity must be seen in the light of a more general hostility to all theories of meaning and value – and in particular, the whole Enlightenment project. In Nietzsche's opinion all the attempts in the Enlightenment to devise a system of morality, such as utilitarianism, constitute nothing less than an attempt to disguise their acceptance of the logic of 'the will to power' – the only logic that could adequately sustain the rampant colonial and capitalist ethos of nineteenth-century Europe. In this context, one could describe Nietzsche's project as a desire to unmask the veil that cloaks the truth, namely that in a world devoid of meaning there is nothing else but the logic of power. In this scenario, his proposal is to liberate modernity to accept its human destiny (*amor fati*); to raze to the ground all of the structures of inherited moral belief and argument and to replace them with the Übermensch or Superman – that unattached solitary individual who knows only one imperative, namely, the will to power.

One of Nietzsche's earliest and most important publications was *The Birth of Tragedy* (1872). Fourteen years later in 1886, he revisited this work; in the course of a short review entitled *Attempt at a Self-Criticism*,[9] he produced a most reflective summary of many of the main ideas of his philosophy. He begins by questioning whether the death of Greek tragedy, the birth of Socrates and the beginning of science marked a critical breakthrough in civilisation or perhaps a decline. As he says, 'might not this very Socratism be a sign of decline, of weariness, of infection, of the anarchical dissolution of the instincts?' (*Self-Criticism*, 18) The meaning of that phrase becomes clear as Nietzsche turns his attention to the belief in science that underpins the very structure of modernity.

> And science itself, our science – indeed, what is the significance of all science, viewed as a symptom of life? For what – worse yet, whence – all science? How now? Is the resolve to be so scientific about everything perhaps a kind of fear of, an escape from, pessimism? A subtle last resort against – truth? And, morally speaking, a sort of cowardice and falseness? Amorally speaking, a ruse? O Socrates, Socrates was that perhaps your secret? O enigmatic ironist, was that perhaps your – irony? (*Self-Criticism*, 18)

In proclaiming his belief in a world of meaning and order perhaps Socrates was just being ironic – motivated by a desire to protect people from the harsh reality of an absurd world. Ironic or just mistaken, Socrates alongside Christ is held up to ridicule. In the place of their belief in a world of order and harmony reminiscent of the cult of the God Apollo, Nietzsche proposes the cult of desire and sexuality associated with the God Dionysus: a craving for beauty, festivals and pleasures marked the Dionysian cult in ancient Greece. In arguing for a rediscovery of this cult, Nietzsche rejects the view that it represents a form of escapism from a decidedly pessimistic world-view. As the following quotation illustrates, it is rather Nietzsche's view that it is the culture of modernity that is guilty of escapism:

> Could it be possible that, in spite of all 'modern ideas' and the prejudices of rationality, practical and theoretical utilitarianism, no less than democracy itself which developed at the same time, might all have been symptoms of a decline of strength, of impending old

age, and of physiological weariness? These, and not pessimism? ... It is apparent that it was a whole cluster of grave questions with which this book burdened itself. Let us add the gravest question of all. What, seen in the perspective of life, is the significance of morality? (*Self-Criticism*, 22)

With this question Nietzsche moves to acknowledge that there is no justification for the world, or to be more precise, 'the existence of the world is justified only as an aesthetic phenomenon' (*Self-Criticism*, 22), but even here, there is no pretence of an objective horizon of meaning that would legitimate the Enlightenment such as the belief in rationality, the acceptance of utilitarianism and even the merit of democracy itself. In Nietzsche's world, there is no place either for enlightenment values or for any other values. On the very idea of morality, he asks, 'might not morality be a will to negate life, a secret instinct of annihilation, a principle of decay, diminution, and slander – the beginning of the end?' (*Self-Criticism*, 23)

In such an unqualified rejection of the whole foundation upon which the history of civilisation was based, it is hardly surprising that Christianity would be attacked. However, the strength of the critique is still interesting to observe:

Christianity was from the beginning, essentially and fundamentally, life's nausea and disgust with life, merely concealed behind, masked by, dressed up as, faith in 'another' or ' better' life. Hatred of 'the world', condemnations of the passions, fear of beauty and sensuality, a beyond invented the better to slander this life, at bottom a craving for the nothing, for the end, for respite, for 'the sabbath of sabbaths' – all this always struck me, no less than the unconditional will of Christianity to recognize only moral values, as the most dangerous and uncanny form of all possible forms of a 'will to decline' – at the very least a sign of abysmal sickness, weariness, discouragement, exhaustion, and the impoverishment of life. Confronted with morality (especially Christian, or unconditional, morality), life must continually and inevitably be in the wrong, because life is something essentially amoral – and eventually, crushed by the weight of contempt and the eternal No, life must then be felt to be unworthy of desire and altogether worthless. (*Self-Criticism*, 23)

While acknowledging that Nietzsche is a critic of the Enlightenment, his assessment of Christianity shows that he is also a creature of the Enlightenment which gave birth to the belief that God is simply an illusory human projection designed to overcome a sense of alienation from life as it is experienced. In the belief that Christianity is a form of escapism that has its origins in a fear of sensuality, Nietzsche anticipates the critique of Sigmund Freud. In their belief that the persistence of Christianity can be explained as a hatred of this world and a craving for an alternative, both Ludwig Feuerbach and Karl Marx have anticipated Nietzsche. All have in common the viewpoint that, in the overcoming of religious belief, one would arrest to a greater or lesser extent the 'will to decline' that they detect at the heart of modernity.

To conclude, Nietzsche's critique of all inherited sources of meaning and values is radical not because of his attack on Christianity, but rather because his critique is anti-social in a manner that is hostile to any possible conception of a community or civil society. The *Übermensch* finds his good nowhere in the social world, but only in himself. It is a conception of a rootless and relativist world-view that could be said to place Nietzsche at the dawn of a post-modern world.

Jean Paul Sartre (1905–1980)

Born in Paris, Sartre studied at the École Normale Supérieure where he obtained an Agrégation de Philosophie. During the Second World War he and other philosophical figures in the Existentialist milieu, such as Albert Camus, became members of the French resistance. In 1964 he was awarded but refused the Nobel Prize for literature. He was a long-time member of the French Communist party from which he resigned in 1968 in response to the Soviet re-occupation of Prague. For the rest of his active life he continued to occupy a controversial role in French political life and, amongst other things, he helped to organise the anti-Vietnam war trials that took place in Paris in the early 1970s.

Sartre's powerful political passions and a remarkable literary gift propelled him rapidly to become the leading exponent in France of Existentialism. In following this philosophical route Sartre was influenced by many well-known philosophers such as Nietzsche and Heidegger; the former providing Sartre with a philosophical rationale for his espousal of atheism, the latter confirming Sartre's view of the correctness of a phenomenological methodology. The most celebrated of his prodigious philosophical and literary output include *Being and Nothingness* (1940), his most well-known novel *Nausea* (1944) and the short philosophical essay *Existentialism and Humanism* (1945). His philosophy revolved around a passionate belief in absolute freedom and a study of the consequences of that stance.

It is Descartes' recognition of the link between human nature and consciousness that provided the building blocks on which Sartre constructed his philosophy of absolute freedom. In the course of his phenomenological analysis of 'being', Sartre discerns two contrasting ways in which 'being' appears, namely, 'being in itself' (*être-en-soi*), and 'being for itself' (*être-pour-soi*). The distinction is between beings that lack a consciousness of their own existence and beings that are conscious, i.e. human beings. As distinct from being as something (*en-soi*) which 'is', being as consciousness (*pour-soi*) is always striving 'to be' – always in a state of becoming – tied to nothing but always desiring to be something. Human beings or conscious beings are literally tied to nothing: they are absolutely free.

Although no more than an extended essay published in response to some critical comments about his philosophy, *Existentialism and Humanism*[10] (henceforth *EH*) offers an accessible entry into the key themes that characterize his philosophy of absolute freedom and his analysis of the consequences of accepting that stance. At the outset, Sartre introduces the distinction between the idea that 'essence precedes existence' and that which holds that 'existence precedes essence'. According to Sartre, the former idea expresses the traditional belief in a creator God, one who from the beginning of time has a blueprint of who I am (essence) just as a paperknife manufacturer has a blueprint of a paperknife before he goes into mass production (existence). In such a scenario, human beings may have the illusion of being free, but just like puppets at a puppet show it is only an illusion. From the outset, God both knows and controls everything relevant about me. The only alternative that allows for a philosophy of absolute freedom is the belief that existence precedes essence. In this scenario, the person is a creator rather than a creature. He/she exists and then creates their essence or defines himself/herself through the exercise of their own free will. As he says,

> What do we mean by saying that existence precedes essence? We mean that man first of all exists, encounters himself, surges up in the world and defines himself afterwards. If man as the existentialist sees him is not definable, it is because to begin with he is nothing. He will not be anything until later, and then he will be what he makes of himself. Thus, there is no human nature,

because there is no God to have a conception of it. Man simply is. (*EH*, 28)

In a reworking of Descartes' celebrated statement of human identity, 'I think therefore I am', Sartre proclaims, 'I choose therefore I am.' The key importance of the distinction between essence and existence is that it allows Sartre a platform on which to proclaim the incompatibility of a theistic world-view with a belief in human freedom. In short, one either accepts that one is a creature or a creator; only the latter stance, which embraces atheism, is capable, from Sartre's perspective, of doing justice to a belief in absolute freedom.

Although Sartre is critical of those who refuse to accept the logic of an atheistic standpoint, he nevertheless reserves his most caustic comments for those of a broadly secular humanist tradition who believe that theism is just an out of date hypothesis that will die away quietly by itself without any consequences. Sartre vehemently rejects such 'easy' atheism. As he says,

> The existentialist, on the contrary, finds it extremely embarrassing that God does not exist, for there disappears with Him all possibility of finding values in an intelligible heaven. There can no longer be any good a priori, since there is no infinite and perfect consciousness to think it. It is nowhere written that 'the good' exists, that one must be honest or must not lie, since we are now upon the plane where there are only men. (*EH*, 33)

As with Nietzsche, Sartre too recognised that the acceptance of the non-existence of God has huge implications in respect of any and every quest for meaning and values. For with the death of God one loses all hope of finding values – any reason to act in one way rather than another. In a continuation of the passage quoted above Sartre gives vent to the radical implications of accepting an atheistic standpoint, one that reaches a memorable climax in the phrase 'man is condemned to be free':

> Dostoevsky once wrote 'if God did not exist, everything would be permitted'; and that, for existentialism, is the starting point. Everything is indeed permitted if God does not exist, and man is in consequence forlorn, for he cannot find anything to depend upon either within or outside himself. He discovers forthwith, that he is without excuse. For if indeed existence precedes essence, one will never be able to explain one's action by reference to a given and specific human nature; in other words, there is no determinism – man is free, man is freedom.... That is what I mean when I say that man is condemned to be free. Condemned, because he did not create himself, yet is nevertheless at liberty, and from the moment that he is thrown into this world he is responsible for everything he does. (*EH*, 33–34)

In the phrase, 'we are left alone, without excuse' one has some sense of a philosophy of absolute freedom. It is a far cry from those who argued that Sartre's stance was irresponsible and would foster a trivialisation of human existence. In fact Sartre goes to some trouble in *Existentialism and Humanism* to point out that the acceptance that one is 'condemned to be free' is a sobering moment that brings with it an acceptance of anguish, abandonment and despair. The call to embrace anguish flows from the acknowledgement that, in a philosophy of absolute freedom, I am entirely responsible for my choices, choices that I make not just for myself but also for all people. Abandonment reminds me that, despite all the advice that I can seek, I choose alone. Even the choice to seek advice, to seek it from a particular source, and to abide or not with the advice given, is something that ultimately I choose alone. Despair draws attention to the futility and yet inescapability of choice in a world where nothing matters – at every instance I must choose, but no choice has any significance; to embrace despair is to be prepared to live without hope.

Like Nietzsche before him, Sartre's human being is one who is destined to create values by his choices in an absurd world, one that cannot support any values. In this predicament Sartre correctly observes, 'Man is a useless passion'. Another way of expressing the human predicament is to acknowledge, as Sartre does, that in the final analysis, human beings desire to be God, 'to be free' and at the same time 'to be' – to be all powerful – to no longer need to desire anything or to find oneself in a constant state of becoming. The desire is to be God because then one would be all-powerful and thus truly free.

As with Nietzsche's *Übermensch*, Sartre's human being is above all an isolated human being – alone and without excuse; in Sartre's memorable expression, 'hell is other people'. Given Sartre's view that freedom is primarily freedom from all constraints, he is correct to proclaim that hell is other people. Relationships even of the most fleeting kind impose constraints on one's freedom. But to suppose therefore that people in relationships are less free than others is to work with a view of freedom that simply does not accord with the way it is experienced. Human experience testifies to another view of freedom – one that is received as a gift in and through a loving relationship. In this scenario, the belief is that it is only in and through love that one can ever become truly free.

Ultimately, the cogency of Sartre's atheistic philosophy hinges upon whether one is prepared to accept the coherence of his view of freedom. If, as Sartre believes, it is only the attainment of power that guarantees freedom then all relationships including one's relationship with God (supposing that there is a God) will inevitably be perceived under the rubric of 'dominate/dominated'. But, as it was suggested above, there is another view of freedom that links it to love rather than to power. If one were to accept this latter scenario, God is not an obstacle to the attainment of freedom, rather it is the existence of a loving God which provides the ultimate guarantee of the possibility of true freedom.

In terms of the quest for meaning and values, there is a fine line but also an immense gulf between Sartre's view of human fulfilment and that proposed by a religion such as Christianity: a fine line in the difference between the desire to be God and the desire to be like God; an immense gulf between the paths of pride and humility or, to put it another way, the paths of power and love.

A secular world-view critiqued

Iris Murdoch (1919–1999)

Iris Murdoch was an Irish-born Oxford-based novelist and philosopher who was the recipient of numerous awards and accolades, including the Booker prize in 1978 for her novel *The Sea, The Sea*. Her husband, John Bayley, movingly described her struggle with Alzheimer's disease in *Elegy for Iris* that was subsequently produced as a film under the title *Iris*. As a philosopher, Murdoch can best be described as a modern day Platonist; human life both can and ought to be lived in the light of the idea of the Good, one that provides an answer to questions concerning both the origin and the goal of human striving. In her reassertion of the objectivity of the Good and her belief that human life is lived in the struggle to overcome attachment to an illusory ego-centric world, her philosophy provides a striking contrast to the expressions of secularity that we have already described.

Her most famous philosophical work entitled, *The Sovereignty of Good* (1970)[11] (henceforth *SG*) is addressed explicitly against what she perceives to be the ethical legacy of empiricism and existentialism. In the former case she focuses upon the logic of a 'behaviourist ethic' that, as we have earlier observed, flows from an empiricist/logical positivist philosophy. As a philosophical theory, behaviourism unhesitatingly accepts the materialist logic of empiricism. It asserts that human beings are simply the products of the material world into which they are born: products of their genetic makeup, the environment, socialisation, etc. Given the determinist character of behaviourism it is difficult to speak coherently of a behaviourist ethic, but it suggests that the quality of a person's life is exclusively determined by their observable behaviour. The idea of existentialism that is the focus of Murdoch's critique is that proposed by Sartre, which as we have observed, acclaims a philosophy of absolute freedom. As a focus for criticism, it is hard to imagine two more unlikely philosophical bedfellows than empiricism and existentialism, the former effectively denying the freedom of the will, whereas the latter sees nothing else but freedom.

The focus for Murdoch's critique of behaviourism and existentialism is to be found in the *The Sovereignty of Good*. She begins her critique with the following passage:

> What seems to have been forgotten or 'theorized away' are the facts that an unexamined life can be virtuous and that love is a central concept in morals. Contemporary philosophers frequently connect consciousness with virtue, and although they constantly talk of freedom they rarely talk of love. (*SG*, 1-2)

The reference to Sartre is unmistakable in the link that she draws between consciousness and virtue and the constant talk of freedom, but what might not be so obvious is the importance that she attaches to the idea that 'an unexamined life can be virtuous'. In her opinion, the rejection of this viewpoint by both behaviourism and existentialism is a key reason why both of these theories are fundamentally flawed. As a materialist philosophy behaviourism can have little concept of the importance to the person of an inner/spiritual life that is not observable. Likewise in the Sartrian existentialism, which travels under the banner 'I choose therefore I am'; what is proposed is a concept of the will that is isolated from any sense of an inner world of beliefs or reasons or feelings that might influence the quality of one's choice.

Rather than the empty external freedom of existentialism, Murdoch looks to an alternative view that places emphasis on the growth in freedom that accompanies a growth in the person and one that shifts the emphasis in morality from the world of action to that of vision. As she says, 'freedom is a function of the progressive attempt to see a particular object clearly'. (SG, 23) And again, 'freedom is not strictly the exercise of the will, but rather the experience of accurate vision which, when this becomes appropriate, occasions action.' (SG, 67)

In stark contrast to the 'optimism' of Sartre that proclaims human beings to be absolutely free, Murdoch is acutely conscious that, most of the time, people are not free in any real sense of the word – free, that is, from the prejudices that attend every generation and every culture. As she rightly observes, it is an immensely difficult task to truly see a person, that is, to perceive him/her justly. We are all too easily imprisoned in a world of illusions or prejudices that prevents us from seeing the world as it really is. In this context, to see a person as he/she truly is counts as nothing less than a moral achievement, one that is difficult because it demands nothing less than to see him/her with eyes of love.

Murdoch's philosophy is one that draws attention to sin or egoism, a characteristic in human nature that needs to be confronted if one is to talk truthfully about ethics or a search for values. The classical Greek and Christian worlds were all too conscious of the selfish or egotistical side of human nature. In Murdoch's view, it has been the legacy of an over-optimistic Enlightenment, both empiricist and existentialist, to lose sight of this sobering fact. Like Plato, Murdoch argues for the importance of the concept of conversion (*metanoia*). As in Plato's allegory of the cave, she recognises that the path of conversion is difficult – it is not easy to confront one's prejudices. The images that Plato uses to describe this journey are all familiar to Murdoch, a journey from darkness to light, slavery to freedom, and an illusory world to the real world.

Her philosophy can be seen as a protest against the illusions that are fostered by the theories of behaviourism and existentialism, and in particular the illusion that there is no objective transcendent horizon of meaning and values. The idea that in the world of ethics there is no standard, no ideal of perfection to which we ought to strive is as senseless as believing that great artists or musicians have neither a standard of excellence nor any idea of perfection to guide their work. If there is a distinction that can be made between an artist and a charlatan there is also one that can be made between an ethical and a selfish person. As Murdoch says, 'the central concept of morality is "the individual" thought of as knowable by love, thought of in the light of the command, "Be ye therefore perfect" (*SG*, 30). She is in no doubt but that there exists 'a moral reality, a real though infinitely distant standard' (*SG*, 31) that guides our path on the journey to see clearly. As with Plato, it is only in the light of the good or the perfect that we can see things in perspective – in their right order. It is only in the light of that journey that one can be said to become free in the true sense of that word.

According to Murdoch, modern ethical theories such as behaviourism, utilitarianism or existentialism cannot account adequately for either moral progress or moral failure because they have no sense of the existence of an appropriate goal towards which they ought to strive and which does justice to the seriousness of the ethical project. As she recognised, it is only an ideal such as love of the Good or love of God that can adequately account for the universal experience of a search for meaning and value. In this scenario, the person is nothing less than a moral pilgrim, one for whom the journey is truly liberating.

Shaping communal values: sources other than religion

Liberal individualism
Communal values in contemporary western societies are shaped to a greater or lesser extent by what is commonly referred to as a liberal ethos. Liberal individualism or liberalism, as a political doctrine and also as a cultural phenomenon, emerged over a relatively lengthy period of history and in distinct phases, the earliest of which saw it develop in parallel with the emergence of a scientific rationality in the seventeenth century. A twenty-first century post-modern acceptance of radical individualism, allied to the rejection of all attempts to question the adequacy of a relativist or subjectivist ethos, may prove in time to be the final celebration of liberalism, or what is more likely, the final collapse of the attempt to shape communal values in a liberal culture.

The emergence of a liberal ethos is closely associated with the emerging stress on the autonomy of the human subject in the writings of Thomas Hobbes and John Locke. That moment in history not only gave birth to the idea of the person as an individual, but more importantly, individualism as a political doctrine. Through the writings of Rousseau and Voltaire in France, this development of liberalism in turn influenced the framing of the American constitution and the subsequent development of a large scale acceptance in the nineteenth and twentieth centuries of the ideal of liberal democracy, one founded on the notion of the person as an individual, and differing fundamentally from the earlier classic expression of democracy which was based on the idea of the *polis* (city or political community) and the shared destiny of people not as individuals but as members of the *polis* or community.

If the origins of liberalism can be traced to the emergence of the autonomous *cogito* of scientific rationality and the rise of modern individualism, it must nevertheless be recognised that liberalism also developed in the context of the break-up of an older world view – the dissolution of the inherited sources of meaning that gave a coherence and a unity to the medieval and early Renaissance cultures. Above all, it was the legacy of the Reformation and the wars of religion that shaped the features of a liberal culture. From as early as the eighteenth century, liberalism took the form of a doctrine structured to provide a way of coping with irresolvable conflict. In this context, two core features of liberalism emerged, namely, tolerance and a belief in the value of pluralism. Liberal democracy is the first political experiment which was not only designed to respect the values of freedom and equality, but primarily sought to promote tolerance and to accommodate, insofar as was practical, a pluralism of values, ideals, religious beliefs, and so on.

Liberalism and the shaping of communal values
Although liberalism had its origins in the context of the development of a system that can cope with conflict, liberalism as a political theory could not espouse unrestricted pluralism, which would be a recipe for anarchy. Consequently, in the course of its development, there have been many attempts to construct some harmonious basis for social interaction. In practice, liberal democracy has tended to embrace an amalgam of two different and in many respects conflicting theories, namely utililitarianism and human rights theory.

Both utilitarianism and human rights theories are classical expressions of liberalism or of the liberal dilemma of how to shape communal values or to order a society where there exists, as in the emerging Enlightenment culture, no longer any shared vision of the Good or purpose (*télos*) to human nature such as was provided by the communal nature of the Greek *polis* of Plato and Aristotle or the community cohesion offered by a religion such as Christianity. Human rights theory is more genuinely liberal than utilitarianism in that it suggests that certain individual rights are inviolable and it attempts to avoid any commitment to a shared notion of the good. Utilitarianism in some respects marks the abandonment or the modification of liberalism in favour of a pragmatic theory of the Good, variously defined as pleasure or utility and more recently in more straightforward consumerist terms. In a capitalist ethos, liberalism is pluralist in theory but pragmatic in practice, and there is nothing more pragmatic in contemporary liberalism than the economic agenda of consumerism. In the last analysis the freedom and equality of individuals is continually at risk of being sacrificed on the altar of economic priorities.

The rise of utilitarianism is associated, as we have observed above, with the writings of Bentham and Hume. Today, it is the influence of the writings of Hume's close friend, the economist Adam Smith, that is more important; his influence continues to be felt on the values of 'the market' that shape so much of the ethics of business in a liberal society.

There are early precedents for the acceptance of human rights based upon the existence of a universal moral order, i.e. in Aristotle's *Nicomachean Ethics* and, most importantly, in the vision of the human person proposed by the Christian religion. Nevertheless, the emergence in the Enlightenment of an emphasis on the concept of human rights is due, as we have observed above, in no small measure to the influence of the writings of John Locke and Immanuel Kant. Along with Emile Rousseau, and to a lesser degree Kant, Locke argued for a 'social contract' theory of the state; a theory that acknowledges the primacy of the individual who is possessed of inalienable rights. In the opinion of Locke, the protection and promotion of individual's natural rights was the sole justification for the creation of government, and furthermore, the natural rights to life, liberty, and property set clear limits to the authority and jurisdiction of the state.

The period since the promulgation of the Universal Declaration of Human Rights in 1948 has seen huge increase in awareness of the way in which human rights theory can help to shape communal values in a liberal society. In this period the western world has gone to some lengths to develop the scope of human rights theory. The result has been to promulgate additional covenants such as The European Convention on Human Rights (1954), the International Covenant on Civil and Economic Rights (1966) and, more recently, the UN Convention on Social and Economic Rights (2000) and to seek government implementation of these covenants in legislation. In our own country, both North and South, independent human rights commissions have been established to ensure compliance with human rights obligations and to promote the idea of human rights. In the culture of contemporary western society there is no question but that human rights theory occupies centre stage in the shaping of communal values.

Shaping communal values: liberal individualism critiqued

Robert Bellah
One of the most respected American sociologists, Robert Bellah, was for many years Elliot Professor of Sociology at the University of California. His most famous publication entitled *Habits of the Heart* (1985)[12] (henceforth *HH*) is devoted to exploring the significance of individualism to the American psyche. The book argues persuasively that the liberal culture of contemporary American society lacks the resources to promote communal values. In holding this viewpoint, Bellah places himself in the company of figures such as the Canadian philosopher Charles Taylor and Scottish-born Alasdair MacIntyre.

In a lengthy preface to the revised edition (1996) Bellah acknowledges that individualism is the first language in which Americans tend to think about their lives, a language that values independence and self-reliance above all else and values them as virtues that are good in themselves. However, alongside an older more traditional version of individualism that placed emphasis on the virtues of independence and self-reliance, Bellah's recent studies have found increasing evidence of what he describes as radical individualism, one that places increasing pressures on individuals to disengage from the larger society and in so doing contributes to creating a crisis of civic membership.

Bellah's most controversial thesis is that this radical individualism has a 'hard' utilitarian shape and a 'soft' expressive form, the former focusing on the bottom line (economics) and the latter on feelings, which, as he suggests, are often expressed therapeutically. His thesis is that at the end of the twentieth century it is the manager and the therapist who have become the role models for American culture. As he says:

> Between them, the manager and the therapist largely define the outlines of twentieth-century American culture. The social basis of that culture is the world of bureaucratic consumer capitalism, which dominates, or has penetrated, most older, local economic forms. It is an understanding of life generally hostile to older ideas of moral order. Its center is the autonomous individual, presumed able to choose the roles he will play and the commitments he will make, not on the basis of higher truths but according to the criterion of life-effectiveness as the individual judges it. (*HH*, 47)

The contemporary world of consumer capitalism is one that operates according to the logic of instrumental reasoning, that form of reasoning that acknowledges only one goal that is, effectiveness – 'it is good if it works'. An alternative form of reasoning that eschews the pragmatism of this utilitarian ethic might argue that something will work only if it is good. In a managerial society that embraces the logic of instrumental reasoning, economic effectiveness is the key that opens the door to social mobility and enhanced status.

If Bellah is correct, the therapist is also concerned with the instrumental goal of effectiveness. In this case, however, the measure of effectiveness is the elusive criterion of personal satisfaction. Everything in the therapeutic patient/client relationship is subordinated to the furtherance of this goal. Transposing this therapeutic model onto the larger canvas of culture it is not hard to see that the goal of personal satisfaction is one that situates a therapeutic culture within the cultural boundaries of expressive individualism. As Bellah states with more than a touch of irony,

> Its genius is that it enables the individual to think of commitments – from marriage and work to political and religious involvement – as enhancements of the sense of individual well-being rather than as moral imperatives (*HH*, 47).

The particular focus that Bellah brings to this issue in *Habits of the Heart* is his analysis of the manner in which expressive individualism has become embedded in American culture through the increasing popularity of the role model of the therapist. In his opinion, radical individualism has taken root in American society with the emergence of a therapeutic culture. As he perceptively observes, therapy has become a cultural phenomenon. Therapy as a general outlook on life has spread over the past few decades from a relatively small, educated elite to the middle-class mainstream of American life.

Many are conscious of the benefits of a therapeutic culture. As Bellah points out, therapeutic relationships provide a kind of training for people to become better communicators: middle-class Americans today are more 'in touch with their feelings', better able to express them, and more able to seek what they want in relationships. (*HH*, 139) Yet there is a cost – the loss of an understanding of human relationships that transcends the realm of individual needs. Despite the emphasis that many therapists place on the importance of friendships – well-connected persons live longer, healthier lives – a therapeutic culture is radically individualistic. Acknowledging that friendships are necessary for good emotional adjustment does not by itself provide an adequate basis for the possibility of friendship. Bellah's rhetorical question says it all: 'Are friends that one makes in order to improve one's health really friends enough to improve one's health?'(*HH*, 135) One does not have to be an Aristotelian to acknowledge that community based on friendship cannot be conceived as a collection of self-seeking individuals. In promoting a culture that sees social life as an arrangement for the fulfilment of the needs of individuals, therapy distances us from particular social roles, relationships and practices; and from their attendant measures of authority, duty and virtue. In such a culture the very language of therapeutic relationship seems to undercut the possibility of other than self-interested relationships – ones that exclude any intrusion of 'ought' or 'should' into the relationship. In this scenario, a therapeutic culture is one that promotes an ethos encouraging friendliness, but it is ultimately at the expense of friendship.

In his critique of a therapeutic culture Bellah lays considerable emphasis on what he describes as the 'giving–getting' contractual relationship. Therapy is a tightly regulated and carefully balanced contractual relationship coordinated by cost-benefit calculation – one's relationship with the therapist is a strictly commercial contractual one. It is this issue rather than an over-emphasis on emotional self-satisfaction that provides the focus of Bellah's reservations about a therapeutic culture:

> The problem posed by therapy is not that intimacy is tyrannically taking over too much of public life. It is rather that too much of the purely contractual structure of the economic and bureaucratic world is becoming an

ideological model for personal life. ... The prevalence of contractual intimacy and procedural cooperation, carried over from boardroom to bedroom and back again, is what threatens to obscure the ideals of both personal virtue and public good. (*HH*, 127)

And he perceptively observes,

By its own logic, a purely contractual ethic leaves every commitment unstable. Parties to a contract remain free to choose, and thus free to remake or break every commitment, if only they are willing to pay the price for doing so. (*HH*, 130)

Therapy is concerned to assist clients to become well-adjusted persons. That in itself is undoubtedly a most worthy goal. However, in bracketing out of consideration any consideration of the ethical character of human flourishing, therapy can never embrace an ideal such as unconditional love or fidelity, virtues which alone will promote a well-adjusted personality. A culture that is too tightly tied to the extrinsic utilitarian goal of effectiveness, too tightly tied to the methodology of cost-benefit analysis, is not one that is capable of transcending the narrow boundaries of self-interest. It is Bellah's contention that such a culture will never overcome the cultural and psychological narcissism that destroys the ideal of civic membership and/or commitment to community.

Alasdair MacIntyre (1929–)
Born in Scotland with Irish ancestry, Alasdair McIntyre is currently teaching at the University of Notre Dame in Indiana, USA, and is widely regarded as one of the most influential living philosophers. His works include *A Short History of Ethics* (1965), *Whose Justice? Which Rationality* (1988), and the celebrated *After Virtue* (1981).

As the title *After Virtue*[13] suggests, it is McIntyre's view that western culture is has lost connection to the idea of virtue and what it means to be a virtuous person or even what it means to aspire to be a virtuous person. It is his opinion that we possess only the fragments of a former conceptual scheme: we possess the words such as goodness, virtue, a virtuous life, and so on, but we have lost our comprehension, both theoretical and practical, of morality. (*AV*, 1) In this context, there is no rational way to gain moral agreement, hence, for all practical purposes, we are living in what we might call an emotivist culture, one which proclaims that all judgments are nothing but expressions of preference, attitude, feeling. (*AV*, 14) In this deeply pessimistic appraisal of the state of contemporary culture, McIntyre proclaims that emotivism, where others are always means and never ends, has become embodied in our culture. What was once morality has to some large degree disappeared, to be replaced by subjective preferences. It is McIntyre's firm conviction that the increasing predominance of emotivism in contemporary western culture represents a grave cultural loss. (*AV*, 22)

If MacIntyre is correct, a liberal individualist culture provides neither a basis for moral discourse nor a context for rationally securing agreement on any moral issue because it cannot sustain the wherewithal to create a moral community. What is necessary for a moral community to exist is that there is some shared sense of what it is to be a human being, some sense that there is a purpose to existence and some level of agreement as to what that purpose might entail. The attempt to divorce values/ethics from any sense of a goal to which humans ought to strive is to reduce it to the *cul de sac* of arbitrary choice. The legacy of the growth of liberal individualism is that there are only individuals, and in such a culture there is no basis for moral discourse, i.e. no sense of the social character of ethics, no shared sense of even who we are as human beings, and no recognition that there is a purpose to life that transcends mere personal preference.

In MacIntyre's opinion, it is not just that we lack a basis for moral discourse today but that the very language of morality seems to lack the resonance that it once had. The contemporary western world may possesses the language of morals, but, in the absence of any sense either that we are social beings with rights and responsibilities to the community or that there is a purpose to human life that is not reducible to personal preference, there is no possibility of even understanding what words such as justice, virtue or values could mean or how they could inform ethical practice. It is MacIntyre's bleak assessment that, in terms of providing an ethical framework for life, the contemporary culture of liberal individualism is an ethical desert that leaves no alternative but the cultural adoption of the so-called ethical theory of emotivism. In the last analysis people don't believe that there is any such thing as an objective good, but rather that everything is all a matter of personal preference.

Where McIntyre's path crosses that of Bellah is in his description of the social context in which this culture of emotivism thrives, namely a society whose cultural symbols are those of the aesthete, the manager and the therapist. As he says,

> In our own time emotivism is a theory embodied in characters who all share the emotivist view of the distinction between rational and non-rational discourse, but who represent the embodiment of that distinction in very different social contexts. Two of these we have already noticed: the Rich Aesthete and the Manager. To these we must now add a third: the Therapist. The manager represents in his character the obliteration of the distinction between manipulative and non-manipulative social relations; the therapist represents the same obliteration in the sphere of personal life. (*AV,* 30)

Leaving aside the aesthete whose intention to satisfy all desires eliminates even the pretence of an ethical stance, one is left with the manager and the therapist. According to McIntyre and Bellah, there is ultimately very little difference between the manager and the therapist. Neither is capable of transcending the logic of instrumental reasoning. In a withering critique of their failure to engage with morality, (AV, 23-25) McIntyre echoes Bellah by observing that what both the manager and the therapist have in common is the goal of effectiveness, one that is ultimately concerned with the achievement of power. He also echoes Bellah's assessment of the increasing success of this cultural model, remarking that 'the therapeutic model would seem to have begun to invade spheres such as those of education and of religion'. (AV, 30) In this scenario, psychological effectiveness all too easily replaces the goal of truth.

McIntyre traces the roots of the managerial model to the influence of the celebrated apologist for nineteenth-century capitalism, Max Weber. As he observes, Weber believes that every bureaucratic organisation (which the manager serves) embodies some explicit or implicit definition of costs and benefits from which the criteria of effectiveness are derived. Bureaucratic rationality is the rationality of matching means to ends, economically and efficiently. (AV, 25-26) In this scenario questions about ends are questions of values, and on values reason is silent. No authority can appeal to rational criteria to vindicate itself except that type of bureaucratic authority that appeals precisely to its own effectiveness. Therefore authority is nothing other than successful power and the only criteria for evaluating between conflicting values is effectiveness.

In McIntyre's opinion the therapeutic model echoes the managerial.

> The therapist like the manager treats ends as given – outside his scope. His or her only concern is also with

> effectiveness in transforming raw materials into final products – neurotic symptoms into directed energy, maladjusted individuals into well adjusted ones. Neither therapists nor managers in their role as therapists or managers do or are able to engage in moral debate. They restrict themselves to the realms in which rational agreement is possible – that is, of course from their point of view to the realm of fact, the realm of means, the realm of measurable effectiveness. (*AV*, 30)

An emotivist culture in which the manager and the therapist can occupy such prominent roles is of course one in which, as both Bellah and McIntyre recognise, personal identity has lost its traditional boundaries, that is, a social identity and a view of human life as ordered to a given end. As McIntyre observes, the self is now thought of as lacking any necessary social identity, because the kind of social identity that it once enjoyed is no longer available. In addition, the self is now thought of as criterion-less and thus incapable of objective evaluation because the kind of *telos*/goal or vision of the good in terms of which it once judged and acted is no longer thought to be credible.

As a philosophical critique of modernity, it is to be expected that *After Virtue* would offer a more comprehensive treatment of the origins of this modern 'Self' and a more complete vision of the complex nature of the contemporary individual than that suggested in *Habits of the Heart*. McIntyre's thesis as articulated in *After Virtue* is that, in contrast to modernity, the classical culture including fifteen hundred years of Christianity was consistently defined in terms of the belief in the importance of the virtues and the idea of a virtuous person. As McIntyre perceptively observes, this classical viewpoint is utterly dependent upon the acceptance of the premises:

- that we are members of a community and accept the practices associated with membership of that community,

namely the particular rights and responsibilities that accompany membership of a community.
- there is an overriding *telos*/goal or good to human nature and that one can discern the nature of this goal or good.
- that this goal or good should be pursued for its own sake rather than for an extrinsic reason. Virtues are only virtues if they are pursued for their own sake.

It is McIntyre's view that the liberal individualism that defines the culture of modernity is characterised precisely by the rejection of all of these related premises. It is also his view that if one attempts to live by a set of moral precepts deprived of their teleological context, a set of precepts attached to a view of human nature as it is, without any view as to how it ought to be, the whole project of morality is doomed. He further believes that the divorce of 'is' from 'ought' – the breakdown of the link between how a person is and how they ought to be – is the principle legacy of modernity, one that effectively reduces the notion of the common good to majority opinion.

Can one succeed in framing an ethical code capable of countering the appeal of emotivism while the divorce between the 'is' and the 'ought' remains in place? McIntyre would answer in the negative. As we have observed above, there exist two well-known ethical theories, which if sustainable in practice would prove that McIntyre's belief is mistaken. These theories are respectively utilitarianism and an ethical theory based on the notion of human rights. As both Bellah and McIntyre have perceptively observed, utilitarianism is not an alternative to emotivism but rather an extension of the principles of emotivism on to the larger stage that is the concern of the common good. The alternative is a theory based upon human rights. There is no doubt that the widespread societal acceptance of some form of human rights ethic acts as an effective break on the pervasiveness of emotivism and, at the same time, offers a way of creating consensus around the idea of a democratic community. McIntyre is however correct to point out that a theory based only on rights will never be able to adjudicate in the case where there is a clash of rights. On what basis do you decide which right is more important? This difficulty can be simply illustrated by observing the classical confrontation between right and left leaning citizens, the former claiming basic rights for all citizens to the fruits of their labour (low taxes) and the latter claiming basic rights for all citizens to be treated equally in the areas of health, education, etc., (high taxes). In the end, one can only judge on the basis of some prior vision of the dignity of the human person – some vision of the common good that transcends, defines and qualifies human rights.

Shaping communal values: a challenge to the Christian community

MacIntyre and, to a lesser extent, Bellah offer a very pessimistic assessment of the possibility of finding resources that will shape communal values in today's world. However, the pessimism is perhaps a little overstated because, for the most part, western society still operates under the fairly widely accepted vision of the common good that has been inherited from a religious, largely Christian, background. Furthermore, there is in fact a widespread acceptance of the large body of human rights legislation that sets out the parameters within which communal values can be constructed. In this context, it should not be forgotten that most accepted human rights are based upon at least a tacit acceptance of basic Christian beliefs about the nature and dignity of the human person. One should not underestimate the importance of this fact when seeking to explain the widespread acceptance of this theory.

In seeking to promote communal values that will make concrete the search for meaning and values, there is a challenge facing those of a theistic and particularly Christian persuasion. On the negative side, there is the danger of Christian Churches seeing themselves as under the rubric of therapeutic communities that in effect abdicate any responsibility to hold an authoritative stance on the goals of the Christian faith.

On the positive side, the challenge for theists of a Christian persuasion is to create and sustain community in an individualist culture. As we have observed, a core theme in *Habits of the Heart* is the need to counter the increasing predominance of a therapeutic culture. In meeting this challenge it is interesting to see the role that Bellah attaches to the Churches. As he says:

> The public church and its counterparts in the non-Christian religions offer the major alternative in our culture to radical religious individualism... All reject the radical self-seeking of utilitarian individualism and none of them is content to be only a (therapeutic) lifestyle enclave of warm mutual acceptance. For all of them, religion provides a conception, even if rudimentary, of how one should live. (*HH*, 239)

Although all of the Churches have suffered to some degree from 'a therapeutic thinning out of belief and practice, a withdrawal into the narrow boundaries of the religious community, or both', it is Bellah's view that they still provide in the American context the best hope for the renewal of interpersonal meaning and civic membership. This is so because in his opinion the Churches embody the view that a community can set standards, adopt values, capture conscience, and become authoritative in the life of human beings. Our culture falls apart without such a vision.

Religion also has the capability of countering an instrumentalist culture that cannot know the meaning of commitment, constancy and fidelity. The challenge facing Christian communities is to provide locations for commitment and thus to offer both an experience of what it means to belong to a community and also an ability to appreciate the commitments of others. Religious communities and schools have the potential to provide an ethos, a sense of community, shared values and a shared sense of the good that alone can critique the radical pluralism and rootlessness of an individualist society. In this context, religion has the capability to bring hope to those who experience themselves as lost or rootless. It also has the capability to bring reconciliation to a world marked by division and to bring forgiveness to individuals who cannot forgive themselves.

Finally, the Christian communities have the potential to challenge the dominance of the individualist ideology of market capitalism. In this context, those involved in Christian ministry have the capability to create social solidarity and to bring compassion to people who are broken, to those who are the losers in a society that sees only winners and losers. Religion has also the capability to bring justice to a world marked too often by division. In the western world the poor suffer twice: they suffer material poverty but more importantly they suffer the poverty of the loss of self-esteem in a culture where one's worth as a person is measured in terms of one's disposable income.

Appendix

Different relations between religions and the secular world
The manner in which religion relates to the secular culture varies depending on the particular political and religious context. At one extreme are those who advocate a theocracy, such as in some Islamic states, and at the other extreme are those who advocate complete separation of Church and state. The following are a few examples of the variety of stances among our near neighbours.

The first amendment to the constitution of the USA states 'Congress shall make no law respecting an establishment of religion, or prohibiting the exercise thereof'. In 1802 President Jefferson was to refer to this provision as 'a wall separating Church from State'.

In the EU the position is almost the exact opposite as that which pertains in the USA. Not only is there a state religion in the UK (Church of England), Denmark (Danish Lutheran Church) and the Netherlands (Dutch Reformed Church) but Greece also legislates in the context of an official religion in the state (Greek Orthodox Church). In Germany, Austria, Italy, Spain and Portugal, the Catholic Church is officially recognised through a series of concordats with the Vatican.

From the point of view of religious education, the net effect of the close legal relationship between Church and state in the

EU means that religious education is supported by the state. France is different; it operates on a strict separation of church and state. There is no religious instruction in state schools and parents must fund a high proportion of the costs in the private religiously run schools. This position is similar to that which pertains in the USA.

In the context of the EU, Ireland would seem to be out of line. There is no state religion, no official religion, not even a concordat with the Vatican, and yet, unlike France (and the USA) religious education at primary and secondary level is fully supported by the state. Unlike other European 'concordat' countries, the Irish state does not subsidise Churches, nor give them the right to levy taxes. No assistance or salary is paid to clergy. There is no ministry for religious affairs. And yet, almost unique in the EU context is the fact that 'religious marriages' are recognised as binding in civil law.

APPENDIX

Notes

1. In the treatment of the theme of happiness in Islam, Hinduism and Buddhism I am indebted to Philip Barnes's excellent summary contained in the book from this series entitled *World Religions* (Dublin, Veritas, 2003, pp.108-111, 130-134 and 150-154.
2. Peter Gay, *The Enlightenment: An Interpretation, Book One: The Rise of Modern Paganism*, London, Wildwood House, 1973, p.8.
3. Gerald Hanratty, *Philosophers of the Enlightenment: Locke, Hume and Berkeley Revisited*, Dublin, Four Courts Press, 1995, p.40.
4. David Hume, *A Treatise of Human Nature*, Book One, ed. D. G. C. Macnabb, London, Fontana, 1962, p.42
5. Ibid. 331.
6. David Hume, *On Human Nature and the Understanding*, ed. Antony Flew London, Macmillan, 1962, p.135.
7. L. Wittgenstein, *Tractatus Logico – Philosophicus*, trans. D F. Pears and B.F. McGuinness, London, Routledge and Kegan Paul, 1970, p.71.
8. Ibid., p.73
9. Friedrich Nietzsche, 'Attempt at a Self-Criticism', in Walter Kaufmann, ed,. *The Birth of Tragedy and The Case of Wagner*, New York: Vintage Books, 1967, pp.17-27
10. Jean Paul Sartre, *Existentialism and Humanism*, trans. Philip Mairet, London, Methuen, 1973.
11. Iris Murdoch, *The Sovereignty of Good*, London, Routledge, 1970.
12. Robert Bellah, *Habits of the Heart*, Los Angeles, University of California Press, 1985, revised, 1996.
13. Alasdair MacIntyre, *After Virtue*, London, Duckworth, 1981, tenth impression, 2000.

Select Bibliography

Annas, J, *Ancient Philosophy*, Very Short Introductions Series, Oxford, OUP, 2000

Aquinas, St Thomas, *Summa Theologiae*, trans, Timothy McDermott, London, Methuen, 1889

Arendt, Hannah, *The Origins of Totalitarianism*, London, Allen and Unwin, revised edition, 1967

—, *The Human Condition*, Chicago, University of Chicago Press, 1998

—, *Love and Saint Augustine*, Chicago, University of Chicago Press, 1996

Aristotle, *Metaphysics*, trans. John Warrington, London, J. M. Dent and Sons Ltd, 1954

Augustine, *Confessions*, trans. R. S. Pine-Coffin, London, Penguin, 1961

Barnes. J, *Aristotle*, Very Short Introductions Series, OUP, Oxford, 2000

Barnes, Philip, *World Religions*, Into the Classroom Series, Dublin, Veritas, 2003

Bellah, Robert, *Habits of the Heart*, Los Angeles, University of California Press, 1985, revised, 1996

Blackham, H. J., *Humanism*, London, Penguin, 1968

Camus, Albert, *The Rebel*, trans. Antony Bower, London,

Penguin Books, 1965
—, *The Myth of Sisyphus*, trans. Justin O'Brien, London, Penguin Books, 1975
—, *The Outsider,* trans. Stuart Gilbert, London, Penguin Books, 1961
—, *The Plague,* trans. Stuart Gilbert, London, Penguin Books, 1960
—, *The Fall,* trans. Justin O'Brien, London, Penguin Books, 1963
Cassidy, Eoin G., 'Modernity and Religion in Ireland' in E.G. Cassidy, (ed.), *Measuring Ireland: Discerning Values and Belief,* Dublin, Veritas, 2002, pp.17–45
—, 'Le Phénomène Érotique: Augustinian resonances in Marion's phenomenology of love', in E.G. Cassidy and I. Leask (eds), *Giveness and God: Questions of Jean-Luc Marion,* in the series 'Perspectives in Continental Philosophy series ed. J. Caputo, New York, Fordham University Press, forthcoming Spring 2004
—, 'Religion and Culture: The Freedom to be an Individual', in E.G. Cassidy (ed.), *Faith and Culture in the Irish Context,* Dublin, Veritas, 1996, 16 –34
—, 'The right notes in the right order: faith and the challenge of a therapeutic culture', in *Milltown Studies,* No. 48, 2001, pp.1–20
—, 'Le role de L'Amitié dans al quete du Bonheur Chez Augustin', in J. Fallon and J. McEvoy (eds), *Actualité de la Pensée Mediévale,* Louvain, Editions Peeters, 1994, pp.171–201
—, 'Pathways to God: the Road Less Traveled', in A. Murphy and E.G. Cassidy, (eds), *Neglected Wells: Spirituality and the Arts,* Dublin, Four Courts, 1997, pp.11–27
—, 'The First of all questions: Heidegger and the Intelligibility of Metaphysic', in M. Hinds (ed.), *REA,* Dublin (2002), pp. 26–46
Chadwick, Henry, *Augustine,* Past Masters series, Oxford, OUP, 1986

Copleston, Fredrick, *Aquinas*, London, Penguin, 1958, 1979
Danto, Arthur, *Sartre*, Modern Masters series, London, Fontana, 1975
Davis, Colin, *Levinas: An Introduction*, Cambridge, Polity Press, 1996
Descartes, Rene, *A Discourse on Method and Other Works*, trans. E. S. Haldane and G.R. Ross, New York, Washington Square Press, 1965
Delius, Christoph, et al. *The Story of Philosophy: From Antiquity to the Present*, Cologne, Könemann, 2000
Dunne, Joseph, *Back to the Rough Ground: 'Phronesis' and 'Techne' in Modern Philosophy and in Aristotle*, London, University of Notre Dame Press, 1993
Dupré, Louis, *Passage to Modernity*, New Haven, Yale University Press, 1993
Eliade, Mircea, *Myths, Dreams and Mysteries*, trans. P. Mairet, London, Collins, 1960, 1976
----------, *Patterns in Comparative Religion*, London, Sheed and Ward, 1969
Erasmus, *Praise of Folly*, trans. Betty Radice, London, Penguin Classics, 1971
Frankfort, Henri, et al., *Before Philosophy: The Intellectual Adventure of Ancient Man*, Maryland, Penguin Books, 1949
Gallagher, Kenneth, *The Philosophy of Gabriel Marcel*, New York, Fordham University Press, 1962, 1975
Gallagher, Michael Paul, *Clashing Symbols: An Introduction to Faith and Culture*, London, DLT, 1997
—, *Free to Believe*, London, Darton Longman and Todd, London, 1987
—, *Struggles of Faith*, Dublin, Columba Press, 1990
Gaarder, Jostein, *Sophies World*, London, Phoenix House, 1995
Gay Peter, *The Enlightenment: An Interpretation, Book One: The Rise of Modern Paganism*, London, Wildwood House, 1973
Hanratty, Gerald, *Studies in Gnosticism and in the Philosophy of Religion*, Dublin, Four Courts Press, 1997

—, *Philosophers of the Enlightenment: Locke, Hume and Berkeley Revisited*, Dublin, Four Courts Press, 1995

Heidegger, Martin, *Being and Time*, trans. J. McQuarrie and E. Robinson, Oxford, Basil Blackwell, 1973

—, *An Introduction to Metaphysics*, trans. R. Manheim, New York, Anchor Books, 1961

Hume, David, A Treatise of Human Nature, Book One, ed. D. G. C. Macnabb, London, Fontana, 1962

—, *On Human Nature and the Understanding*, ed. Antony Flew, London, Macmillan, 1962

Kant Immanuel, Critique of Pure Reason, trans. Norman Kemp Smith, London, Macmillan, 1973

—, *Critique of Practical Reason*, trans. L. W. Beck, New York, Library of Liberal Arts, 1968

Kearney Richard, *Dialogues with Contemporary Continental Thinkers* Manchester, Manchester University Press, 1984

Kung, Hans, *Christianity and World Religions*, trans. Peter Heinegg, SCM, London, 1986

Levinas, Emmanuel, *Totality and Infinity*, trans, A. Lingis, Duquesne University Press, Pittsburgh, 1969

McCarthy Fachtna and McCann Joseph, *Religion and Science*, Into the Classroom series, Dublin, Veritas, 2003

MacIntyre, Alasdair, *After Virtue*, London, Duckworth, 1981, tenth impression, 2000

McLellan, David, *Marx*, Modern Masters series, Fontana, London, 1975

McQuarrie John, *God Talk*, London, SCM Press, 1967

—, *Heidegger and Christianity*, London, SCM Press, 1994

Marcel, Gabriel, *Mystery of Being, Vol. 1*, South Bend, Indiana, Gateway, 1950

Marion, Jean Luc, *Prolegonmena to Charity*, trans, S. Lewis, New York, Fordham University Press, 2002

—, *Le Phénomène érotique*, Grasset, Paris, 2003

Marx, Karl, *The Essential Writings,* (ed.) R. Bender, New York, Harper and Row, 1972

Moran, Dermot, *Introduction to Phenomenology*, London, Routledge, 2000

Murdoch, Iris, *Sovereignty of Good*, London, Routledge, 1970

------------, *Metaphysics as a Guide to Morals,* London, Chatto and Windus, 1992

Nietzsche, Friedrich, 'Attempt at a Self-Criticism', in Walter Kaufmann (ed), *The Birth of Tragedy and The Case of Wagner* New York, Vintage Books, 1967

Pears, David, *Wittgenstein*, Modern Masters series, London, Fontana, 1971

Plato, *The Last Days of Socrates*, trans. Hugh Tredennick, London, Penguin Classics, 1954

—, *Gorgias*, trans. Walter Hamilton, London, Penguin Books, 1960

—, *Symposium,* trans. Walter Hamilton, London, Penguin Books, 1951

Polkinghorne, John, *Science and Creation*, London, SPCK, 1988

Pritchard James B. (ed.), *Ancient Near Eastern Texts,* New Jersey, Princeton University Press, 1955

Purcell, Brendan. 'In Search of Newgrange: Long Night's Journey into Day', in Kearney, R. (ed.) *The Irish Mind,* Dublin, Wolfhound Press 1985

Sartre, Jean Paul, *Existentialism and Humanism*, trans. Philip Mairet, London, Methuen, 1973

Singer Peter, *Marx*, Past Masters series, Oxford, OUP, 1986

Steiner, George, *Heidegger,* Modern Masters series, London, Fontana, 1978

Stern, J. P., *Nietzsche*, Modern Masters series, London, Fontana, 1978

Taylor, A. E. *Plato: The Man and his Work,* London, Methuen, 1926, 1986

Taylor. C, *Socrates*, Very Short Introductions series, Oxford, OUP, 2000

Taylor, Charles, The Ethics of Modernity, Cambridge, Mass., Harvard University Press, 1991

Touraine, Alain, *Critique of Modernity*, trans. David Macey, London, Blackwell, 1995

Van Bavel, T. J., *Christians in the World: Introduction to the Spirituality of Augustine,* Catholic Book Publishing Company, New York, 1980

Voegelin, Eric, *Order and History (vol. one): Israel and Revelation*, Louisiana, Louisiana State University Press, 1956

Wittgenstein, Ludwig, *Tractatus Logico – Philosophicus,* trans. D F. Pears and B.F. McGuinness, London, Routledge and Kegan Paul, 1970